62½D

27th June.

14.12.71

THE TEACH YOURSELF BOOKS

CONTEMPORARY MUSIC
An Introduction

Uniform with this volume

and in the same series

The Teach Yourself Guidebook to the Ballet

Teach Yourself to Compose Music

The Teach Yourself Concise Encyclopedia of
General Knowledge

The Teach Yourself Guidebook to the Drama

The Teach Yourself History of Music

Teach Yourself Jazz

Teach Yourself Music

Teach Yourself Orchestration

Teach Yourself the Organ

Teach Yourself to Play the Piano

Teach Yourself to Sing

Teach Yourself Songwriting

Teach Yourself the Violin

CONTEMPORARY MUSIC

An Introduction

FRANCIS ROUTH

THE ENGLISH UNIVERSITIES PRESS LTD

ST PAUL'S HOUSE   WARWICK LANE

LONDON E.C.4.

for Diana

Copyright © 1968
Francis Routh

SBN 340 05940 0

*Printed in Great Britain for the English Universities Press Ltd
at the Pitman Press, Bath*

CONTENTS

ACKNOWLEDGEMENTS

IN writing this book I have been greatly helped by many friends and colleagues, whose advice, criticism and suggestions I am very glad to acknowledge. Several ideas are here developed which originated in discussion or correspondence, and I am particularly indebted to those musicians who have made available to me in this way the fruit of their experience: Miss Noelle Barker, Dr. Andrew Byrne, Dr. Erik Routley, Sir Michael Tippett, Mr. Ernest Tomlinson. Nor must I forget to mention my pupils, since few things help to crystallize an idea more than attempting to teach it.

I am grateful for many specific kindnesses; to Dr. M. A. Baird, Music Librarian, University of London, for so readily making available many books, scores and records belonging to the University Library; to Mrs. Vanessa Cunningham, for her painstaking editing of the typescript; also to Mr. David Hughes and Mr. Michael Pope.

Also I record my gratitude to the following, who have read the manuscript in whole or in part, and have made most valuable comments and suggestions: Mr. Tristram Cary, Dr. Hans Heimler, Mr. Robert Sherlaw Johnson, Mr. Hans Keller, Dr. A. S. Osley, and Professor Hans Redlich, University of Manchester.

I acknowledge with much appreciation the cooperation of the following publishers, in allowing me to examine scores which they publish:

Boosey and Hawkes Ltd.	— works of Stravinsky and Copland
G. Ricordi & Co. Ltd.	— works of Varèse
Schott & Co. Ltd.	— works of Tippett
Universal Edition Ltd.	— works of Schoenberg, Berg, Webern, Boulez, Stockhausen

Grateful acknowledgement is made to the following for their kind permission to reproduce copyright material:

Literary quotations

(Permission has been given by the publisher unless otherwise stated.)

Page

12   *A survey of contemporary music* by Cecil Gray. Oxford University Press

14–15   *The Republic of Plato*, trans. Cornford. Clarendon Press, Oxford

19   *Delius* by Philip Heseltine (Peter Warlock). The Bodley Head

21   *Hear me talkin' to ya*, edited by Nat Shapiro and Nat Hentoff. Copyright 1955 by Nat Shapiro and Nat Hentoff. Reprinted by permission of Holt, Rinehart and Winston, Inc., Publishers, New York

42, 55 *Conversations with Igor Stravinsky.* Faber & Faber

126   *Memories and Commentaries*
        Expositions and Developments
        Copyright Igor Stravinsky, reprinted by permission.

48   *Life with Picasso* by Françoise Gilot and Carlton Lake. Thomas Nelson

52   *The Poetics of Music* by Igor Stravinsky. Harvard University Press

52   *Chronicles of my life* by Igor Stravinsky. Victor Gollancz
        Copyright Igor Stravinsky, reprinted by permission.

64   *Les fondements de la musique dans la conscience humaine* by Ernest Ansermet. Editions de la Baconnière

69–71   *Olivier Messiaen* by Claude Rostand. Ventadour, Paris

95   *The path to the new music* by Anton Webern. Universal Edition (Theodore Presser Co.)

121   *Composer in residence* by Ross Lee Finney. *Composer*, No. 15 (April, 1965)

181–183 *Essays before a Sonata* by Charles Ives. Dover Publications Inc., New York

Page

197, 207   *America's music* by Gilbert Chase. McGraw-Hill Publishing Company Ltd.

199   *Ferruccio Busoni* by Edward J. Dent. Oxford University Press

201   *Introduction to contemporary music* by Joseph Machlis. W. W. Norton & Co. Inc., New York

215   *Words for prepared discourse* by John Cage. American Composers Alliance Bulletin, Vol. II, No. 2, page 11

267   *An autobiography and other essays* by G. M. Trevelyan. Longmans, Green & Co. Ltd.

The quotations on pages 243/4, 247, 248 are by permission of the *New Statesman*, *The Guardian*, and *The Observer* respectively.

Musical quotations

Ex. No.	Publisher
1	Breitkopf and Haertel, Wiesbaden; reproduced by permission of British and Continental Music Agencies Ltd., London.
3 & 4	Editions Jean Jobert, Paris.
5	Durand & Cie., Paris.
6b, 7	J. & W. Chester Ltd., London, E.C.1.
8, 9, 11a	Copyright 1960 by Hawkes & Son (London) Ltd.
12–18	Alphonse Leduc & Cie., Paris.
24	Copyright 1924 & 1952 by Wilhelm Hansen, Copenhagen.
22, 25, 31	Universal Edition (Alfred A. Kalmus Ltd.)
33	Universal Edition (London) Ltd.
34, 35	Oxford University Press, London.
37–44	Schott & Co. Ltd., London, W.1.
46–48	Copyright 1932 by Boosey & Hawkes, Inc.
49a, 49b	Copyright 1942 by Boosey & Hawkes, Inc.
50, 51	Copyright 1947 by Boosey & Hawkes Music Publishers Ltd.
52–54	Copyright 1945 by Boosey & Hawkes, Inc.

PREFACE

CERTAIN assumptions underly this study of contemporary music. The term set is Europe and America in the twentieth century, starting with Debussy and Busoni; yet of the many hundreds of composers who fall within this period only a handful are mentioned; of a truly immense quantity of material only a tiny fraction has been selected, and several trends and fashions have been excluded. Even about a single composer, if he is a figure of importance, omniscience is impossible; still more is this the case when so many are involved. And so this is neither an encyclopaedia about the composers of the contemporary period, nor does it make any claims as history; rather is it a study in aesthetics, which may be said to take up where encyclopaedias and histories leave off, and for which a certain factual knowledge about the most prominent contemporary composers, and their works, is assumed. It is in the light of his aesthetic intentions, and against the background of his tradition, cultural context and ethos, that a composer's work is best seen. Therefore the question underlying this study is not so much who wrote what, as what is the essential musical environment in contemporary Europe and America?

In so far as criticism is taken to mean the expression of value-judgements, I have not sought, in the first instance, to present the reader with criticism. It is no function of a practising musician to pronounce judgement on his colleagues. The nearer they are to him in time and place, the more is this the case. Any price-tags he puts on the work of his contemporaries are no one's concern but his own. But this general absence of pronouncement on the work of contemporaries is by no means to be confused with having nothing to pronounce about. On the contrary; every musician needs a reasoned viewpoint of the events surrounding him, for such a viewpoint will be a cultural life-line to help him through the mêlée that makes up our present musical situation. But as far as the events of today are concerned, he is himself part of them; he belongs to a living organism. It is only towards the events of yesterday, in so far as they have a bearing on today, that he can hope to achieve a more objective stand-point; and this is not because he is outside them, or because they do not concern him, but because their outcome is no longer in doubt.

Two examples will illustrate this important point; jazz and serialism. These two forces, which exert a gravitational pull, each in its own direction and contrary to the other, have long since ceased to be novelties, and have become established facts; they are no longer the exclusive preserve of a minority, but are now common property, and—very nearly, at least—respectable. As long as their nature, purpose and aesthetic *raison d'être* were a matter of some doubt, and their future contribution to the musical common cause was ambiguous, there was room for polemics on either side; but now that the dust of battle has cleared somewhat, and we can see these two phenomena more clearly for what they really are, it is possible to consider their effect on the *materia musica* more as a matter of fact, and less as a cause for alarm and histrionics.

Since jazz is one of the very few spontaneously active forces of the twentieth century, and has lent colour and influence to a wide range of compositions, it would be short-sighted to omit it from a consideration of contemporary music. "Pop" music however presents a very different picture. Its purpose is chiefly, if not entirely, commercial, and its effect is a negation of that active function of the composer and that active response by the listener which an art-work presupposes. It is, in a word, non-art, and would be out of place in a discussion such as this about music.

No composer today can be considered *in vacuo*, without reference to his artistic point of departure. The year 1900 makes a suitable starting-point for historical as well as musical reasons. In the twentieth century a handful of works stand out as being of the most positive and seminal importance. It will be of greater use to consider a few of these works in some detail than to glance cursorily either at the total range of output of their respective composers, or at the more derivative works of their profuse and miscellaneous progeny.

In any verbal *exposé* of a subject as elusive and indefinable as music, it is necessary to define the function, and the limitation, of words. As far as this study is concerned, they are not used as a means of communicating ready-made value judgements, but rather to suggest some objective means whereby the listener may form his own. The devaluation of the listener's function is one of the least desirable characteristics of an *admass* age. In no sense is a verbal description of music a sufficient substitute for active musical experience. Nor, by the same token, is a menu a sufficient substitute for a good dinner. There is a case to be made out that music is self-sufficient, and that verbal description is irrelevant; yet, even if we do not go so far as this, we must admit that the function of music is one thing, and that the function of words is almost totally different and distinct. It is interesting to note that although there has been a large quantity of art criticism, and numerous writers have devoted themselves to the study of the visual arts—to say nothing of literature—the number of writers of corresponding calibre who have devoted themselves to music has been comparatively small. Music has no Ruskin or Herbert Read.

The musical phenomenon is here treated in a three-fold way; which is itself a reflection of the creative process. After an attempt to set the scene in historical perspective, the facts of some of the outstanding landmarks of contemporary music are presented. The composers, as it were, state their case. This we shall call the Thesis. Next, those factors are considered which have a bearing on the listener's receptivity to what the composer has to say. Six such factors chiefly impress themselves on the student of the contemporary scene. There are in addition several problems of criticism presented to the listener by the diverse styles adopted by contemporary composers. This aspect of the matter we shall call the Antithesis. These two sections would be incomplete without a third, that concluding Synthesis, which is a basis for the listener's reasoned aesthetic.

Some of the material of this study was first used in lectures given between 1964–1966 at the Battersea College of Technology, now the University of Surrey; some is condensed and shortened from a broader, more detailed enquiry, *The Aesthetics of Music*. The work as a whole may be considered as an introduction to contemporary music, whose purpose is to suggest a link between the contemporary composer and his audience. Something of this nature is meant by Aaron Copland when he refers to the "gifted listener".

FRANCIS ROUTH

CHAPTER ONE

INTRODUCTORY:
THE PROBLEM STATED

FEW WOULD DISPUTE the lack of understanding that exists between many contemporary composers and their audience. Artistic confusion exists on both sides. The difficulties and complexities of certain schools of composition appear to be arbitrary and inexplicable to the listener, who is often left instinctively and intellectually uninvolved. Any interest he had is soon replaced by indifference, annoyance even, that the composer should place such hindrances in the way of his enjoyment. Moreover composers are often at variance with each other.

Yet the composer needs to establish some sort of *rapport* with the listener and with his fellow musicians; without at least a potential audience, art dies, and disintegrates into mutually exclusive factions, whose dogmatism and intolerance are related inversely to their impact on an audience in the concert hall. It is all too easy to make sweeping and exaggerated claims on behalf of a composer, or a school of composition, which has not been heard or assessed to any large extent. But the more it becomes known, the more difficult such polemics become; the listener, by then, has begun to form his own aesthetic assessment.

The problem of contemporary music is partly aesthetic, partly sociological: how is a new and strange composition to be evaluated? What is the usefulness and the rôle of the composer in our contemporary society?

(i) *Aesthetic*

The aesthetic judgement of all music, new as well as old, that is to say the intelligent, humble, cultured attitude to a composition, is of prime importance if music is to have a positive value to our society. Let us therefore not underestimate the importance or the relevance of aesthetics, though let us remember that such a way of thinking rarely enters into the musical scheme of things today, hardly figures as a University discipline, and is generally dismissed as too vague a thing to be worth serious consideration. Aesthetics begins where history and musicology leave off; it asks the question not why, when or where a work was written, but what is the effect of that work on a listener. It is a creative, essentially active, response to art. It is concerned not so much with what is good or bad; that is the field, strictly speaking, of ethics. Nor is it concerned with what is true or false; such a line of enquiry is, basically at least, scientific and factual. It is concerned solely to establish what it is that makes a work beautiful or ugly, effective or ineffective, interesting or boring.

The three goddesses of Beauty, Truth and Goodness are independent and jealous ladies, each with her own particular sphere of activity; and though it may well be the case, as Plato put forward, that in a healthy community they interact, and that the influence of one may extend into the domain of the other two, nevertheless we must clearly differentiate their distinct rôles if we are to lay the basis of a valid aesthetic judgement; and it would be perverse to allocate music to any except the first. This does not mean that we entirely disregard the other two; heavy would be the divine nemesis for such human presumption; but it does mean that the primary question about a musical composition is about its beauty; other considerations are therefore secondary.

Let us be quite clear about this from the outset. The sense or faculty with which we judge music is on a different intellectual level from that with which we decide whether an action or institution is good or bad, or whether a scientific theory, or religion, or philosophical system, is true or false. Certainly an aesthetic judgement is based on a consideration and analysis of the facts; indeed to be valid it must; and the "facts" of a composition—that is to say the notes, sounds, or other factors that go to make it up—can be scientifically verified. The link between science and aesthetics is by no means tenuous. If wrong notes are sounded in a performance, thereby making a false image of the work, this can be checked simply by reference to the score. There is nothing complicated or subtle about that. But, as we shall see later, music does not live by notes alone; and the moment the listener forms an aesthetic judgement of a work, he exercises a different intellectual faculty. He substitutes one way of thinking, the factual and deductive, with another, the imaginary and associative.

Whether an aesthetic judgement is fair or unfair depends on the training, experience and cultural make-up of the person making it, to say nothing of his psychological maturity. It is surely indisputable that we should be particularly careful only to praise, or condemn, for the right reason a composition that is new to us. It may be considered in two stages; first the formative stage, next the executive. Mistakes and misjudgements may be made by the composer at any point in either stage, which may bring about some artistic shortcoming in the finished work. The listener must ask himself not only whether the music successfully communicates the effect the composer intended, but also whether his artistic purpose and intention was honest and valid in the first place. If it was shortsighted, or for any reason mistaken, or, again, if his intentions, though excellent in themselves, were frustrated by his technical failure to realise them, then there are valid grounds for an adverse aesthetic judgement of his work.[1]

In attempting to define, we must guard against an over-simplification. Whatever else the contemporary situation may be, it is certainly not simple. There is an infinite variety of sound-possibility open to the composer today, and in one sense his most important work is done at the preliminary, formative stage, when he clarifies his intentions to himself and selects his material. No matter how technically expert he may be, an error of judgement at this stage will spoil the artistic effect of the finished work.

The formation of an aesthetic judgement by the listener is an indispensable stage in the creation of a new composition. Composer and audience, creator and listener, each have a function in bringing to life a new work. This function cannot be delegated. For a composition to become fully alive, it is necessary that it should be not merely performed, but also assessed, by an audience. This assessment must be on the aesthetic level, and, until such an assessment is made, the

[1] Cf. St. Augustine's definition of music as *Ars bene modulandi*; the art of making a controlled variation of sound in an effective way. The word "bene" covers both the intention behind, and the execution of, the composition. And who is to decide whether it is "bene" or not?

composition remains ideal, not actual. The ability to communicate his inspiration is just as much part of a composer's technique as the ability to write notes, or symbols, on paper, and to manipulate his *materia musica*. Indeed, one might reasonably ask, what is the use of any idea, however brilliant, unless it can be shared with others?[1] In his turn, the listener needs an openness to all manifestations of musical imagination, an informed receptivity, an ardent curiosity. He will thus be a partner in building a musical tradition that is alive and active, not complacent and conservative. This can be observed to happen or not to happen, as the case may be, at various stages of musical history.

In just the same way as a composer's technique is directed towards communicating his ideas, which will necessarily remain abstract until they are communicated, so the listener's aesthetic judgement will remain insubstantial and ineffective until it is verbally expressed. Certainly instinct and intuition may attract or repel at the initial hearing of a new work, but this is by no means an adequate substitute for aesthetic judgement. Far from being a general, somewhat vague attitude, as is sometimes thought, such a judgement should be a highly disciplined and rigorous intellectual process. It is the very reverse of speculation. The choice and use of words needs to be most exact, in proportion as their subject-matter is the reverse. Criticism of this sort is creative writing of the highest importance, and its author becomes not merely the composer's advocate, but an artist himself.

Unfortunately this rarely happens. One aspect of the problem facing the contemporary composer is that *for the most part* his work is not aesthetically assessed. Not only has there been an almost total breakdown in communication between himself and his audience; there has been an almost total failure of creative criticism. One of the most potent factors governing our society is its preoccupation with science and technology; and the scientific attitude and method has permeated our thinking in artistic as well as material matters. As far as contemporary music is concerned, this tendency has produced two main results. First, analysis has taken the place of criticism, and the terminology used to describe

[1] Cf Einstein: *Greatness in Music*, p. 163.

certain music, particularly *avant-garde* music of the serialist and electronic schools, has become highly technical and specialist, derived as it is from the language of physics and mathematics. Second, the scientific method applied to historical research has resulted in a pronounced increase of interest in early, mediaeval and pre-classical music. This is the age of the musicologist. Diligent research is carried out; authentic, practical editions are produced; old notation is laboriously transcribed, and most careful attention is paid to detailed points of scholarship. In fact we may say that one of the most marked features of the mid-twentieth century is the energy and the address with which musicians have sought to rediscover and recreate not merely the letter, but the spirit, and the cultural ethos of earlier historical periods. The Mediaeval and Baroque traditions in particular have exercised a peculiar fascination over our contemporary musical scene. In a word, our age is Alexandrian.

Unfortunately, all this work and energy, highly laudable in itself, has a debit side, which is that *for the most part* little or no attention is paid by trained musicians—particularly in Colleges and Universities—to contemporary culture, and in particular the contemporary composer. One is as likely today to hear not just a performance, but a reasoned assessment, of Perotin or Ockeghem, Willaert or Schütz, as one is of their contemporary equivalents. Byzantine Church music, or the mediaeval motet, appear to be no less relevant and familiar to the scholars of today than the contemporary serial or electronic techniques; in fact, probably more.

I have said *for the most part* advisedly, because there is a highly important exception to this general trend; that is that composers themselves have seen the need for the advocacy and assessment of their work, and have set about meeting it, partly by writing books themselves, partly by the dissemination and discussion of ideas in conferences, lectures and summer schools. Most of the important composers of this century have expressed their thoughts verbally in some form or another, and have considered it important to keep themselves informed by means of such gatherings with other composers and musicians. The Charles Eliot Norton lectures, given at Harvard University, are most notable; the international seminars at Princeton University in America, and the gatherings at Darmstadt and Donaueschingen in Germany, symbolise this desire to re-establish the link between the composer and his audience, without which no contemporary music can be written that is not merely experimental, derivative or ephemeral.

But if a composer's work is to be fully accepted, and acceptable, it is a necessary prerequisite that he should belong, in the deepest sense, to his environment. He cannot work in isolation. Yet you cannot make yourself "belong" to a society simply by holding a summer school, or by writing a book. Now it is commonly accepted that in the first decade of this century certain radical changes took place in all fields of intellectual thought—scientific, philosophical, theological, as well as artistic. Existing ideas were challenged, existing systems questioned. It is important to realise that this upheaval had two sides to it. It was partly a revolutionary throwing overboard of ideas and attitudes handed down from the nineteenth century that were considered outmoded and unacceptable; partly also an exploration into the whole nature of man. Among the composers of this period, of whom we may chiefly mention Busoni, Debussy and Schoenberg, there was not only a growing dissatisfaction with the existing techniques of composition, but also an overwhelming desire both to discover new ones, and to re-think the most fundamental premises underlying all music—the reasons for it, and the purpose of it. If we are to understand fully the spirit and ethos that governs composers in the mid-twentieth century, we must take into account this duality of purpose that manifested itself at the turn of the century, the revolutionary on the one hand, the exploratory on the other. The years before the first world war are the period when modern music begins; present-day developments have their origin in work written then. Moreover, the changes in all aspects of life brought about by the 1914–1918 war are difficult to exaggerate.

Unfortunately, the dynamic and radical re-appraisal of the musical art that was carried out by composers in the early years of the twentieth century was not balanced by any equivalent change of attitude on the part of the listener. This resulted in a lack of understanding, and produced a rift which has lasted ever since. The isolation surrounding the contemporary composer is a problem which has its origin in the lack of a reasoned advocacy on the part of the listener over a period of some fifty years. Trained and informed musicians who might have been expected to give a balanced judgement of the developments that were taking place under their noses were, for one reason or another, reluctant to do so. Some were too academically conservative to be interested in such things; some were nothing more than militant partisans of this or that protagonist, and their judgement was thus biased; some, as we have already observed, opted out of the uncongenial task or interpreting the present in favour of the much safer one of delving into the past; they became musicologists and left the work of criticism to others.

(ii) *Sociological*

The isolation of the contemporary composer, the fact that he no longer belongs integrally to his environment, is also a sociological matter of the greatest importance to our understanding of contemporary music. Many composers are thrown back onto themselves, and work in their own private world. Adorno has called it a "detached inwardness".[1] The point at issue now is not so much the quality, the technical expertise of a particular composition, which may well be excellent, but the position of the composer in society. Generally speaking he is beholden to no man, subscribes to no common philosophy, and takes employment where he finds it. In a word, he is free-lance, and has felt at liberty to write and to experiment as his temperament dictates. The result, as anyone could have foreseen, is the plethora of conflicting styles that we see today, a wide spectrum of differing idioms, ranging from the ultra-conservative to the *avant-garde*. The disappearance of the true patron, and the necessity felt by most composers to develop an individual, and probably novel style, so as not to be confused with any other composer; also the devaluation of music to the level of a commercial product, and part of the "entertainment industry", are all familiar and characteristic features of our society. Contemporary music is not a spontaneous growth; it is certainly not the natural expression of the spirit and aspirations of Western civilisation today; nor does it spring from the cultural soil of the people. Rather is it a

---

[1] Quoted by Wildgans, *Anton Webern*, p. 170.

carefully nurtured hothouse plant, which having been produced then has to be "sold". Its roots are shallow; it does not endemically belong. How often have we not heard a composer, or his partisans, chiding an audience for being so stupid as not to appreciate his work?

This is not to say that the composer is idle, that his work is not heard. Far from it. Indeed the more actively he markets his product, the more performances he will achieve, the more he will be in demand. It is the *admass* principle, that a market exists if you make it. But although this may be desirable commercially, it is artistically upside-down; he who shouts loudest does not necessarily have the most to say.

One may well ask whether this has not always been so. If it is agreed that the composer today does not belong to his environment, has there ever been a time in the past when he did? In what way can a composer be said to "belong"? A brief glance at some of the main periods of musical history will help us to see that the present situation was not always so. A sense of historical perspective will help us to see our century in its true light; an awareness of what has happened in the past can be a contributory factor to an assessment of the present.

There are three ways in which composers of the past have "belonged" to their society.

(a) The first was the direct composer-patron relationship. Direct patronage is now practically a thing of the past, though the three chief examples in our century have been the stipend granted to Sibelius by the government of Finland, the commissioning of Russian ballets by Serge Diaghilev, and the commissioning of compositions from many composers, including Schoenberg, Bartok, Casella, Malipiero, Piston, Copland and Prokofiev by the American benefactress Elizabeth Sprague Coolidge. The commissioning of individual works is a fairly common practice today, for instance, in Europe by German Radio Stations, by the Dutch Government, and, in England, by Sadler's Wells Opera, by some Universities, by the B.B.C. But examples of direct patronage in an earlier age are too numerous to name. European courts were incomplete without their musicians-in-residence, and kings and princes, particularly in the Baroque period, were both zealous and competitive in their patronage. Music's gain was incalculable. If we today,

with our highly complex laws of copyright, and our sophisticated means of communication, tend to look with superiority
or complacency at the rough-and-ready society that faced
Bach or Mozart, we should reflect that no composer, of
whatever period, has a greater need of anything than en-
lightened patronage; and this today is not often found.

(b) The second way in which a composer can be said to
"belong" is if his work is seen and felt by his contemporaries,
in other fields as well as music, to be a full and natural
expression of a generally-felt mood, or *zeitgeist*. Two factors
will allow the composer to bring his skill to fruition; the
knowledge that his music has a necessary and important
place, and a period of time long enough to allow the process
to work. The history of music provides two outstanding
examples of this phenomenon; the first can be seen in the
gradual flowering of polyphony in the centuries of the
Renaissance; the second can be seen in the Romantic movement. In the first case, the origin was primarily religious, or
at least church-dominated; in the second case, it was literary
and intellectual. In both cases a spirit of high endeavour and
aspiration governed the thoughts of the leaders and foremost
thinkers of the time. In both cases the composer was entirely
at one with the ideals and wishes of his society. He thus
"belonged" in a very deep sense.

The Renaissance. The heaven-aspiring quality of the thought
of the Middle Ages can be seen in Gothic art, whether expressed in the traceries and lofty arches of the mediaeval
architect, or the broad structure and ingenious interplay of
part-writing of the polyphonic composer. The culmination
of the work of this period was reached in the sixteenth century,
and was shared by composers in four countries: the Englishman Byrd, the Flemish Lassus, the Italian Palestrina, and the
Spaniard Victoria. Their work was a truly universal musical
expression of the European ideal of the Renaissance.

The Romantic Period. Two centuries later, beginning at the
end of the eighteenth century, the Romantic movement was to
colour the work of all artists, writers, painters and composers
alike. Frequently it is said that twentieth century music is a
reaction against nineteenth century Romanticism. If this is
so, it is as well that we should have an idea of what it is that
is being reacted against.

Romanticism was a mixture of many apparently contradictory elements: a search for the universal beauty of form,
architecture, design, coupled with a desire for personal and
introspective utterance; a feeling for the universal brother-
hood of man, coupled with a gradually developing sense of
nationalism; a susceptibility to the bizarre, the abnormal, the
picturesque, coupled with a precise, scientific sense of enquiry.
Romanticism is by no means to be confused with Victorianism,
although they occur partly at the same time. The development
of science from the seventeenth century onwards had led to
rationalism, the age of Enlightenment. Things were questioned
which previously had been accepted. In France particularly
this was the time when research was carried out into the
physical nature of musical sounds, and discoveries made
which were to have very far-reaching consequences for music.
In 1722 Rameau published his four-volume *Traité de
l'Harmonie*, which had a profound impact.[1] It contained the
scientific and theoretic justification for composition in triads,
and described the harmonic series, the nature and function
of chords, and major and minor tonality. It is interesting to
note that by a strange coincidence the year 1722 also saw
the publication of the first book of Bach's *48 Preludes and
Fugues*.

Thus were laid the foundations of the harmonic style,
which characterised the Romantic composers. The point
where the old contrapuntal style and the new harmonic style
meet is the music of Bach. The composers who followed him
were quick to realise the immense potential contained in the
new discoveries, and the most immediate developments were
twofold. First the notes of the scale were thought of vertically
as part of a chord, and not just horizontally as part of a
melody; they thus assumed a totally fresh significance, and
a new relationship to each other. Second, arising out of this
relationship, a new formal structure for a movement was
worked out. A secondary theme could be given extra colour
and contrast if the composer changed the music into a

---

[1] Though Rameau's book won wide acceptance, and was used as a
textbook for at least the next 100 years, it provoked some opposition,
notably from German theorists, such as Mattheson and Kirnberger,
to say nothing of Bach himself. Up to the time of Brahms, theoretical
teaching remained centred round the Figured Bass.

different key from the one he started with. And whereas the *materia musica* of the polyphonic composers had been the traditional ecclesiastical modes, now it became the scales—one major, and one minor, which, since the introduction of equal temperament, were available at twelve different pitches.

So we see that, at the dawn of the Romantic movement, the composer was in a far stronger position than just that of a colleague of the writer or the painter, even though he was inspired by the same ideal as they. He had something his colleagues had not, namely a totally new technical apparatus ready to hand. He was filled with all the excitement and freshness of a new discovery, which appeared to him as patently and logically the way forward in musical composition. And in the event, the new harmonic style was to prove an immensely rich and exciting store-house of inspiration for over a century. The first-fruits of success, as it were, are the works of the first Viennese school, Haydn and Mozart, which are separated from Rameau's treatise by some fifty years.

Little wonder then that the Romantics looked to music as their most natural, and fullest form of artistic expression. The poet and critic Baudelaire saw an indissoluble link between words and music. Goethe, Hoffman, Schopenhauer even use words in a musical sense; music was so closely linked with literature that it was looked on as a language itself, with grammar and syntax just like any other language, and with the harmonic relationships of notes corresponding to the meaning of words. The music of Schumann, Berlioz or Liszt is such a compound of the literary and the musical that it is almost impossible to say where the one begins and the other ends. With perfect naturalness and ease the Romantics invented new forms of composition which were an amalgamation of the two arts: *Symphonic Poem*, and *Song without words*. Moreover so close a correspondence was seen between music and visual art that keys were thought to represent colours, and tonality to represent perspective.

It has been aptly summed up by Cecil Gray: "Music is the Romantic art." He might have added *in its harmonic aspect*, as the one thing that singled out music during the Romantic period was the exploitation of harmony. Cecil Gray unfortunately ends his excellent *exposé* of Romanticism (in *Contemporary Music*) with a fantastic *non sequitur*, as illogical as it is sweeping: "It follows that the greatest music has been, is, and always will be romantic, in the widest and indeed only legitimate sense of the word."

It does not. What follows is that as the Romantics developed and exploited harmony to the extent they did, any future music written on a harmonic, chordal basis, is bound to sound romantically derived. But this logical *faux pas* hardly detracts from the excellence of the essay as a whole.

Diatonicism led perfectly naturally to chromaticism; they are simply opposite sides of the same coin. Once having established your rules, it is then only natural to see how far you can stretch them. The system appeared entirely right and logical, based as it was on irrefutable scientific facts; and the seed of these developments can be seen in Rameau's treatise. Moreover, whatever the contributory factors may have been, the ideas and ideals that characterised the Romantic period found their fullest and most natural expression in music. The Romantic composer not merely belonged to his society; he was central to it. His art grew and burgeoned during this time, and was the central source of inspiration from which other artists drew theirs.

(c) The third way in which we observe that composers in the past have "belonged" to their environment is an extension of the examples just given. It is when a society, in seeking to find a means of the corporate, artistic expression of its philosophy and aspirations, looks to music to help in providing it.

It is important to differentiate between a state, or society, which thus includes music among its assets, and looks to the composer as a positive force for good, and, on the other hand, a state which seeks to exercise control of its composers, and to curb the development of music in directions which it considers undesirable; this is clearly a negative trend.

An extreme case of such state tutelage is provided today by Soviet Russia, where a very watchful eye is kept on composers' works and style. Commissions and performances are controlled through the Union of Soviet Composers, which numbers some 1,400 members, and the penalty for the composer who infringes the requirements of the Communist Party, is denouncement. The most severe period followed a decree of 10th February, 1948, when many leading Soviet composers, including Shostakovich, Prokofiev, Miaskovsky and Popov, were accused of "formalistic distortion and anti-democratic tendencies". For the next ten years an iron curtain descended on Soviet music, though Stalin's death in 1953 brought a slight relaxation. Since 1958 a more liberal policy has been adopted, though the Soviet commandment to the composer appears to be still a negative one; positive suggestions are mainly limited to the encouragement of the use of folk-song material. It was unfortunate that the period of most rigid control coincided with the period of awakening in Europe after 1945. The result is that Soviet composers are in a position of officially enforced isolation, and the Russian tradition is receiving no injection of fresh ideas from outside.[1]

Yet in the traditions of the Classical and Romantic periods, no country pays greater attention than Soviet Russia to the education and training of musicians. The capital of each Republic has its Conservatoire, from which the most talented proceed to Moscow or Leningrad. There the course is of five years' duration, and of a thoroughness comparable only with Vienna. Certainly in England it is not found. Perhaps it is not surprising that many of the world's most brilliant executive performers are Russian; also that of the two most original contributions to musical theory in the twentieth century, one of them, Schenker's *Harmony* (1906), was the work of a Viennese; the other, Serge Taneiev's *Convertible counterpoint in the strict style* (1909), was the work of a Russian.[2]

But "belonging" is a positive, not a negative relationship. Naturally the composer would be expected to share a common integrity of purpose, and identify himself with the ideals of the spiritual leaders of a particular society; his creative impulse and the general *zeitgeist* would thus fuse and become one. He might be required to subordinate his personal whims to the wishes of the majority—a thing which musicians are usually loth to do; in many cases he might well remain anonymous; but his gain would be a deep and lasting sense of belonging.

Let us then consider four examples of this third category of "belonging", taken from the whole range of musical history. These are: Greek music, Gregorian plainsong, the Lutheran

---

[1] See *Soviet music since the second world war*, by Boris Schwarz (*Musical Quarterly*, January 1965).

[2] See *Composer* No. 17, October 1965.

Chorale, and jazz. Three of these are historically factual; one (Greek music) is frankly speculative, though based on a high degree of probability.

(i) *Greek music*. The cultural tradition of classical Athens in the fifth and fourth centuries before Christ was such that not merely music but all arts were placed automatically at the service of the city-state. Poetry, drama, sculpture, architecture were all united in one single purpose—to make the city of Athens an "education for all men". And so indeed it has proved ever since. Countless are the people to whom she has held up an ideal, right down to our day.

Our direct knowledge of Greek music is hampered by the fact that very few records remain; we can only conjecture what the actual sounds were like. But because we lack direct evidence is by no means sufficient reason for our ruling out the possibility of the existence of music in a developed art form. In fact the Greeks not only felt for music instinctively, they developed it practically. They worked out a tablature system of notation[1]; they had string, wind and percussion instruments; they understood scales; they discovered melody and rhythm (which, incidentally, are Greek words); they developed solo and choral singing, and poetry and music were for them indivisible. Their characteristic spirit of logical enquiry produced the inevitable theories about music, those of Pythagoras being the best known to us. But the strongest evidence of all is provided by the writings of Plato, who felt obliged to take music into account as a force to be reckoned with in his ideal republic. He would not have done this unless he felt that music had reached a mature stage of development, pregnant with possibilities for the future. The following quotation shows Plato's concern that music should form an integral part in the education of the "Guardians" of his ideal city:

' "Hence, Glaucon", I continued, "the decisive importance of education in poetry and music: rhythm and harmony sink deep into the recesses of the soul and take the strongest hold there, bringing that grace of body and mind which is only to be found in one who is brought up in the right way. Moreover,

---

[1] See Curt Sachs, *The Rise of music in the ancient world*.

a proper training in this kind makes a man quick to perceive any defect or ugliness in art or in nature. Such deformity will rightly disgust him. Approving all that is lovely, he will welcome it home with joy into his soul, and, nourished thereby, grow into a man of a noble spirit. All that is ugly and disgraceful he will rightly condemn and abhor while he is still too young to understand the reason; and when reason comes, he will greet her as a friend with whom his education has made him long familiar."

"I agree", he said; "that is the purpose of education in literature and music." [1]

This is not the place to enquire into the nature of Greek music. Our concern is the importance attached to music, and the composer, by Athenian society. For the Greeks, in particular the Athenians, a composer fulfilled an essential social and religious service. Music included poetry and dance, and was required as a matter of course whenever there was any public festival or celebration. The victor in the Olympic or Pythian games was rewarded with a choral ode; and the highest place afforded to music was in the dramatic performances which marked the climax of the religious festival of Dionysus. Song and dance were the basis of comedy as well as tragedy, and the Choruses were a subtle blend of poetry, dance and music, reflecting the mood of the play in antiphonal movement and choral singing. The composer had considerable scope for melodic ingenuity and rhythmical complexity in the Strophe and Antistrophe, the Mesodos and Epodos. As Lowes Dickinson says, "the nearest modern analogy to what the ancient drama must have been is to be found probably in the operas of Wagner, who indeed was strongly influenced by the tragedy of the Greeks." [2] So, we would add, are Stravinsky, Tippett and others today.

What we can say with absolute certainty is that it is entirely consistent with the known facts for us to suppose that the composer was most highly honoured in Greece, and that he had an integral place in Greek society.

(ii) *Gregorian plainchant*. The function and importance of the composer in pagan Greece was remarkably similar to his

[1] Plato: *Republic* III, 401, translated by F. M. Cornford.
[2] *The Greek view of life*, p. 240 (1st ed. 1896).

rôle in early Christian Italy. He was required to express and to unify the mood of the people; typified, in this case, by the Christian church.

The Romans had tended by nature to tolerate religious sects, provided that the security of the empire was not threatened. They were even prepared to accommodate Judaism. But Christianity was different. The first serious persecution under Nero in 64 A.D. was followed by intermittent, local persecution. By the year 300 the situation had changed considerably. The Roman empire was on the verge of political and financial collapse, while the Christian church had established a more stable organisation, and thought out its beliefs. It appeared to the emperor Domitian as not just a religious sect, but a state within a state. This, particularly when he was desperately trying to prevent the break-up of the empire, he could not tolerate, and he set about a deliberate campaign to eliminate Christianity. He and his colleague Galerius were nothing if not thorough, and the edict of the year 303 marks the beginning of the "Great Persecution". This lasted till the death of Galerius in 311, and the final liberation was marked by the accession of Constantine, who became the first Christian emperor in 312, and officially put an end to all persecution by the Edict of Milan in 313.

We can well imagine the deep-felt emotions, the surge of popular feeling, that such a deliverance sparked off. The dark years of cruelty and butchery were now a thing of the past; all the energy and activity which had hitherto been repressed could now be directed openly towards the unconcealed glorification of God on this earth through the church.

It was certain that this spirit of the times should seek artistic, and particularly musical, expression. The first *Schola Cantorum*, or song-school, was founded in Rome by Pope Silvester (314–336), and the long process began of collecting together and unifying the diverse musical traditions that existed. The chief elements came from Greek, Hebrew, Latin and other Mediterranean cultures, and the climax was reached under Pope Gregory (590–604), in the complex system that bears his name.

The Gregorian repertoire of Introits, Tracts, Responsories, Graduals, Offertories, Alleluias, was a truly immense musical achievement, the work of countless musicians over many centuries, notably Ambrose (333–397), Bishop of Milan, and Pope Damasus I (366–384). Nor did this cumulative process cease with Pope Gregory; indeed the earliest Roman chants of which manuscript sources are extant date from 50–100 years after his death. What we know today as "Gregorian chant" is a later (8th/9th century) synthesis, the final stage of an evolutionary process of which the formative beginnings are obscure.[1] Every part of the Mass, every Sunday of the year, was taken into account; the purpose was to achieve a unified, homogeneous and logical design for the music of the universal church. That this purpose was fulfilled, and that the principles were sound, may be judged by the fact that Gregorian plainchant remained in general currency at least until the development of polyphony, some 800 years later.

It may perhaps be objected that the Gregorian system was inimical to change and experiment; that once having formulated a system the church authorities were reluctant to admit any variation of it. This is, broadly speaking, true. It is the nature of authorities to be authoritarian; nevertheless it is also true that the Church, personified by Pope Gregory, gave music first place as the greatest unifying and expressive force in Christian worship. The composer thus not merely "belonged"; he was essential. We may note also that Plato's forebodings turned out to be entirely correct, when he expressed the view that music more than any other art has the power, for better or for worse, to move men's souls.

(iii) *The Lutheran Chorale*. We today are reluctant to think much less to speak, of contemporary music in such terms as the corporate expression of an ideal, or of the spirit of our period; some might even add, with a touch of irony, that commercial jazz or a "pop group" give a much truer and more colourful reflection of all that is *ersatz* and phoney in our culture, than a symphony concert or the music in a church service give of what is not. But for all such moments of pessimism, which come to the best of us, when we doubt not merely the relevance of music in our scheme of things today, but also whether it can ever again have more than peripheral entertainment value, it is a certain and most salutary remedy to consider the Reformation period in Europe, and in par-

[1] See Willi Apel *Gregorian Chant*, pp. 74–83.

ticular its driving force in Germany, Martin Luther. Under his inspiration, and during the ensuing centuries, music, in the form of the Chorale, became not only the centre of Protestant worship; it was the very expression of the German soul.

Martin Luther fought passionately as a reformer on two fronts simultaneously; on the one hand against the humanism of the Renaissance, its concentration on purely human effort in Science, Literature and the arts, its rejection of spiritual values; on the other hand against the excesses of the mediaeval Roman church. On both these fronts he stood for the ordinary folk; he wanted their religious worship to be both genuinely spiritual and popularly based. To this end he allowed services, and particularly hymns, to be in their native language; and he gave them tunes, simple and direct, which he taught them to sing.

Like all churchmen for a very long time, he valued music extremely highly, and the Chorale was the means that he employed in his struggle. The first collection of his Chorales was published in 1524. Their origin lay in melodies from the Roman Church, as well as in secular folk tunes; some of them were original. It is a mistake to attribute to Luther a higher level of musical attainment than in fact he reached. The Chorale was a slow growth, and could not be weaned quickly from the polyphonic tradition. Services continued to be written in Latin. But the Lutheran system (like the Gregorian system 1000 years earlier) made use of existing musical traditions, and created that atmosphere in which the composer could work. It gave him both place and purpose, and made possible that musical tradition which was to reach its culmination two centuries later in the work of Bach.

(iv) *Jazz*. Over some three centuries, until the abolition of slavery in the mid-nineteenth century, more than ten million Negroes had been shipped across the Atlantic from Africa; roughly the population of Great Britain as it was in 1800. Sold into bondage, and denied every freedom, they nevertheless retained the characteristics of their race, and did not entirely lose the memory of what they had left behind. Even after their emancipation, following the end of the American civil war in 1865, their lot continued to be a wandering loneliness, a social isolation. So music was for them a much-needed folk art, a solace in adversity, a search for identity in a strange land. Simple, untutored and unsophisticated it certainly was; yet a rich harvest was soon reaped in the Spiritual, and later the Blues. Ragtime and jazz were the instrumental developments of these earlier vocal styles, and from about 1915 onwards the form and style of jazz began to be established, its potential realised. The advance of jazz to its present position of influence in American, and hence in world music, is one of the most remarkable stories of our age. Rarely has there been a more striking instance of what Horace meant when he wrote:

> *Graecia capta ferum victorem cepit et artes*
> *Intulit agresti Latio.*

'Captive Greece took captive her fierce conqueror, and brought her arts into rustic Latium.'

We are not concerned so much with the later developments of jazz, which continue up to the present, as with the nature of the original phenomenon, and its meaning for those among whom it first appeared. Its nature was folk art,[1] and the names we associate with it today are performer/composers— Louis Armstrong, Duke Ellington, Charlie Parker, Thelonius Monk, Ornette Coleman—who use familiar material to express common sentiments; its meaning lay in the bond that united the listener with the performer. They shared the same situation and the same spiritual yearning.

A certain well-known visitor to Florida in 1884 could not help being most forcibly impressed by the marked characteristics of the Negro. He records their

> "longing melancholy, intense love for nature, childlike humour, and innate delight in dancing and singing."[2]

One could also mention a fervour and intensity, an entirely unselfconscious identification with the performance of music. Their strong religious tendency was only in small measure due to the influence of missionaries; much more was it due to their situation, that of a captive people in a strange land.

---

[1] Finkelstein *Composer and Nation*, p. 307.
[2] Peter Warlock *Delius*, p. 113.

It was remarkably similar to the Israelites. Moreover is not the Bible itself an account of suffering in this world, and an expectation of better things in the next? What was more natural than that the biblical characters should appear as more than merely historical figures?

Thus the Spiritual contained an emotional element which all could understand. It far outweighed the intellectual element; and the style can best be described as free polyphony, without any influence of musical 'theory'. One singer would give out a line of melody, which the rest then picked up; the harmony, the words, the order in which the parts entered, were improvised. The Negro's instinctive sense of rhythm ensured that the timing was not lost, and that there was no discordant element; and the extension of this technique to instrumental music led to jazz. It is only in the harmony that we can detect the influence of the missionaries; certain suave and glutinous progressions are used which we recognise as originating in the 19th century hymn book.

The secular equivalent of the Spiritual were the Blues. Of all jazz forms this is the most characteristic, while at the same time the most difficult to define; though many have tried. It is perhaps strange that all vindictiveness and hatred of the white man are entirely absent from the Blues. Instead there is a profound sorrow, a nostalgia, tempered with a satirical wit and humour.[1] The Blues *motif* was 12 bars; three statements, each contained within four bars. The singer would start, followed by an answering *obbligato* on the accompanying instrument, to complete four bars. The bass would provide the basic rhythm, and the "blues chords", while the melody would either lag behind or anticipate the beat. Numerous slurs, and the use of the interval of the third and seventh which were poised precariously between the major and the minor, characterised the harmony.

It is one thing to describe certain outward features of the Blues; it is quite another to describe its nature. It has proved an inexhaustible vein from which later composers have drawn. W. C. Handy, who first wrote Blues in 1909, "Jelly Roll" Morton, Alberta Hunter, the legendary Bessie Smith, and innumerable others, could hypnotise an audience with their

[1] See the account of the Cakewalk in Finkelstein *Op. cit.*, p. 304.

singing of the Blues. The following first-hand accounts may show something of the emotional content:[1]

T-Bone Walker: The blues? Man, I didn't start playing the blues ever. That was in me before I was born, and I've been playing and living the blues ever since. That's the way you've gotta play them. You've got to live the blues . . . Blues is all in the way you feel it . . .

Alberta Hunter: The blues? Why the blues are a part of me. To me the blues are—well, almost religious. They're like a chant. The blues are like spirituals, almost sacred . . . As for musicians who could play the blues? Well, the ones that didn't know music could play the best blues. I know that I don't want no musicians who know all about music playin' for me . . .

W. C. Handy: The blues is a thing deeper than what you'd call a mood today. Like the Spirituals, it began with the Negro, it involves our history, where we came from, and what we experienced . . . The blues came from nothingness, from want, from desire. And when a man sang or played the blues, a small part of the want was satisfied from the music.

Negro music has consistently been imitated and exploited by white men, at least since the Minstrel Shows of the early nineteenth century. And white musicians were quick to learn the style of jazz. The first to acquire the jazz idiom successfully was "Bix" Beiderbecke. But whites could not play in the same bands as Negroes, and the first white band, the Original Dixieland Jazz Band, appeared in Chicago in 1914. Jazz was commercially profitable, and has now become so much a part of American music, and shared equally by Negroes and whites, that its origin may seem unimportant. Yet through all the development of jazz up to the present—its gradual absorption into industrial America, its splintering into Traditional, Classical and Modern—it is the Negro performer/composer who has consistently maintained the artistic initiative. Jazz remains his creation, which the white musician has copied, plagiarised and exploited, but rarely originated, and certainly never surpassed. As a living example of the expression through music of a corporate philosophy, the story of jazz has no parallel.[2]

[1] *The story of jazz*, ed. Shapiro and Hentoff, p. 243/8.
[2] See Wilfred Mellers, *Music in a new found land*, p. 262 foll.

2

New Orleans was a cultured city, and had been famous for its French opera since the end of the eighteenth century. It was also a segregated city, and on the other side of Canal Street, in the famous Creole "red-light" district of Storyville, music of a very different sort was played. Every brothel, sporting house and clip joint provided music, in addition to other forms of diversion; and as a brisk business was carried on round the clock, the musicians were in continuous demand. A pianist, "treating" a dance-tune or operatic aria, would play against a background of drink, gambling, prostitution, and dope-peddling; also occasionally of violence and sudden death, until "the district" was closed in 1917. Thus originated the jazz style, with its characteristic loudness, and accentual rhythm. After all, it is no use playing too quietly or too timidly if you wish to make yourself heard through the din of a public bar.

But it was the band which was so decisive a factor in the birth of Ragtime and Jazz; and frequent opportunities for band music were provided in this crowded, brash, fantastic city by house-parties, banquets, balls, country hay-rides, picnics, marriages, funerals. "Gay New Orleans, the city of pleasure. For the least significant occasion there would be some music."[1] Even at a funeral this spirit of gaiety was irrepressible. On the way, there the music would be suitably solemn and lugubrious; on the way back, the band would break out into something more characteristic, and a lot less inhibited.[2]

Everywhere there was music; inside the dance halls and cabarets, as well as outside on the sidewalks, everyone played; the Mississipi river-boats were no exception. One musician recalls the feeling of misery he experienced as a schoolboy when he sat in a classroom and heard the band go past outside, but could not watch the parade.

The Ragtime band had six players—Clarinet, Trombone, Cornet or Trumpet, Guitar or Banjo, Drums, Bass. There was no shortage of instruments; the junk stores were full of them, left over from the civil war. The bands would play marches by Sousa, dating from those days; or they would play dances.

---

[1] Shapiro and Hentoff, *Op. cit.*, p. 39.

[2] "Jelly Roll" Morton's description of funeral music is quoted by Mellers *Op cit.*, p. 283.

More often than not, being unable to read the music, they would improvise. From these bands grew jazz, and the term was first used by "Red" Brown's Ragtime Band in Chicago, 1916.

So the jazz musician had a position of central importance in the Negro community; in a sense he was their spokesman. But there is another factor for us to consider, since jazz is a twentieth century phenomenon of the greatest significance; that is the influence that it has exerted over composers of widely differing creeds. That this Negro folk art should contain within itself the seed of such potential growth is a very remarkable fact. Jazz has a creativity, a dynamism all its own. The freedom of the jazz performer is the counterpart to that very lack of freedom that has been the Negro's political and social fate; hence derives the unique vitality of jazz.

Many have been the copies and the adaptations of Ragtime or the Blues. The whole range of American popular music, (very different from commercial 'pop' music), has been coloured by them to some extent, ranging from the artificial, if homely, crooning of Bing Crosby or Frank Sinatra, to the Broadway musical and folk-opera. Jerome Kern's *Showboat*, Gershwin's *Porgy and Bess*, Bernstein's *West Side Story* and Copland's *The Tender Land* are notable examples of this development.

Among symphonic composers, Dvorak introduced the Spiritual "Swing low sweet chariot" into his *New World* symphony,[1] while Debussy's *Children's Corner Suite* for piano contains a Golliwog's Cakewalk. Delius, during his visit to Jacksonville in Florida, was particularly impressed by the work-songs and Spirituals, and his choral work "Appalachia" is built round the song "Oh Honey, I am going down the river in the morning"—the river being the symbol of separation of a slave from his family. Michael Tippett, in *A child of our time*, uses Spirituals in much the same way as Bach used Chorales in his Passions; and Tippett has captured exactly the right mood, for example, in "Steal away", by the use of a solo voice followed by the rest of the chorus;

[1] See John Clapham *Antonin Dvorak—musician and craftsman*, pp. 86 foll.

also by the harmony, which is basically diatonic, though blurred and clouded over.

Stravinsky's *Ragtime* and Milhaud's Ballet Nègre *La Création du monde*, head a long list of works directly jazz-inspired. The instruments used by Stravinsky in *Histoire du Soldat*[1] very nearly constitute a Ragtime Band. American composers have been particularly influenced, including Roy Harris, Virgil Thomson, and Aaron Copland. It is recorded[2] that Milhaud "felt that playing jazz was an expression of American culture. He felt a musician born in America should be influenced by jazz."

* * *

These diverse ways in which composers of the past can be said to have "belonged" integrally to their environment are highly relevant and instructive to us in our present-day situation, when the composer is more isolated. Each example illustrates an identification of the composers' creative impulse with the spiritual dynamic of his age, to produce an active musical culture and tradition.

There are certain common factors; for instance, in each case the corporate will of a society was directed towards some spiritual or intellectual aspiration; the Greeks sought to realise the ideal of the good and the beautiful in their public festivals; Pope Gregory and the Roman Church sought to unify the worship of Christendom; the Lutherans sought to involve the ordinary people more directly in their church; the American negroes sought an identity and a solace in adverse circumstances. Music, it would seem, was welcomed and used because of its power to unify, to aspire, to excite, to bring solace. It represented a generally, if not universally, felt mood; the composer, because he was accepted, spoke for, and to, his contemporaries, and his work was seen as part of a wide, general pattern of living.

Conversely, the music of any of the traditions or cultures mentioned had to be the work of composers who were born into that tradition, and were part of it. In other words the composer was automatically a 'contemporary' composer. This was not necessarily because of any *advance* in musical

[1] See page 45.
[2] Shapiro and Hentoff *Op. Cit.*, p. 376.

technique—we must be careful in the use of such words—but simply because, in order to express fully the mood of an age, a composer had to belong to it; also because the requirements and ideals of one period were not necessarily shared by another. For instance the characteristic style of Gregorian chant, and the spirit that informed it, were different from the style and spirit of the Protestant Chorale. They sought to express different ideals. Again the polyphonic technique, which was so excellent a thing to express the aspirations of the mediaeval church, was not at all suitable for the needs of composers in the Romantic period, when the mood and temper of the times was so utterly different.

Two further principles may be deduced from these historical examples. The first is that an endemic musical tradition takes a considerable period of time to grow and flourish; several centuries in the examples mentioned, though in the case of Greek music we ought to add 'probably'. And though we talk about *Gregorian chant* or the *Protestant Chorale*, we must always remember that these are really composite terms to express the result of a continuous process involving numerous composers over a long period. The second principle we can deduce is that underlying each of these traditions is the fact that not only was the composer a contemporary, but he occupied an integral part in his society. His work was anything but a decoration, or an accessory. As we have seen, since the development of a musical tradition requires a continuous effort and a sustained sense of purpose, it follows that the working out of technical problems is only possible if the composer is given a place at the very centre. You cannot isolate him if you wish to establish a musical culture; and you cannot establish a musical culture if you look on music merely as an entertainment or a diversion.

Music is, after all, a thing of the spirit. Its means may be clumsy, its technique constantly changing and difficult to define. But the basic origin of a musical culture, if it endemically belongs to a society, is some spiritual aspiration on the part of the leaders of that society. Certainly a composer may speak with an individual voice and in his own style. The fact that he occupies an important position in the life of his society does not necessarily spell uniformity. Rather the reverse, since by a strange paradox it is only when he is set a limitation, a goal, that a composer's creative genius can fully find itself.

It is, at first sight, strange that, in spite of the sheer quantity of music played today, the contemporary composer does not belong to his society. Yet he enjoys neither patronage nor tradition. The very term *contemporary music*[1] serves to highlight the fact that there exists a *corpus* of music that is not contemporary. This has been true in previous periods as well, but it is even more true today. There is available to us a truly immense quantity of music of the past; Romantic, Classical, Polyphonic, Mediaeval. Indeed so much music has already been written, and is waiting for performance, and so many past composers and historical problems await investigation by the musicologist, that one may well question the need for any new music at all. Why not abolish the contemporary composer, and let us simply enjoy what we have already? And before dismissing as incredible and ridiculous the possibility that any age should be so short-sighted and philistine as to live off its past capital in this way, we should recall how quite recently Nazi Germany attempted to do just that, and what grim and tragic consequences resulted. The work of contemporary German composers, such as Fortner, Hartmann, Henze, Stockhausen, can only be fully assessed against the background of chaos and emptiness in their country following 1945. The broken thread had to be repaired; the former splendour of German music had to be lifted up from the ruin of the war.

The situation today as we have said is a criss-cross of many different styles, categories and influences; and it is important that we should establish just which ones are to consider, and which not. One thing is certain; never before has there been such a flood of music pouring down on us wherever we turn, cascades of sound of every sort and description. One might indeed say that "the name of it is called Babel". There is also an equal variety of idioms, and for this reason it is impossible to generalise about contemporary music under one all-inclusive heading.

But we can establish the sort of background against which

[1] The term may be said to have come into official use in 1922, with the foundation of the International Society for Contemporary Music (I.S.C.M.).

to consider the contemporary composer. If we have suggested that he does not belong to his society in quite the same way as his forbears did, we next need to ask just what are the circumstances that prevail today, and which are peculiar to our age. If the contemporary composer has no patronage and no tradition, what has he to take their place? If we accept that

"the basic origin of a musical culture ... is some spiritual aspiration on the part of the leaders of a society" and if we also accept that no such aspiration is generally felt today, where then do we find the origin of our contemporary musical culture?

Where a corporate ideal has been lacking, composers have substituted an individual one. The music of the contemporary composer is essentially a personal testament. Some of his contemporaries may understand and appreciate his work—or they may not. But his acceptance by the generality of his society is not normally the pattern today. Instead of directing his attention outwards towards the ultimate purpose of his work, its contribution to a society's culture, its significance for the listener, the composer tends instead to direct his attention inwards towards himself, the means he employs, his instrumentation, his technique; his music as a result becomes inhibited, experimental, neurotic. Instead of drawing his inspiration from an active tradition, he attaches himself to this or that group; his music becomes labelled.

The listener's approach to contemporary music is materially affected by this, his judgement modified accordingly. Whereas the music of the polyphonic or Romantic period is assessed by the way in which a particular composer makes use of an accepted idiom and a handed-down technique, a piece of contemporary music will be assessed by the way in which the composer invents and develops his own. If he is not able to make use of an accepted idiom to express the generally felt aspirations of his society, we can only ask whether, and to what extent, he has succeeded in inventing his own idiom to project a personal *credo*. Moreover, it is extremely unlikely that a work written in such circumstances will have a wide, let alone a universal appeal. If it does so this will probably be due to some other extra-musical considerations.

The gradual lowering of an active public response to contemporary music is clearly related to this increasingly inward-looking tendency of the contemporary composer. The more he concerns himself with the minutiae of his own technique, the less he interests his audience. But it is also the direct result of one of the most characteristic products of our age, the motion picture. Hollywood, and the cinema generally, with its celluloid world of make-believe, and its publicity-born film stars, providentially endowed with fame, glamour and other desirable attributes, has had a pervasive influence over most artistic matters. People are taught to look for the Big Name; and once established, this habit is not confined to films. Moreover background music, by its very definition, hardly suggests an active response on the part of the audience. One is not required to listen to film music; it is enough if one is merely aware of it.

And so the background to twentieth century music is basically one of uncertainty between the composer and the listener; an uncertainty affecting the listener's response to new developments. But it will soon become apparent that the story of contemporary music is one of high ideals, not, as in previous periods, on the part of a society as a whole, but on the part of a handful of composers, whose personal endeavours have been met, generally speaking, with a gradual lessening of public response. These composers therefore must be our next consideration.

THESIS

CHAPTER TWO

THE FORERUNNERS

(i) *Ferruccio Busoni* (1866-1924)

The problems facing the twentieth century composer are summed up in the work of Ferruccio Busoni. His work rests on that questioning of past traditions, which are no longer accepted by him automatically. In this he was chronologically first. His musicianship was many-sided; he was a composer, a pianist, an editor, a teacher, and a man of letters. In all these fields his achievement was both distinguished and significant. The questions that he raised are the sort of questions every composer today must also raise; and we shall see that the pattern of his career is to be often repeated in that of subsequent musicians. He was personally acquainted with many of the important composers of the early 1900's, such as Mahler, Delius, Schoenberg, Sibelius; he was misunderstood and abused by the press, particularly in Germany; he was a cosmopolitan, continually searching, striving. His life and career epitomise the only true solution to the problems facing the twentieth century composer, namely the breaking down of music to its constituent parts; he therefore represents an inspiring example to us, as well as a starting-point for study.

He was an entirely dedicated artist, utterly opposed to amateurism in all its forms. He pursued his aims even at the cost of denying himself the success and worldly esteem to which his prodigious talents entitled him. He never envied the apparently greater success of some of his contemporaries; on the contrary, he considered, entirely correctly, that they had obtained their comfortable position only by renouncing any more lasting claims. His ideals earned him intense hostility and prejudice in his lifetime; only after his death did he find an advocate outside his own immediate circle.

As a composer, he soon acquired a fluent mastery of conventional technique, and his compositions up to the Piano Concerto (1904) bear the influence of Brahms, Wagner, Liszt.

Yet he was very conscious of the deadening inertia of German traditionalism, and the soporific effect exercised over later composers by Wagnerian opera. While admiring certain of Wagner's acoustical discoveries, and felicities of scoring, he was averse to the heroic style. Wagner represented an end, not a beginning; nothing further could be done in that direction. Busoni however was searching for a new beginning. New problems had to be faced, and one could not tread the established nineteenth century path. He was dissatisfied with the work of Brahms precisely because of the latter's "comfortableness", his apparent failure to face new problems (Bequemlichkeit).[1]

So Busoni's music, and his thoughts on music, are the starting point for our study of the twentieth century. He understood and thought about the musical situation on a deep and profound level. He would ponder about harmony, form, orchestration, opera, and his ideas would find expression in his own composition, in an article, in a letter. He was thoroughly conversant with the broad stream of the European musical tradition, while at the same time accepting unequivocally the artistic necessity of seeking new paths of expression. Though possessed of an immense musical heritage, he refused to live off it parasitically. He placed his gifts at the service of his contemporaries, many of whom received first performances through him. His series of orchestral concerts in Berlin (1902–1909) are a model of artistic adventure coupled with integrity. He even went so far as to consider that any knowledge he might have was only useful if it could be given back to others in good measure. In short, he was a born teacher, and among his most distinguished pupils were the composers Kurt Weill and Edgard Varèse, the pianist Egon Petri.

As a performer Busoni was severely analytical, and the experience he thus gained of the use of various forms, he put to use in his own compositions. He attempted to infuse into his work all that was assimilable of the composers he admired most and loved best.[2] These were Bach, Mozart, Beethoven,

---

[1] This view was not shared by others; for example, Schoenberg described Brahms as "progressive" (See *Style and Idea*).

[2] For the idea that the artist needs to assimilate the tradition of the past, cf. T. S. Eliot's essay *Tradition and the individual Talent* (1919).

Liszt, Verdi; also Saint-Saens, Berlioz, Bizet, Bellini, Meyerbeer, Chopin, Franck, and a score of others. Tradition for him was something to be respected, not feared; but one should learn positive lessons from it, not slavishly follow it. It is by no means to be confused with traditionalism, with which he had nothing but impatience.

What singled out Busoni from other pianists of his time, and made his playing so distinctive and memorable, was not merely his knowledge and technique, but also his attitude towards the printed score. Certainly he was both virtuoso and scholar, yet he viewed the actual notes of a composition with anything but antiquarian reverence or musicological purism. What interested him was the music itself, as it pre-existed in the composer's imagination, and of which the printed notes were a very imperfect representation. Therefore, he felt, what music loses through notation should be restored by the interpreter. He would see through the score, as it were, and aim to reproduce in his playing the pristine freshness of the musical idea as the composer heard it before he wrote it, entirely untouched and unspoilt by traditions, whether good or bad. Clearly, to do this successfully your mind must be on the same plane as the composer's; you must in effect compose the work while you play it. Busoni's success and impact as a pianist confirms that this is precisely what he did.[1] Intense feeling marked all his playing. For him, intellectual analysis, which can enable one to pick out ideas and progressions in a composition that may or may not have been consciously put there by the composer, was as nothing compared with the feeling and emotion engendered by a work. Analysis may indeed tell you something about the composition; but what is that compared with what the composition itself can tell you about the spiritual inspiration of the composer? True feeling was what mattered to Busoni; true feeling coupled with knowledge and imagination. Technique was invariably his servant, not his master.

The same principles guided him in composition as in his other activities. His work reflects the contradictions that are inherent in European music itself since 1900, as well as the Italian/German dichotomy in his own make-up. He could not

[1] See the description by the pianist Claudio Arrau in the Journal of the British Institute of Recorded Sound, vol. 1 No. 8 (Autumn 1962).

blindly take over already-formulated laws; equally he could not simply break the rules for the sake of it. A style is just as derivative if it slavishly copies a system as if it consciously and deliberately disobeys it; neither approach can masquerade as true creativity. Moreover the profound experience of music which he obtained as a pianist made it impossible for him to compose spontaneously. He was even inhibited from using the word *Sonata*, since he felt that his works in this category hardly bore comparison with those of Beethoven. Indeed, his very knowledge prevented the wide acceptance of his compositions. The complexities and the elliptical allusions, both musical and literary, of the operas *Die Brautwahl* and *Arlecchino* overtaxed his audience, who did not share his cultural background and erudition. By the time of the *Berceuse* (1910) he had broken with the traditional conception of consonance and dissonance; he was not, however, consciously preoccupied with originality, and he tended to mistrust those who were. The true creator, he felt strives not so much for originality as for perfection. Therefore, it will be both salutary and stimulating for us to take note of some of the main tenets of his musical faith; for by doing so we shall see that he anticipated in a number of ways the trends of later composers, whose originality is purported to be their chief, if not their only, claim on our attention.

Harmony was for him the result of polyphonic movement, the interplay of melodic parts. A preoccupation with chromaticism had led some composers to lose sight of this historical fact, and to consider harmony as consisting mainly of chords, interesting or otherwise, which are imposed on the music as it were from outside. For Busoni, however, harmony was only logical if it arose out of the melodic movement; it could not precede the melodic movement, let alone dictate to it, as certain academic textbooks suggest. However strange a harmony may appear, as in the second *Sonatina* (1912), it will be perfectly logical if it is seen as the result of an extension of polyphonic movement.[1]

Arising directly out of this was his use of an orchestra of solo players, which is one of the most familiar characteristics of twentieth century music. So far from grouping the instruments together *en bloc*, and doubling where necessary, he

[1] See Ex. 1.

looks on orchestral sound as the weaving together of individual tonal strands. In short he looked on technique as entirely
subservient to the search for the expression of new ideas. He
attempted to widen his musical speech to the very utmost,

Andante tranquillo   Busoni
dolce, senza accenti   *Second Sonatina*

Note: Accidentals apply only to one note.

Ex. 1

to a universality that should adequately express whatever
presented itself to his imagination.

And many things did. His literary output was considerable,
and represents an attempt to find a rational and theoretical
anchor in a sea of experiment and uncertainty. He certainly
asked the right questions, though some would disagree with
his answers. His aesthetic may best be described as Platonic.
Freedom was his watchword, which is not the same thing as

licence; nor is freedom of form the same as formlessness.[1] He saw[2] all music as one, infinite and eternal. A composition existed before it was written, and continued to exist after its last note had died away. The composer simply attempts to capture an infinitesimally small particle of that vast range of music which exists in the world of eternity. Tonality, the difference between consonance and dissonance, and all the other arbitrary distinctions we draw between the notes of the scale, are only one diffracted ray from the sun of music, in the empyrean of the eternal harmony. Change and energy are what characterise life, and in this respect the composer copies nature.

Music sets in vibration our human moods—excitement, tranquillity; it neither represents nor describes their specific

Busoni

Background chords

Varied scale patterns referred to in *A New Aesthetic*
(cf. *Berceuse élégiaque*, bar 54 foll.)

Ex. 2

cause. Thus in an opera the music's concern is with the state of mind of the characters, not with a description of what is already being represented on the stage. That would be merely

[1] See *The Essence of Music*, p. 27.
[2] In *A New Aesthetic*.

'programme' music. There is in any case no need to duplicate the action. Music is concerned with the spiritual and the eternal, not with the actual and the ephemeral.

For this reason emotion and humanity are what count. The form a composition takes is of secondary importance to the spirit that gives it birth. Music was born free, and to win freedom is its destiny. Experiment therefore to escape from the arbitrary limitations of tonality and scales, bars, notation and the rest, is to be welcomed. But the experimental discovery of new effects, and new sounds,[1] is not to be confused with art. It is the means, not the end, and requires taste, emotion and artistic intent before it has any musical worth.

(ii) *Claude Debussy* (1862–1918)

Although Debussy's *Prélude à l'Après-midi d'un Faune* was heard in 1894, few would dispute that this work belongs in essence and significance to the twentieth rather than to the nineteenth century. The aesthetic that informed Debussy's style, both in that work and at least up to and including *Pelléas et Mélisande* (1902), was that of the French Symbolist movement in literature, rather than the Impressionist movement in painting. The Symbolist movement had been foreshadowed by Edgar Allen Poe, with whose writings Debussy was well acquainted, and was centred round the poet and philosopher Mallarmé. It had a widespread influence, literary, theatrical and musical, in many parts of Europe; in France itself we think of Rimbaud, Verlaine, and several others; in Germany, of Stefan George, Rilke; in Belgium, of Maeterlinck; in Great Britain, of Yeats.

The guiding principle of the Symbolists was that the imagination of the listener is captured by the use of suggestive verbal imagery, dream-like and evocative, which calls into being the sensitive, associative attributes of the unconscious mind. Words are to poetry what notes are to music; and they are made to aspire towards the condition of music by means of what Poe called a "suggestive indefiniteness". Symbolism was primarily a literary movement, though Mallarmé

---

[1] For Busoni's new scale divisions, see Ex. 2. He also experimented with the tripartite division of the tone, instead of the two semitones; but such theories remained unrealised in his compositions, and only became practical possibilities with the rise of electronic music (p. 116).

attempted, not entirely successfully, to extend it to the theatre, and Debussy extended it to his own compositions. His two works which may be called directly Symbolist are his settings of Mallarmé's *Prélude à l'Après-midi d'un Faune*, and his operatic treatment of Maeterlinck's *Pelléas et Mélisande*. Many other works, *La Mer* for instance, were Symbolist-inspired.

The Symbolists were less concerned with the nature of poetry, or art generally, than with the way in which it affects the listener. The associative force of words (or music) calls for a response in the listener that is not merely an automatic appreciation of a word- (or sound-) pattern, a passive reflex-action of the auditory sense, but is rather an acutely felt identification of self with the action or situation portrayed; what is more, it is all the stronger for being unconscious and imaginary. For who can doubt the elemental force of the fantasy-world, particularly if it is conjured up by an acute sensibility? This was the source of power which the Symbolists sought to harness to the artistic requirements of poetry and drama, and which Debussy sought to harness to music. It is moreover interesting to note that the theories and ideas of the Symbolists were the artistic equivalent and counterpart of the work of Freud, whose discoveries into psychoanalysis, and particularly into the working of the unconscious, and the significance of dreams, were taking place at precisely the same time.[1]

Symbolist verse has indeed all the attributes of music, as can readily be seen from the number of composers who have been drawn to it—Fauré, Delius, Schoenberg, and many others: evocative, dream-like imagery, the juxtaposition of contrasting ideas, the symmetry of a formal scheme, all these are musical attributes. Moreover the association of words corresponds most closely to the association of music. Water, for example, a favourite theme of Debussy, can be associated with tears, rain, death, the sea. And since the image may be literary, pictorial, dramatic or musical, it will be immediately apparent that the Symbolist aesthetic had a strong tendency to bring all the arts together into one. It has already been mentioned[2] that music itself has strong unifying tendencies.

[1] Freud's *Interpretation of dreams* appeared in 1895.
[2] p. 17.

It was Debussy's vision, as it had been Wagner's, to make use of this fact and to compose a work, that is to say an opera, which should combine drama, poetry, music and other arts, and in which none should predominate. He chose Maeterlinck's Symbolist play *Pelléas et Mélisande*, and the violent reception which greeted its first performance suggests not only that Debussy succeeded in his artistic purpose of portraying the world of shadows and twilight, of sensuous imagery and the reality of the unconscious, but also that his audience was not psychologically ready for such an experience.

As with most composers of his time, the ghost of Wagner hung heavy over Debussy, and exerted an influence even over such comparatively later works as *Le Martyre de Saint-Sebastien* (1911). Indeed Wagnerian ideals were very much in the air at this period, and it may even be said justifiably that in *Pelléas et Mélisande* Debussy succeeded in putting into practice Wagner's theory of a fusion of music and drama. Certainly Debussy was well acquainted with the bulk of Wagner's work, and was particularly attached to *Parsifal*. Nevertheless, the essential clue to Debussy's style, as indeed to that of most important composers of the twentieth century, is the extent to which he succeeded in establishing his individuality over the conflicting influences and tensions that were rife at this time, and in achieving a unity of idiom, when the prevailing tide of fashion was towards a breaking up of the accepted musical language, and its dichotomy into two opposing halves, the experimental on the one hand, the academic on the other. If he is to be of any lasting importance, a composer will be concerned to break free from academic traditionalism, to achieve the emancipation of harmony, and the extension of traditional tonality. Of Debussy's achievement in this direction there can be no question.

To what extent may we speak of his style in terms of Impressionism? He himself objected to the word. Derived as it is from the school of painting of Monet and Renoir, it might be thought suitable to describe those works of Debussy which contain a strong pictorial element. Yet the description is too loose to be of much assistance in our understanding of his music; moreover, it implies that Debussy sets out to portray a landscape or a seascape, and this is not exclusively so. It would be much more accurate to refer to his style also in terms of Symbolism.

The essential elements in his style are already clearly apparent in *Prélude à l'Après-midi d'un Faune*. He uses short melodic phrases, often of two bars, and avoids unrelieved length. This may be seen not only in the flute solo with which the work opens (Ex. 3), but also in the oboe passage at 4

Debussy
Prélude à L'après midi d'un Faune

Ex. 3

(Ex. 4). Another example of this characteristic is the famous tune which occurs in *La Mer* at 60 (Ex. 5); there are many others. The origin of *Prélude à l'Après-midi d'un Faune* lies in a dream-like world of fantasy, and this is perfectly matched by the ambiguous harmony that Debussy uses throughout. From the very opening notes of the first phrase, he suggests,

Ibid.

Ex. 4

in a single melodic line, many different tonal centres. They are implicit, not explicit; there is an absence of specific key, and the uncertainty of progression is admirably suggestive of

Debussy
La Mer

Ex. 5

the total freedom of the imaginary world, and of the total reality of the present moment, as something separate from the past or the future. This is further enhanced by Debussy's blurring of cadences. What appears, speaking conventionally, as a dissonance, is built up and sustained well beyond the point at which one would expect a cadential resolution.[1]

Of the influence of Debussy, there can be no doubt. That is to say that his aesthetic intentions found an echo in others, not that others copied his style. Many indeed criticised him; Busoni, for example, while approving the attempt to break down the traditional distinction between consonance and dissonance, and the use of new scales, thought the whole-tone scale, and the resulting chords that went with it, an unnecessary stylistic limitation. But many composers were influenced by the whole-tone scale, though they might use it in a very different way; Schoenberg for instance,[2] and Berg,[3] who

[1] It is interesting to note in passing that Busoni gave the first Berlin performance of *l'Après-midi* on 5th November, 1903, to the horror of the German press. The concert was part of the series already referred to (p. 32).

[2] E.g. Chamber Symphony, Op. 9, oboe phrase at ⟨106.⟩

[3] E.g. String Quartet, Op. 3, 1st movement, 1st violin, bar 7.

studied Debussy closely, and was much influenced by him, particularly in his early songs.

But it is in the work and thought of Stravinsky that Debussy's influence can be clearest seen—and hence his commanding position in the twentieth century. His later sonatas, in which he turns away from the literary and pictorial images of earlier works, and writes 'absolute' or 'pure' music, foreshadow Stravinsky's neoclassical works of the 1920s; and there are a number of references in Stravinsky's own writings to his contact with, and his debt to, the older composer. They shared a common patron, Diaghilev, and thus may be said to have faced common aesthetic problems; for Diaghilev's ballets drew together painting, dancing and music in much the same way as the Symbolists visualised a union of drama, poetry and music.[1]

Debussy and Stravinsky first met in 1910, after a performance of the latter's *Firebird*; and though their friendship later degenerated, Stravinsky was well aware of the far-reaching significance of Debussy's work. Each influenced the other to some extent. Stravinsky's influence can be discerned, as might be expected, in Debussy's ballet score *Jeux*; traces of Debussy can be heard in Stravinsky's *Le Rossignol*, and parts of *Le Sacre du Printemps*. Referring to the first of these, Stravinsky says:[2] "Why should I be following Debussy so closely, when the real originator of this operatic style was Mussorgsky?" He refers[3] to the first time he heard *l'Après-midi* as "among the major events of my early years." He attended the first performance of *Le Martyre de Saint-Sebastien*; he was bored by *Pelléas*; he conducted *Nuages* and *Fêtes* at a concert in Rome in 1932; he even wrote a cantata for Debussy, *Le Roi des Etoiles*, to words by a symbolist poet, Balmont; he also wrote the *Symphony of Wind Instruments* to his memory; the two composers played through *Le Sacre* together at the piano, both being highly accomplished pianists. In short, as Stravinsky aptly sums it up:[4] "The musicians of my generation and I myself owe the most to Debussy."

---

[1] Diaghilev commissioned Debussy's *Jeux* in 1912.

[2] *Memories and Commentaries*, p. 133 For the similarity of *Le Rossignol* to Debussy's *Nuages*, see Lambert *'Music Ho!'* p. 26.

[3] *Expositions and Developments*, p. 59.

[4] *Conversations with Igor Stravinsky*, p. 48.

CHAPTER THREE

COSMOPOLITAN COMPOSERS

(i) *Igor Stravinsky* (*b.* 1882)

From Debussy to Stravinsky is, as we have seen, but a short and logical step. Historically and aesthetically the one follows the other, however great the difference in style may be between the two. Indeed we may say that the whole course and pattern of twentieth century music is summed up and epitomised in the many-sided career of Igor Stravinsky. The complete cosmopolitan, as much at home in any European capital as he is in a Hollywood studio or University campus; as much concerned with the experimental and the *avant garde* as he is with the music of the universal Church; as much conversant with the primitive and the exotic in art as he is with the sophisticated or the traditional. Though his career appears to be divided, somewhat suspiciously, into mutually exclusive phases, this is in fact, as will be seen, a dangerous over-simplification, as certain characteristics of style appear in all phases of his work, and the basic principles of his creativity have remained remarkably constant throughout his life. We must at all costs avoid any tendency to minimise the scope and range of his output by placing his music into compart-ments, or pigeon-holes.

Over a period of sixty years his creativity has ranged from primitive exoticism to ascetic experiment; from the full-blooded orgy of *Le Sacre* to miniatures of only a few bars' duration; the composers who have attracted him, taken from the entire range of musical history, are too numerous to mention; formative influences in his style include jazz in the twenties, serialism in the late fifties. He has always been a most energetic and successful promoter of his own music, and has documented his own career with great thoroughness, both by means of books, and by recordings which he himself has directed.

In his formative period, which coincided with the all-important opening decade of this century, his aesthetic approach to the musical art was basically different from that of Busoni or Debussy in that he viewed the mainstream of Western European music from the point of view of an outsider, an onlooker. His traditional world was Glinka, Tchaikovsky, Rimsky Korsakov; not so much Haydn, Beethoven and Wagner.[1] As a result the Western tradition was for him an object of enquiry, of the closest interest, and he was led by a spirit of discovery not only into the world of the Classical, pre-Classical and Medieval composers, but also into the developments of his own day. The music of Wagner, Beethoven, Bach, Purcell, Monteverdi, Gabrieli, Ockeghem, Josquin, came to him with just as much directness and novelty as the most recent innovations of Boulez or Varèse. Each one of the composers named has influenced him either directly or indirectly. Indeed the motivating impulse of his neo-classical compositions was not so much a desire to escape from the literary and pictorial influence of the Romantics as a desire to synthesise the structural and formal principles of the past with the harmonic and rhythmic style that is so much his own.

His career is marked by one or two seminal works, which represent as it were artistic points of no return. *Le Sacre* is

Stravinsky
La Sacre du Printemps
Rhythmic patterns in "Spring rounds"

Ex. 6a

plainly one; *Oedipus Rex* and *Movements* two more, which mark his neo-classical and serial style respectively. Stravinsky himself, in his writings, keep referring back to *Le Sacre*; it

---

[1] cf. *Poetics of Music*, p. 58 for the relationship of *Mavra* to the tradition of Glinka and Dargominsky. Also Ch. 5 *passim*.

obviously meant a great deal to him; and the fact that this particular score has subsequently been used as a kind of glossary of twentieth century musical effects by many a hack

Stravinsky
Histoire du Soldat
The Soldier's March

Ex. 6b

composer should not cause us to lose sight of the true nature of its originality, which lies partly in the formal construction and cohesion of the various movements, partly in the substitution of motivic for thematic development, partly in the subtle exploitation of rhythmic patterns (Ex. 6a). Its direct successor was *Histoire du soldat*, composed in 1918, which, because of its very reduced scale of instrumentation, and the shortness of its movements, makes a more convenient study.

Histoire du soldat

It is scored for only seven players: clarinet, bassoon, cornet, trombone, violin, double-bass, and various percussion instruments. Each category thus has a treble and a bass instrument. As theatre music, the work is entirely original, and is intended to be narrated, danced and played. The music by itself also constitutes a Suite.

Histoire du soldat continues the exploitation of rhythm where *Le Sacre* left off. It may best be described as rhythmic counterpoint, that is to say the superimposition of one rhythm upon another, or of variable rhythmical patterns upon an invariable metrical pulse. Metre is the regular division of music into small pulse-units; rhythm is the grouping together of these units into patterns. By superimposing varied rhythmical patterns over a constant, basic metre, Stravinsky achieves a tension, and hence an expressive dimension, that has no precedent.

An example occurs at the very opening of the work, The Soldier's March; the metre is $\frac{2}{4}$, played *staccato* by the double bass. Over this there are rhythmical patterns of $\frac{3}{4}$, $\frac{2}{4}$ and $\frac{3}{8}$, played by the cornet and trombone (Ex. 6b). Of the two beats that constitute the *basso ostinato*, the first is naturally the stronger, since in $\frac{2}{4}$ time the first beat is strong, the second weak; it will be noticed how this strong pulse occurs on different unaccented beats of the following bars: the third crotchet beat of $\frac{3}{4}$ time, the second crotchet beat of $\frac{2}{4}$ time, the third quaver beat of $\frac{3}{8}$ time.

The composition abounds in subtle and complex applications of this principle. In the *Royal March*, between $\boxed{11}$ and $\boxed{12}$, the metrical $\frac{2}{4}$ is handed from the blatent trombone to the more mellow double-bass, while the rhythmical patterns of the melody pass from the cornet to the bassoon. It is obvious that the shorter the metrical division, and the smaller the pulse-unit, the greater will be the sense of urgency and restlessness. This is admirably shown in the *Devil's Dance*, in which the metre is as short as $\frac{2}{8}$.

In the *Little Concert*, at $\boxed{21}$, three simultaneous metres occur: $\frac{3}{8}$ in the violin, $\frac{4}{8}$ in the double-bass and bassoon, $\frac{3}{4}$ in the cornet. Against this are set changing rhythmical patterns ($\frac{5}{8}$, $\frac{3}{8}$, $\frac{4}{4}$) in the clarinet and trombone. Occasionally, Stravinsky introduces a succession of differing metres instead of one constant one. In the Tango, at $\boxed{4}$, there is an interchange of $\frac{2}{8}$ with $\frac{4}{16}$ (Ex. 7). In this example the antithesis and the tension between the rhythm and the metre is made more marked by the introduction of bitonality, or the simultaneous use of two tonal centres—in this case B flat minor in the violin, and A major in the clarinet.

In short, Stravinsky uses the instruments of his little orchestra with an independence of each other that recalls the vocal technique of the polyphonic period, particularly of Ockeghem. Counterpoint in each case is the blending of contrasting parts.

What matters in Stravinsky's music is his aesthetic attitude, his artistic intention; and in this respect a most important

ibid., Tango

Ex. 7

and instructive comparison may be made between him and
Busoni. Both aimed at the same thing; that is to say they both
approached the work of past composers in its pristine
originality and freshness, and disregarded the dead weight of
traditionalism that had since grown up around it and con-
cealed its true nature. Whether it was a work of Bach or
Pergolesi, Wagner or Gesualdo, what mattered to them was
the original spark of inspiration, the emotive reality that
compelled the composer to create it the way he did. Both
Busoni and Stravinsky saw the necessity for the twentieth
century composer to consider his art *de novo*, to rid himself
of the stultifying and oppressive conventions of academicism,
if music was to belong to the present.

The diatonic scale was by no means the only possible one;
however great the achievements of the past were, they must
not become ossified into an academic tradition. Stravinsky
has most aptly described what he means by academicism:[1]

'Academicism results when the reasons for the rule change
but not the rule . . . though by "rule" I mean something
nearer to "principle" '
What then is to be the creative artist's attitude to tradition?

[1] *Memories and Commentaries,* p. 113.

This question has been powerfully answered by Picasso, who was a close collaborator and friend of Stravinsky, and did several portraits of him:[1]

'Since Van Gogh we are all self-taught—one might almost say primitive-painters. Since our tradition has foundered in academicism, we must recreate a whole new language. Every painter of our day is free to recreate this language from A to Z. None can apply to him an *a priori* criterion since the fixed rules are no longer valid. From one point of view it is a liberation, but it is at the same time a terrible limitation. When an artist begins to express his personality, what he gains in liberty he loses in discipline, and it is extremely bad not to be able to attach oneself to a rule.'

Later, in the same vein, we read:

'Modern art is on the road to decline because there no longer exists any powerful academic art. A rule is needed, even if it is a bad one, because the power of art is affirmed by the rupture of taboos. Removing obstacles is not liberty, it is licence: it is a sickness which makes everything spineless, shapeless, meaningless, a cypher.'

If we substitute Debussy for Van Gogh, and the word *composer* for the word *painter*, what Picasso says is precisely and devastatingly true for music.

Up to this point Busoni and Stravinsky were entirely at one in their intention. The distinction between them lies in the fact that, whereas Busoni sprang directly from the European tradition, Stravinsky did not. What the former felt and understood instinctively, the latter had to discover for himself. Stravinsky refers to his 'discovery' of Sonata form, which could not have been said by a composer brought up on it. The process of his discovery is described by himself:—[2]

'The artist imposes a culture upon himself, and ends by imposing it upon others.'

If Busoni was to succeed in reaching outside and beyond his tradition, he could only achieve this by a conscious intellectual effort on his part; for Stravinsky there was no such

[1] *Life with Picasso*, Françoise Gilot, pp. 67, 187. See also T. S. Eliot's essay *Tradition and the individual artist*.
[2] *Poetics of Music*, p. 56.

necessity, as he was already outside it before he started. We would therefore expect him to be accused by conventional Europeans, critics and writers, more than composers, of lapses of academic taste; and to be informed that he shows no decent respect for the conventions, and that his "classicism", as shown in his neo-classical period, is spurious and only skin-deep.[1] He would probably be delighted to hear it, though it shows a total misunderstanding of his deep sense of creative purpose. What concerned Stravinsky, as it did Busoni, and indeed any composer of note today, was not so much the assimilation or the imitation of the outward form of a past, or present, style of composition, as the understanding of its inner reality and structure, its spirit and ethos. Has he not always shown a mistrust of the traditional Sonata form? His purpose was creative not academic, active not passive. Nothing, he felt, could be accepted on trust, secondhand, by the creative artist; he must work out his own methods and style for himself.

As we have already seen, the various phases of Stravinsky's work are marked by certain seminal, if not terminal, compositions. Underlying this diversity of output is the creative spirit of which we catch a glimpse in that most illuminating essay in self-analysis, *The Poetics of Music*. This consists of six lectures, the second and third of which, 'The phenomenon of Music' and 'The composition of Music' are of the greatest importance to our understanding not only of Stravinsky's own musical purpose, but also of the essence of our contemporary situation.

The composer's environment in the early twentieth century was a mixture of intellectual anarchy and individual freedom. The breakdown of restraints and conventions imposed on the artist the great psychological burden of almost limitless freedom to express himself in any way he chose, as well as the immensely complicated intellectual task of formulating afresh the basic principles of his art. His search into the nature of music caused Stravinsky first to rule out absolutely certain

---

[1] Criticism of this nature is very common, particularly among English writers; e.g. Constant Lambert *Music Ho!*, p. 74, Cecil Gray *Contemporary Music*, p. 149. Similarly, the critic Donald Mitchell, referring to the English Composer Peter Warlock, talks about the "dubious character of his Elizabethan dress", (*Daily Telegraph* 5.xi.63).

specious ideas. Music for him was not "imitation"; the synthesis of the arts which Debussy put forward represented an aesthetic cul-de-sac; Wagnerism, and the idea of music-drama, had done untold harm to the understanding of music, and 'endless melody' was a contradiction in terms, since the word 'melody' meant a cadenced phrase; melody was simply one of several irreducible elements of the *materia musica*; moreover as soon as song is subordinated to expressing the meaning of words, it loses contact with true music. True music is sovereign.

Allied to the absolute sovereignty of music is the fact of the composer's having to choose. At the very root of the creative process lies a "speculative volition", which makes an artist choose one course rather than another. Creating is finding; you cannot know what a composition will be until it is finished. All you can regulate is the direction in which you apply your creative volition, according to the priorities you set yourself in your task. Stravinsky accepted entirely the need for constraint, for only within a limitation does a composer find himself. There is nothing more damaging to his creativity than limitless, apparently infinite, freedom.

He was struck by the somewhat paradoxical dual nature of the musical phenomenon. First there was the obvious distinction between Classicism, with its disciplined restraint, and Romanticism, with its self-assertive freedom. Yet Classicism only attains artistic meaning and beauty when it is apparent where the restraint lies, and when it is quite clear how the composer has subordinated his creative will to a higher artistic necessity; otherwise the adoption of Classical procedures becomes mere formalism. In the same way, the freedom which we designate as Romantic is only artistically tolerable if it is defined, and confined, within formal limits. Absolute freedom is an illusion.

Music's duality also has more subtle aspects. A composition requires variety; it also requires unity. Consonance and dissonance are equally fundamental elements to the life of a composition, though the dividing line between these two forces has become more and more blurred in proportion as the diatonic system has become less and less accepted as universally valid. The means of music are on the one hand mechanical, mathematical (in one word, *Pythagorean*), and on the other hand emotive, associative (in one word, *Platonic*). Or, to use another illustration from the Greeks, a composition may contain elements of primitive and unrestrained instincts, which we call Dionysian, as well as ordered and controlled restraint, which we call Apollonian. This distinction is made by Nietzsche. Moreover Hindemith used to designate chords containing tritones as Dionysian; chords built on fourths or fifths as Apollonian. Tension and contrast are the very stuff of music.

Stravinsky was particularly fascinated with the time element in musical composition, as we have already seen from *Le Sacre* and *Histoire du Soldat*, and was influenced by the work of the Russian philosopher Pierre Souvtchinsky, whose theory on this matter is quoted in the *Poetics of Music*.[1] All music, after all, makes use of time, and sets up a relationship between its own metrical progress, and the never-ceasing temporality of the physical world, which is measured by the hands of a clock, and which Stravinsky calls 'ontological'.

No other human art or activity, not even poetry, is related to ontological time in quite the same way as music is, which is so much a 'chronologic' art. Now the movement of rhythmically organised musical time, or 'chronos', can be either regular or irregular. If it is regular, it will move parallel to ontological time; if it is irregular, it will move counter to it. The first case will produce a feeling of euphoria in the listener, which Stravinsky calls a 'dynamic calm'; the second case will produce the opposite effect, namely one of tension and contrasts. The second of these is more adaptable to the realisation of the composer's emotive impulses, since it corresponds to the effect of different psychological or emotional experiences. As everyone knows, actual, or ontological, time can seem to pass slowly or quickly depending on the state of mind one happens to be in at any given moment. If one is bored or unhappy, time seems to pass slowly; if one is experiencing pleasure, it seems to pass more quickly. In fact, of course, the movement of actual time is entirely constant and invariable; the variations in psychological time are perceptible only in relation to the sensation of real time. Let us allow Stravinsky himself to sum up the argument:[2]

[1] pp. 30–32.
[2] *Poetics of Music*, pp. 31–32.

'Music that is based on ontological time is generally dominated by the principle of similarity. The music that adheres to psychological time likes to proceed by contrast. To these two principles which dominate the creative process correspond the fundamental concepts of variety and unity.'

'For myself, I have always considered that in general it is more satisfactory to proceed by similarity rather than by contrast.'

'Contrast produces an immediate effect. Similarity satisfies us only in the long run. Contrast is an element of variety, but it divides our attention. Similarity is born of a striving for unity. . . . Variety surrounds me on every hand. So I need not fear that I shall be lacking in it, since I am constantly confronted by it. Contrast is everywhere. One has only to take note of it. Similarity is hidden; it must be sought out, and it is found only after the most exhaustive efforts.'

These words were written in 1939, and certainly in the aesthetic of neo-classicism, similarity and unity triumph over contrast and variety. But the same cannot be said about earlier works, such as *Le Sacre* and *Histoire du soldat*, to which we have already referred. His claim to prefer unity to variety must be treated in its context. In the same way, his celebrated dictum[1] that:

'Music is, by its very nature, essentially powerless to express anything at all. . . . Expression has never been an inherent property of music.'

must be considered only with reference to his use of the words of Russian poems. Like most general statements about music, its application is limited; a change of opinion is by no means unknown among artists, particularly over such a rich and varied career as Stravinsky has had.

An example of such a change may be seen in his verdict on Schoenberg's *Pierrot Lunaire*, of which he heard the first performance in Berlin in 1912. In 1935, when he wrote 'Chroniques de ma vie', he showed no sympathy for the aesthetic of the work, though he found the instrumentation

---

[1] *Chronicles of my life*, p. 91.

praiseworthy. In 1962, when he recorded his views in 'Expositions and developments', he looked back on his hearing the work as a "great event", and refers to his "enthusiasm". This is not so much an inconsistency as a change of creative perspective, largely brought about by his adoption in the late 1950's of the Schoenbergian 12-note technique; and, although *Pierrot Lunaire* is not a 12-note work, Stravinsky's opinion of Schoenberg obviously underwent a subtle modification, whether consciously or unconsciously, over the period of 50 years. It is the greatest mistake for us to refer at whatever point in his career to an artistic turnabout by Stravinsky. Certainly it might appear that his *Symphony in C*, written in 1940, with its thematic development, was a contradiction of those formal, constructional principles that he had used in previous works, for example the *Symphony of Psalms*; certainly it might appear that his adoption of the 12-note style was a reversal of everything he had previously stood for. But might it not be that, by thinking in this way, we are considering his music from too narrow and rigid a viewpoint? One can only refer to a contradiction or reversal of style if one looks on a composer's work as being in the nature of a once-for-all revelation, and his style as something sacrosanct, untouchable. Such is by no means the case, as even the most cursory study of any important composer will show; and today in particular we need to remember not only the blood and sweat involved in the actual work of composition, but also the uncertain status of the composer in our society—a factor which positively invites him to experiment, to change and to adapt. Moreover, a composer who ceases to develop has also ceased to create; there is never a point at which he can call out "eureka"; those who do are invariably of secondary importance. And was there ever a creative artist who was less inclined to remain stationary than Stravinsky?

His ardent curiosity about musical techniques of all periods makes it difficult, if not impossible, to list those composers of whose influence he is consciously aware, to say nothing of unconscious influences. They include Wagner, in the *Scherzo Fantastique* (1908); Bach, in the *Piano Sonata* (1924); Beethoven, in the *Symphony in C* (1940); also Mozart, in *The Rake's Progress*, and Machaut in the *Mass*; in more recent works Purcell, Monteverdi, Gesualdo, Josquin;[1] and so on.

Not only, as we have said, did he derive significance from earlier styles and techniques; he recast them and rethought them to suit his own purpose. To take just one example, the Piano Sonata does not use the conventional Sonata form; rather does Stravinsky use the principles of Sonata form to present a free association of contrasted ideas. 'Sonata' he took to mean something sounded, as opposed to 'Cantata', meaning something sung; the basic implications of the term were more to him than the tradition which had grown up round it. The same applied to his interpretation of the term 'Symphony'.

Seen in the perspective of his creative career, Stravinsky's adoption of the 12-note technique[2] was entirely logical. Contrapuntal and rhythmic complexity had always been an integral part of his technique, and he approached the problems of serialism with precisely the same creative curiosity as he brought to a Mass of Josquin or a Sonata of Beethoven. He was drawn more to Webern than to Schoenberg, and into the apparent rigidities of the Viennese system he infused his own characteristic melodic sense, and his own subtleties of rhythm. His first essays in the 12-note style were gradual and hesitant; the Septet and Cantata (1952), Canticum Sacrum (1956), Agon (1957). It is not until Threni (1955) that the style has become an inherent part of his musical thought, as distinct from a technical experiment. Threni, or the Lamentations of the prophet Jeremiah, is severe in style, yet surprisingly triadic, for all its serialism,[3] and represents Stravinsky's attempt to synthesise the 12-note technique with the principles of sixteenth century polyphony. It is immediately followed by an orchestral composition of much greater intricacy—Movements, for piano and orchestra. This work marks a turning point, not only in Stravinsky's output, but in the history of contemporary music; it is in this work that we see the principles of serialism put to the test, and followed through to their logical conclusion. For this reason, and

[1] Curiously, it would appear that the later the work of Stravinsky, the earlier the influence tends to be.
[2] See below, page 88 foll.
[3] Memories and Commentaries, p. 107.

because we shall have reason to refer to the work later, a close analysis of this composition will be relevant to our inquiry.

> *Movements* for piano and orchestra (1958/9)
> (references are to the Hawkes pocket score)

The orchestra used is as follows:—

2 Flutes	2 Trumpets
Oboe	2 Tenor Trombones
Cor Anglais	Bass Trombone
Clarinet	Harp
Bass Clarinet	Celesta
Bassoon	Strings (6, 6, 4, 5, 2)

Since it is a purely instrumental composition, its formal construction is in no way dictated by the requirements of a literary text, as is the case with most of Stravinsky's other serial works. Rather does the composer discover for himself the sort of constructional shape that is best suited to an instrumental work in the serial style.

The duration of the work is only ten minutes, and the five short movements are played without a break. They are related, as Stravinsky says,[1] "more by tempo than by contrasts of timbre, mood or character". The work is highly intricate, involving not only the contrapuntal manipulation of the note-row, and the exploitation of its melodic and harmonic possibilities, but also polyrhythmic combinations. In spite of the use of pedal-points, trills and held chords, there is not the faintest trace of any key. Every aspect of the combination has been to some extent determined by serial forms. The confining of the short orchestral interludes each to a defined timbre may also be considered as a "serial orientation", as Robert Craft says.

The series on which the work is based (Ex. 8) has pronounced melodic and sequential features. It consists essentially of four groups of three adjacent notes, each a semitone apart. It will be noticed that notes 7–9 of I are the same as notes 10–12 of O; and vice versa. Because of this characteristic, the interval of the minor second is prevalent throughout the work,

---

[1] *Memories and Commentaries*, pp. 106–7.

as well as its corollaries the minor ninth (which marks the opening of the first movement), and the minor sixteenth (with which the first movement ends). Numerous grace notes occur, mainly in the piano part.

Stravinsky
Movements for piano and orchestra

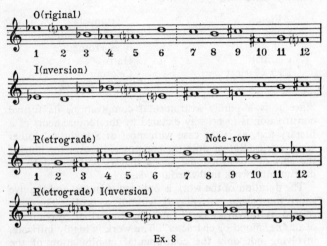

Ex. 8

Each of the four possible versions of the series (O, I, R, RI) has eleven possible transpositions—the equivalent of modulations in harmonic composition—and these can best be shown diagrammatically (see p. 57).

In the widest sense, of construction and rhythm, the five movements may be said to bear the same sort of relationship to each other as the movements of a classical symphony or sonata.

I. The first movement is quick, and contains just a suggestion of some of the main features of traditional Sonata form. The opening section is repeated, like an Exposition. This is followed by a slower passage, reminiscent in mood of a "second subject", though of course we must be careful not to press the analogy. Then at bar 42 the series appears again

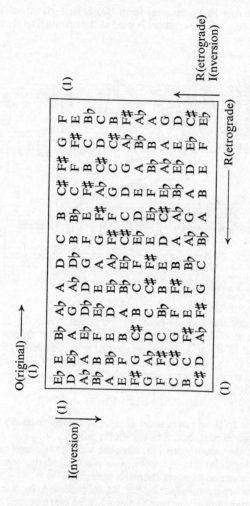

untransposed in its original form (O), to represent a Recapitulation.

The row in its original form (O) is first given out by the piano (Ex. 9). The trumpet is used at the opening, as elsewhere,

Stravinsky
Movements I, bars 1–6

Piano

C. Bass
(sounds 8va lower)

Ex. 9

to mark the starting-point of the series, while the first flute gives out the all-important interval of the minor ninth, coloured by a dramatic *crescendo*, which is really the hallmark of the work. At bar 3, the trumpet plays F to announce the Retrograde statement of the series, with the note order varied:—

$$1 \quad 7 \quad 12 \quad 11 \quad 10 \quad 9 \quad 4 \quad 3 \quad 2$$

The missing notes soon appear in bar 6, notes 5 and 6 in the piano part, and 8 in the violin part.

At the second-time bar, after the repeat, the piano has RI_7,[1] starting with the 7th note, and played quietly, *legato*, and with more even notes than the opening.

The recapitulation at bar 42 is preceded by a complex two-bar phrase, starting at bar 40. Bass clarinet and bassoon

[1] See p. 90.

give out I, the flute gives out RI_9, the violins in augmentation have the first six notes of R, while the cellos, supplying a sort of *basso continuo*, have a sustained part consisting of the first two notes of R (G and F). The piano then follows immediately at bar 42 with the recapitulation of O (Ex. 10a).

Stravinsky
Movements I, bars 40–42

Harp. *f*

Ex. 10a

The first movement ends as it began with a flute *crescendo* extended over a minor sixteenth.

The polyrhythmic combinations, such as occur in bar 40 and elsewhere, are meant to be heard vertically, not horizontally. There is a parallel to this to be seen in the second 3-part

Agnus Dei from Josquin's Mass *l'Homme armé* (Ex. 10b). In the short extract given, it will be noticed how the value of the notes in the Tenor is twice that of the notes in the Bass, while the notes of the Bass are one and a half times the value of the notes in the Cantus, since the Cantus part is in $\frac{3}{2}$ time,

Josquin des Pres
Agnus Dei from *Missa l'Homme armé super voces musicales* (1502)

Ex. 10b

against the duple time of the other two parts. The poly-rhythmic effect is achieved by the vertical combination of these parts, with their three-against-two beats.[1]

II. In the second movement the series is O_7, the first note (A) being given to the trumpet in the fourth bar (bar 49). The movement is played predominantly by piano and strings, and the notes of the series are distributed between the instruments, in contrast to the more independent treatment of Ex. 10.

III. The third movement, on the other hand, consists primarily of piano and wind, with the brass alone in the last four bars. The series is O_6, with the second note of each half, namely B (note 2) and F♯ (note 8), displaced and sounding at the end of each half-series. When O_6 is repeated at the end

---

[1] A striking instance of the device known to theorists as *hemiola*.

of the movement (bars 92–95) by trumpets and trombones, B (note 2) is once again displaced, but in the second half of the series both G and F♯ are displaced (notes 7 and 8), and these are played instead in the final chord.

IV. The fourth movement contains the only orchestral *tutti*. It concludes the movement, and is a short *ff* (bars 137–140). Starting in bar 136, the lower strings give out R_{12}; starting in bar 137, all the violins, *ff* and *pizzicato*, play R. Meanwhile longer notes, minims and crotchets, make up the wind parts. The two trumpets share I_3 between them, the first playing notes 7–12, the second notes 1–6. The flutes play the same notes as the second trumpet, but in a different order; the oboe and Cor Anglais play a retrograde version of the flute part. The characteristic *crescendo* effect is given to all the wind in the last bar; the leap also appears, though varied. It appears as an augmented octave downwards in clarinet and bassoon, and as a major ninth, minor ninth and minor seventh upwards in trombones and first trumpet respectively.

V. In the last movement Stravinsky reverts once more to the segmentation of the orchestra, using all the instruments separately except the oboe and bassoon. At the end (bar 183) he adds celesta.

The piano gives out I_9, broken up after the first four notes; once more the trumpet marks the first note of the series (G). The central point of the movement, indeed the culmination of the whole work, is reached in bar 180, with a restatement of the original series (O). The first four notes are given to the trombones, playing *f*, the remainder to the violas and cellos. This final statement of the series is introduced by a measured *accelerando* for two flutes, which play once again the augmented octave, over a chord held by three cellos. The model for this passage (Ex. 11a) is a madrigal by Monteverdi, "Sfogava con le stelle" (Ex. 11b). It will be noticed how the notes of the one coincide with the syllables of the other.

Stravinsky deliberately avoids calling this work a concerto. It is more a study in the grouping together of various instruments with the piano, which plays very nearly throughout. It is as if the composer is piecing together his orchestra instrument by instrument. But as he says,[1] for him form is

---

[1] *Expositions and Developments*, p. 103.

everything, and the form of this entirely serial, entirely
instrumental work, is decided by nothing apart from musical
considerations; there is no literary or dramatic influence. Like
Histoire du soldat it sets the seal on a phase of Stravinsky's
development; but *Histoire* was representative; the violin

Stravinsky
Movements V, bars 177–179

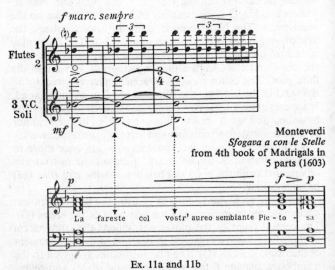

Monteverdi
Sfogava a con le Stelle
from 4th book of Madrigals in
5 parts (1603)

Ex. 11a and 11b

represented the soldier's soul, the percussion represented the
devil and all his machinations; in *Movements* there is no such
representation. There is however a marked similarity between
the two works. In *Histoire* Stravinsky aimed to synthesise new
rhythmic discoveries into his style. Variable rhythmic patterns
were set against invariable metrical units. In *Movements* he
aimed to synthesise new serial discoveries, the constant
element being the series on which the work is based, and of
which he introduced innumerable variants.

The discussion of Stravinsky's music is never-ending. Never
was there a composer whose achievement it is more difficult,
or indeed more pointless, to attempt to summarise. His

approach to music, that is to say the objective, aesthetic approach, is a constantly self-renewing appetite which can never be satisfied. It presupposes a source of material external to the composer himself, and in this sense the content of Stravinsky's music is impersonal; it is only the manner which is personal. His art contains no trace of sensuality, and is in no way an expression of himself. "*Si je le veux, je le peux*" he once said in a revealing moment. Others may seek new means of expression; Stravinsky has always sought new ideas to represent, whether they are derived from classical Greece (*Oedipus Rex, Apollo Musagetes*), religious ecstasy (*Symphony of Psalms*), or simply a sense of aesthetic, formal beauty.

There are, as Schweitzer has said,[1] two types of composer, the subjective and the objective; those who discover their own means, and those who adopt already existing means. Stravinsky, like Bach, assimilated different styles from other traditions than his own; unlike Bach, however, and more like his contemporary Picasso, there is in his make-up something of the destructive *pasticheur*. He will take a stylistic feature of another tradition and modify it to suit his wish; he will take the elements of a language that others have worked out, and make it speak with his individual voice, and in his individual style. So far from his development being marked by contradictions and inconsistencies, there is in fact over his whole output a quite remarkable unity of purpose. The unifying thread is a spiritual one. Like all who are aware of the driving force of tradition, Stravinsky has a fundamental humility which, as with Bach, is basically religious. He has always been concerned to write music for the universal Church—which is by no means the same thing as "church music"—and his understanding of the debt owed to the Church by music is frequently apparent in his writings. His *Mass*, for instance, was intended for liturgical use; indeed most of his later works are settings of biblical texts. *The Flood* (1962) has a text arranged by Robert Craft from the Book of Genesis, and from the York and Chester mediaeval mystery plays. *Abraham and Isaac* (1965) was written for the people of the State of Israel to words, in Hebrew, also from the Book of Genesis. The strong religious leaning of this period

[1] *J. S. Bach*, Vol. I, p. 1.

is further in evidence in his transcription of Bach's canonic variations for organ on the Christmas tune "*Vom Himmel Hoch*", and his completion of Gesualdo's *Sacrae Cantiones* (1603).[1]

It would perhaps be appropriate to finish this brief survey with an impression not of Stravinsky's music but of his personality, by someone who worked closely with him, Ernest Ansermet. He says.[2]

"During my long collaboration with Stravinsky I have learnt from him to be conscious of the basic principles of music—tone-quality, chord, tonality—in a different way from that in which I was conscious of them from the standpoint of my own development. These elements, for me charged with meaning, a meaning derived from usage, were for him, as it were, stripped of their heredity, and returned to the state of perfectly unspotted principles of sensibility."

(ii) *Oliver Messiaen* (*b*. 1908)

When considering the contemporary French scene, over which Messiaen occupies such a commanding position, we must remember that France has always been not only a nation of individualists—such a thing is unremarkable in a composer —but also the most musically insular and self-supporting of countries—which is a matter of rather more importance. For while a resistance to outside pressures and styles may be desirable in certain circumstances, it has meant in the case of France that of the long line of French composers, there have been but few whose music has shown that universality, that cosmopolitanism, which will carry it beyond its native frontier. Messiaen is one of the few. What ensures for his music a hearing that is denied to others is partly that his technique represents a more complete synthesis of the divergent tendencies in present-day styles, partly that his musical curiosity extends far beyond his immediate environment, partly that he has a highly dynamic and personal vision

---

[1] See also *Expositions and Development*, pp. 104–106 (*Monumentum pro Gesualdo*).

[2] Ernest Ansermet, *Les fondements de la musique dans la conscience humaine*, Vol. 2, Notes, p. 266.

of the purpose of his composition, and a burning sincerity, which impresses itself on even the most reserved Anglo-Saxon.

Shutting the door against external trends, which is the usual French characteristic, betrays an attitude which is diametrically opposite to the cosmopolitan aesthetic of Stravinsky, whose attitude, as we have seen, so far from being suspicious and exclusive of innovation, was one of insatiable curiosity. Debussy, however, described himself, with complete satisfaction, as "musicien Français"; and twice in the last forty years has French *amour propre* been defended, the barricades manned against the intruder; first by *Les Six* after the first world war, then in 1936 by *La Jeune France*. This group included Messiaen, Jolivet, Daniel-Lesur, and Baudrier, and though their technical equipment and achievement were very different, they shared a common aim, which they set out in a manifesto *Jeune France*. This was the re-humanisation of music. Theories and abstract systems, they felt, tend to stifle the human creative spirit; music can be a liberator. What matters, therefore, is not so much technique or aesthetic intention as the human content of a composition. Shades of Busoni!

Two main trends of composition were in vogue at this time; on the one hand, an adherence to one of the mid-European systems, such as dodecaphony; on the other hand, a reversion to classical principles. You either went forward with Schoenberg, or back to Bach. *La Jeune France*, however, showed a middle way. So did Hindemith (see below, p. 84). The problem for them was not so much one of resolving the musical language, which in any case is only a means to an end, as of understanding the nature of man; in a word, humanism.

But "humanism" can mean different things to different people; and *La Jeune France* were no exception. To Baudrier and Lesur it has meant that, because man is complete in himself, music is self-expression. Theories and systems are both harmful and superfluous, and what the composer should do is to give musical expression to extra-musical experiences. Obviously the sort of music you write will then depend solely on what experiences you have had, on your environment and psychological make-up.

To Messiaen and Jolivet, on the other hand, man is part

of something beyond himself: universal man; eternal, spiritual man. Music is therefore not limited to the expression merely of a personal experience; it must not be tied down to the technical problems of a particular age, still less to the arbitrary solution of a particular composer. Rather the way to re-discover the one universal, human music, whose thread had been broken, was to retrace one's steps to the beginnings of human consciousness; to primitive and oriental civilisations, exotic modes and rhythms, the world of nature, belief in God. Music seen thus becomes not so much self-expression as an expression of a vision of the world; indeed the spiritual and ethical foundations of such composition are of equal impor-tance to its technique, as we shall see.

The second view, that of Messiaen and Jolivet, has proved the more fruitful; and in concentrating our attention on one, Messiaen, let us not forget the link between the two com-posers. Both did formative, research work in the 1930's, both were profoundly disturbed by the war in 1939, both assimi-lated serial techniques, both stem from Debussy, both acknowledged a great debt to the other.[1]

The music of Messiaen, like that of Stravinsky, is a creative synthesis of various elements—oriental modes and rhythms, bird song; but, strange though it may sound, the Frenchman shows a lower degree of sophistication, a greater freedom of instinct, than the Russian.[2] He is a man of wide culture; his early musical influences included (directly) Debussy, Stravin-sky and Berg; possibly also (indirectly) Delius. He has always shown a marked leaning towards poetry, doubtless derived from his mother, the poetess Cécile Sauvage. Among his teachers at the Paris Conservatoire were Marcel Dupré, Maurice Emmanuel and Paul Dukas. He returned later to the Conservatoire as a Professor, and has subsequently exerted almost as much influence as a teacher as he has as a composer.

His pupils have included Pierre Boulez, Serge Nigg, Jean Barraqué, Karlheinz Stockhausen, and many others; also Yvonne Loriod, the pianist, who later was to become his wife. The nature of his teaching method, which was as wide-ranging

[1] E.g. Messiaen's praise of Jolivet's 6 piano pieces *Mana* (1935).
[2] The reception given to *Trois petites Liturgies de la Presence Divine* in 1945, resulting in the "cas Messiaen", cannot fail to remind us of that afforded to Stravinsky's *Rite* 30 years earlier.

as it was unorthodox, can be considered under three main headings; first, an exploration into unknown regions of music, such as Eastern music, Hindu rhythms, African music—in a word, ethnomusicology; second, the study of harmony, from the early days of Plainchant and Renaissance polyphony right through to the present; third, and perhaps the most important and characteristic aspect of his teaching, since it reflected his own creative thought, his class in "Aesthetics, Analysis and Rhythm". His classroom was the meeting-place for composers, whatever their idiom and inclination, to study the development of their technique. Particularly stimulating was his analysis of Stravinsky's *Rite of Spring*.

Another potent factor in forming contemporary trends, certainly in France, was the arrival in Paris in 1945 of René Leibowitz, whose teaching of the 12-note technique made such a wide impact. He was the first to realise the essential gulf between Schoenberg and Webern at a time (1945 onwards) when the works of Webern were scarcely available, and very little known.

Messiaen has been a frequent performer of his own music. A culminating point was reached in 1956, when he made a complete recording of his organ works on the instrument of Saint-Trinité, the church to which he was appointed organist in 1931. These records, for sheer virtuosity and authenticity of performance, are a most brilliant landmark in the history of the gramophone.

Sometimes he introduces a composition with a preface, setting out his intentions; for example *La Nativité*, *Vingt regards sur l'Enfant Jésus*, and some other works. His technical discoveries are described in a treatise he wrote in 1944, *The Technique of my musical language*. His music can be understood only by means of a dual assessment; on the one hand through the many-sided aspects of his psychology, on the other hand through his technique.

(i) *Psychology*

His psychological make-up is extraordinarily varied and intense; from this stems the richness of his musical language. Though Messiaen's music has a mystical meaning and significance, he himself describes his thought as being more 'theological' than 'mystical'. So far from being somewhat vague, and more or less interchangeable, these two conceptions may be very precisely and exactly differentiated; and the difference is crucial. Mysticism is a state of mind in which, by contemplation, a man seeks to reach outside and beyond the confines of his human state, and thus experience contact with the Divinity. Theology on the other hand is the science of religion, and is very much concerned with man's human condition. Its function is to reconcile the imperfections of this world with the Divine glory—which is precisely Messiaen's purpose. His creative thought is entirely conditioned by a poetic Catholicism. That is to say he first interprets theologically a visionary or mystical theme; he then expresses this poetically in its different aspects, so as to give a series of ideas, or pictures, which will make a framework for the movements, or sections, of a composition. The commonest themes in his work are love, death, bird-song, and the chief festivals of the Christian Church, such as Christmas, Ascension, Pentecost. The underlying meaning of these timeless themes is contemplated, developed, one might almost say 'composed' by Messiaen. For his songs, and song-cycles, he himself wrote the poems.

To take just one example, the theme of love dominates much of his work, but particularly work written between 1944 and 1948, as this list shows:

1944 *Vingt regards sur l'Enfant Jésus*. In this long piano piece, Messiaen has tried, as he says in the preface, to find the language of mystical love, varied and rich.

1945 *Harawi*. A song of love and death, for dramatic soprano and piano. The poem, by Messiaen himself, tells of a Peruvian Tristan and Isolde, whose love, irresistible and profoundly passionate, leads to the death of the two lovers. The text, highly symbolic, is largely derived from Peruvian folklore.

1946/8 *Turangalila—Symphony*, for full orchestra. The title, Hindu in origin, means 'love-song', and although the main interest of the work is technical, and lies in its audacious use of instruments, cyclical structure and development of rhythm, its musical basis is the violent contrast between passionate, physical love, and an ideal, tender, mystical love.

1948　　*Cinq rechants*, for twelve mixed voices. The word
　　　　means 'refrains', and the musical sources are the
　　　　French *troubadours*, Peruvian folk-song once again,
　　　　and Hindu music, particularly rhythms. The "five
　　　　poems of carnal love", by Messiaen himself, express
　　　　the physical union of two lovers, and are partly in
　　　　French, partly in a pseudo-Hindu, with the words
　　　　chosen not so much for their meaning as for their
　　　　sound or rhythm.[1]

In the first three of these works, and indeed throughout his
music generally, bird-song is integrally used[2]; even in purely
technical pieces, such as *Ile de feu*, from the *Quatre études*
(1949). It is an intrinsic part of his musical aesthetic. Music
is not confined to man; we must look for it all around us.
Man's music is not the true music, since it is too much the
result of calculation, systems, conventions.[3]

"Nature, the songs of birds! That for me is the home of
music. Free, anonymous music, improvised for pleasure."

Thus he arrived at the *style oiseau*, systematically worked
out until it became part of his musical thought, its melodies
and rhythms transcribed with a natural realism. This is an
act of faith. As he says,

"All my works, religious or not, are an act of faith, and
glorify the mystery of Christ."

In the magazine *Contrepoints*, March/April 1946, some
questions were put, and Messiaen's answers are highly relevant
to our enquiry:—[4]

Q.　　What are the "canons" of your aesthetic, and of the
　　　technique which serves as the basis of your style?

A.　　I have tried to be a Christian musician and to sing my
　　　faith, (but) without ever reaching that goal. Without
　　　doubt because I was not worthy to do so (this is said
　　　without false humility!). Pure music, profane music,
　　　above all theological music (not mystical, as most of my
　　　listeners think) alternate through my works. I do not
　　　really know whether I follow any "aesthetic" pattern,
　　　but I can say that my preferences are for music that

[1] For the use of this device by Stockhausen and Berio, see p. 129.
[2] Ex. 12a, 12b.
[3] cf. the ideas of Busoni, p. 36.
[4] Quoted in Rostand *Olivier Messiaen*, p. 19 foll.

Messiaen
Harawi
II Bonjour toi, colombe verte

Ex. 12a

Messiaen
Messe de la Pentacôte
IV Communion (les oiseaux et les sources)

Stops used are of 4', 1', and 1⅗'
(tierce) pitch.

Notes sound at the intervals of the
octave, seventeenth and twenty-
second.

(rossignol)

Ex. 12b

glistens, that is refined, and even voluptuous (but definitely not sensual!). Music that sings (all honour to melody and the melodic phrase!). Music which has new blood, which has the stamp of a master, an unknown perfume, a never-sleeping bird. A music in stained-glass, a swirling round of complementary colours. A music that expresses the end of time, ubiquity, the blessed saints, the divine and supernatural mysteries. A "theological rainbow". When, commenting on my '*Vingt regards sur l'enfant Jésus*', I said as much in the Salle Gaveau, the critics ridiculed me. Justifiably perhaps? In religious matters a good deed is worth more than a symphony, a pure life more than a work of art.

Q.   In every work of art there is the element of 'craft' and the element of 'art'; the aspect of technique and the aspect of "expression and meaning"; there is the musical "architecture" of which you are the architect, and there is the musical "magic" which you submit to even though you give it form; how do you reconcile these elements in your music?

A.   Your last question is the most difficult of all. It is concerned with Inspiration. Inspiration is like death: it is with us wherever we are. In a mountain-range, a stained-glass window, a book of medical science, of astronomy, of physics. Some seek it by praying to God, others by embracing a woman's body. The musician finds music all around him. For the lover, all objects have the colour of the same face. And what hidden vibrations and mysterious symphonies there are in a cloud, a star, a child's eye! I believe in musical inspiration, though I don't think it to be a Pythian delirium. It is rather a slow work which takes place in spite of ourselves and of which we are unaware. It haunts us, takes possession of us, like an *idée fixe*, like love. "Inspiration is like love". Occasionally it laughs at us. One sets out with the intention of writing theatre music and one finds oneself with 20 pieces for the piano. One intends to write songs and one eventually writes a symphonic poem or an act of an opera. But why try to investigate the light and its secret jokes? The only thing I can affirm is that I can write nothing that I have not lived through.

The essence of Messiaen is to be found in the organ works. In these, naturally, the themes he treats are specifically religious; they thus form a direct vehicle for his personality. The instrument itself he treats with a scientific precision, as Dr. Erik Routley has pointed out. *Les corps glorieux* consists of "seven short visions of the life after death", and contains many points of structural interest, particularly the cross-reference of thematic ideas between the movements, to give an overall symmetry. As an example of his method, let us consider one work in some detail: *La Nativité du Seigneur*. Although this is an early work, the elements of his maturity are here apparent. It was written in 1935, when he was only 28. It consists of nine "meditations", which are the theological interpretation of the Nativity of Jesus. Each movement is headed by a quotation from scripture. The movements are:

1 The Virgin and the Child   6 The Angels
2 The Shepherds   7 Jesus accepts sorrow
3 Eternal purposes   8 The wise men
4 The Word   9 God among us
5 God's children

The range of mood is wide; an alternation, as he says, of the "profane" and the "pure"; the temporal and the eternal; the human and the divine. There are three 'nativities'; the historical incarnation of Christ (No. 1), the eternal Word (No. 4), the spiritual birth of the Christian church (No. 5); also the colourful characters in the familiar Christmas story; the shepherds (No. 2), the angels (No. 6), the wise men (No. 8). These comparatively external features of the event are offset by thoughts of inner significance; our predestiny is realised by the incarnation of the Word (No. 3); God alive in the world (No. 9) nevertheless accepts human suffering (No. 7).

How does Messiaen relate this imaginative vision to his music? To take just two examples:

God's children (No. 5)   A *crescendo* in the manuals over held pedal notes represents the Church gradually evolving on its one sure foundation. The quiet section at the end, consisting of slow chords over a B major tonality, suggests the stillness in which the Word is born, amid the uncertainty in the world today.

The wise men (No. 8)   A melody in the pedals, but sounding a high pitch, shines out, like the star that the wise men follow. The rhythm suggests the slow, laborious progress across desert. At one moment there is a slowing down; we imagine the wise men losing heart, becoming exhausted. Then they proceed. Finally they reach their goal. The star comes to rest, and Messiaen takes us into the presence of the child Jesus with a very quiet flute chord of F sharp major, the key to which the movement has tended from the beginning, but which has not been explicitly stated until this moment.

(ii) *Technique*
(*all examples quoted are taken from 'La Nativité'*)

Messiaen's style has developed from the highly personal use of tonality in the early works, through the gradual abandonment of it in the *Liturgies* (1943) and *Vingt regards* (1944), to the adoption of total chromaticism in works composed since about 1950. The central, and crucial, period of his creative life, which ends with *Turangalila* (1948), was marked by many technical discoveries, which he has summarised in a treatise *The technique of my musical language* (1944). We may consider his technique under two main headings; the first melodic and harmonic; the second rhythmic.

Melody and Harmony

Messiaen's technique is the result of his extension of the traditional musical language. The addition of notes to a basically simple chord, to give it extra harmonic colour, has always been a stock-in-trade of composers. We recall the "added sixth" as being peculiarly characteristic of Debussy and Ravel. Again, it was the traditional practice of counterpoint to hold over a note from one chord, to which that note belonged, into the next, to which it was foreign. This produced a dissonance, called a suspension, which would then be resolved. In time composers gave this "suspended" note an independent life of its own, and produced the *appoggiatura*, or accented dissonance. The underlying process was three-fold: Preparation—Dissonance—Resolution.

Messiaen extends and exploits this process, so that it becomes: Upbeat—Accent—Termination (or Cadence). What were formerly single notes he extends into groups of notes, which in their turn may be given an independent life of their own. This practice frequently results in polytonality and polyrhythm. Instead of pedal notes, we find pedal groups; instead of passing notes, passing groups. Embellishments are of integral importance to his style.

It is impossible to summarise the chapters of *The technique of my musical language*, which are already in summary form, and any one of which would form the basis of a detailed course of study. They give us an insight into the creative process unequalled by most other writings.

What chiefly give Messiaen's music its harmonic and melodic character are the 'modes of limited transposition'. Of these, there are seven, though the second and third are used most often. The modes are formed of several symmetrical groups, the last note of each group always being the same as the first note of the following group.[1]

The first mode is nothing more than the whole-tone scale. This is transposable twice; the third transposition gives exactly the same notes as the first transposition, the fourth the same notes as the second, and so on. This mode is too well-known to require an example.

The second mode is divided into four symmetrical groups of three notes each. Each group contains a semitone and a tone. The mode is transposable three times; the fourth transposition, starting on E flat, gives exactly the same notes as the first (Ex. 13). An example of the use of this mode, and a cadence that is typical of it, is found at the opening of the first piece of *La Nativité*, *The Virgin and Child* (Ex. 13d).

---

[1] The basic position of each mode, starting on C, is referred to as the first transposition. Moreover, enharmonics are interchangeable as with Schoenberg's 12-note system.

Messiaen

(a) Melodically (1st transposition)   2nd Mode of limited transposition

Ex. 13a

(b) Harmonically

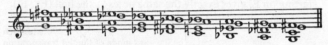

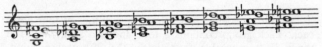

(Each voice realises the mode, starting on a different degree)

Ex. 13b

(c) 2nd transposition.   (d) 3rd transposition

Ex. 13c

La Vierge et L'enfant
(*No. 1 from La Nativité*)

Use of mode in 1st transposition

Ex. 13d

Notes sound at the intervals of the octave lower, octave higher and twelfth higher.

Ex. 13d (contd.)

The third mode is divided into three groups of four notes each. Each group contains a tone and two semitones. The mode is transposable four times; the fifth transposition, starting on E, gives exactly the same notes as the first (Ex. 14).

Messiaen
3rd mode of limited transposition

(a) Melodically (1st transposition)

Ex. 14a

(b) Harmonically

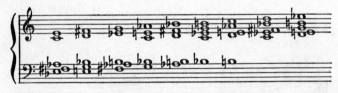

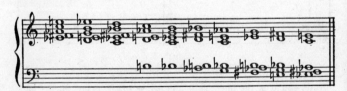

Ex. 14b

(c) 2nd transposition **(d)** 3rd transposition

(e) 4th transposition

Ex. 14c, d, e

(f) Use of mode in transposition

Douloureux, presque vif.

Jésus accept la souffrance
(No. 7 from La Nativité

Ex. 14f

There are four remaining modes, each divided into two symmetrical groups (Ex. 15). These modes are all transposable six times, and for that very reason are of less interest than the other modes. The fifth mode is the same as the fourth, but without D natural and A flat. The seventh is the most chromatic. Examples of the use of the sixth occur in the first piece, *The Virgin and Child*; it appears in its first transposition in the middle section, marked *un peu vif*. In the second piece, *The Shepherds*, it appears in its fifth transposition in the section after the second double bar, marked *modéré, joyeux*.

Messiaen's modalism is a coherent system. His modes are based on rigorous and logical harmonic thought, and in the resulting chord system all the notes appear which belong to the mode used. Each mode thus has its own harmony, and is not harmonised by chords made up of notes foreign to it.

Messiaen
Modes and Rhythms

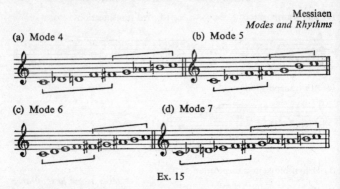

(a) Mode 4   (b) Mode 5

(c) Mode 6   (d) Mode 7

Ex. 15

Messiaen's modes have a polytonal flavour; for this reason,
they can be combined with a tonality, or with one of the
traditional ecclesiastical modes. (An example of this occurs
in the last section of the fourth piece, *The Word*.) They have
nothing in common with Indian, Chinese or ancient Greek
modes; nor with Plainchant. They can alternate, they can
modulate, they can be combined to produce polymodality.
Their use led Messiaen inevitably to the abandonment of
tonality.

Rhythm

To Messiaen rhythm is something autonomous; he treats
it contrapuntally in a way which recalls Bach, or the earlier
madrigal composers. His rhythmic principles are threefold:
(1) Rhythm is entirely free from the domination of the bar-line.
His music is ametrical, and very exactly notated. He will add
to any rhythm a small pulse-unit which will transform its
balance. This addition may be by means of a dot (Ex. 16a),

(a)

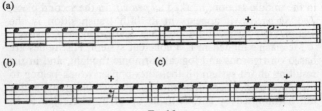

(b)   (c)

Ex. 16

a rest (Ex. 16b), or a note (Ex. 16c). In each example the added value, marked by a cross, transforms a basically simple rhythmic pattern into something subtle and refined.

Messiaen
Les bergers
(*No. 2 from La Nativité*)

Ex. 17

The melodic process already referred to, Upbeat—Accent—Termination, has its rhythmic counterpart. Rhythmic preparation corresponds to the melodic upbeat; rhythmic descent corresponds to melodic termination. Ex. 17 shows how the effect of the preparation (A), accent (B) and descent (C) is enhanced by the added note-values, marked by a cross, as well as by the varied phrase-lengths.

(2) Rhythm can be augmented or diminished by fractional amounts. Bach's technique was either to double or to halve

note-values; but Ex. 18a shows a case of augmentation by the addition of a dot, while Ex. 18b shows a case of diminution by the withdrawal of the dot. Notes can be augmented by a quarter, a third, a half, twice, three times or four times their value, or by the addition of a fixed short duration (e.g. ♪). Diminution can be by inverse proportion.

Messiaen
Dieu parmis nous
(*No. 9 from La Nativité*)

a) Augmentation

La Verbe
(*No. 4 from La Nativité*)

(b) Diminution

Ex. 18

(3) Just as a certain 'tonal ubiquity' results from the modes of limited transposition, so a certain unity of rhythmic movement is the result of the use of non-retrogradable rhythms; these are rhythms which have the same order of note-values in the retrograde, or reversed, form as they do in their ordinary form (Ex. 19).

Non-retrogradable rhythms

Ex. 19

These three principles are contained in the Hindu rhythm *Ragavardhana* (Ex. 20). The retrograde form (Ex. 20b) is shown with the first note made up of its constituent crotchets (Ex. 20c). It will be seen that the second half of the rhythm (B) is a diminution of the first half (A), made inexact by the insertion of a dot; also that the second half (B) is a non-retrogradable rhythm.

Polyrhythm results from the imposition of one rhythm upon another. A simple example occurs in the fourth piece, *The Word*, at bar 32, marked *Plus vif*. An extension of this principle is chromatic rhythm, which is the result of the advance or retardation of time-value, according to a pre-ordained arithmetical progression. A rhythm can be combined with its augmentation, its diminution, or its retrograde.

Messiaen, Rhythms

Hindu rhythm Ragavardhana

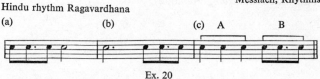

Ex. 20

Rhythmic canon is also possible, as well as rhythmic pedal, or *ostinato* figure, which is repeated without reference to its surrounding context.

The modes of limited transposition and the non-retro-gradable rhythms complement each other. The rhythms realise in a horizontal sense what the modes realise in a vertical sense. The modes cannot transpose because they already contain transpositions; the rhythms cannot reverse because they already contain reversions. As a result the modes have a ubiquitous tonality, the rhythms a temporal unity, in which Messiaen sees a reflection of the divine glory. Thus he comes to describe his musical language as a "theological rainbow".

In 1949/50 Messiaen wrote a work, which was to have very far-reaching influence on subsequent developments in serial and electronic composition, particularly among his pupils. This was the work for piano *Etudes de rhythme*, which consisted of four pieces of musical investigation into melody, duration, intensity, attack, and of which the second piece *Mode de valeurs et d'intensité* uses a serial method throughout. It was not strictly speaking a composition at all,[1] but a serial

---

[1] The same may be said of Bach's *Art of Fugue*, which was also a study in technique.

experiment which took certain musical constants, never transposed or altered, and grouped them into three series of twelve notes (which Messiaen calls *modes* and not *series*) whose tessitura overlapped, and each term of which was given a coefficient of intensity and attack.

This study sees a logical extension of Messiaen's personal musical language. The nature of his modalism was such that it could be developed serially, and thus form a link between the pre-war and the post-war generations. *Mode de valeurs* is the starting-point for Boulez, Stockhausen, Barraqué, and others of the *avant-garde* today.

CHAPTER FOUR

COSMOPOLITAN COMPOSERS: THE SECOND VIENNESE SCHOOL

(i) *Arnold Schoenberg* (1874-1951)

Never has there been a composer whose creative motives are more difficult, yet at the same time more essential, to understand than those of Arnold Schoenberg. It is the greatest mistake to look on his development of the 12-note technique as a consummate achievement, the climax of his life's work. It was not; Schoenberg himself did not consider it as such, and nor must we. It was a means, not an end.

He was concerned with the whole technique of composition; his approach was through philosophical enquiry and exercise of the intellect, and it is therefore on this level that we should assess his work.[1] He moved logically, step by step, dealing with problems as they arose; and as Hercules found, in his struggle against the Lernean Hydra, the apparent solution of one problem simply gave rise to more. Schoenberg consistently warned against the dogmatic approach to composition; he was himself the least dogmatic of teachers. Nothing, so he felt, destroys the spirit of intellectual freedom more than dogmatism, or self-satisfaction. Yet nothing inspires it more than creative energy; and not the least of Schoenberg's achievements was his power to attract to himself, and to form into a 'school', composers and musicians who responded to his technical enquiries by following them up in their own work. This group included Alban Berg, Roberto Gerhard, Karl Rankl, Josef Rufer, Nikos Skalkottas, Erwin Stein, Anton Webern, Egon Wellesz, and several others.

What they investigated and discussed theoretically they put into effect practically. Under Schoenberg's presidency, they formed the Society for Private musical performances, *Verein fuer musikalische Privatauffuehrungen*. It lasted for

[1] See below, p. 228.

three years, 1918–1921, and its purpose was to perform new music adequately and professionally, after lengthy and precise rehearsal. The same work would be played many times; no critics were admitted. The immediate benefits of this unique venture were twofold: first, the work of new composers gradually became known, not merely theoretically or cursorily, but as actual musical experience; second, links were re-established with other countries that had been severed by the war.

In the first decade of the twentieth century, Vienna was the home of the most radical thinkers, and of the intellectual *avant-garde* in all the arts; of Kokoschka, Loos, Hofmannsthal, Freud, to name only four. Later also, in 1922, there flourished the 'Vienna Circle' of philosophers, with which we associate the names of Schlick, Carnap, Waismann, as well as Wittgenstein and Ayer. Against this background of intellectual radicalism Schoenberg developed his technique of composition.

The outward facts of his life can be briefly told. He worked in Vienna until 1901, when he moved to Berlin to teach at the Stern Conservatoire. He stayed for twenty months, but returned nine years later, in 1911. The outbreak of war in 1914 disrupted his work, and after a period of military service he returned to Vienna. In 1922/3 the 12-note style first appeared, though it had germinated several years before then. In 1925 he again went to Berlin, this time to take over the master class in composition at the Prussian State Academy which had formerly been under Busoni's direction. The years which followed saw a steady and consistent development of Schoenberg's newly-discovered technique.

Berlin was indeed the focal point of contemporary European music in the days of the Weimar Republic. Hindemith taught at the *Hochschule fuer Musik*; Klemperer was musical director at the *Krolloper*; Schoenberg himself received pupils from all over Europe and America. The first really international recognition for the work of the Schoenberg 'school' came with the première of Berg's opera *Wozzeck*, conducted by Erich Kleiber at the *Staatsoper* in December 1925.

Hitler's accession to political power in 1933 put an end to this work, and along with a number of other musicians and artists, particularly those of Jewish extraction, Schoenberg left Germany. He stayed for a while in France, though he was unable to find a living there. England he appears not even to have considered, though he had visited this country in 1912. He finally went to America, first to the Malkin Conservatory in Boston, then in 1936 to Los Angeles. In 1940 he became an American citizen.

So much for his career. As for his output, this may be divided roughly into three phases. The first or tonal phase lasts up to 1908 (2nd String Quartet); the second or 'atonal' phase lasts up to 1923, and culminates with *Pierrot Lunaire* in 1912; the third phase, from 1923 onwards, is a development of the 12-note technique.

The first phase begins with works whose harmonic conception is tonal, but then sees a progressive denial and exclusion of tonality. The use of a key-signature became redundant, and it was omitted from the last movement of the second String Quartet (1908); and thereafter until the Serenade (1923) Schoenberg wrestled with the formal and structural problems that resulted from the absence of tonality.

His works of this period, of which *Pierrot Lunaire* is the most striking, are sometimes called "atonal", and represent a search for an alternative form of structure that would be as logical and as powerful as that built on the traditional harmonic scheme, which he had by this time discarded. The freedom of atonality meant, among other things, that an individual note lost its direct harmonic relationship to a chord; also that chords lost their direct harmonic relationship to each other. Some other unifying factor had to be found if a composition was not to be formally incoherent, a mere juxtaposition of logically unrelated ideas.

As we saw with Stravinsky, a certain consistency of style runs through all his compositions, of whichever phase, and it is therefore not correct to make too rigid or complete a distinction between them. Typical of his characteristics are the creation of melody by (orchestral) tone-colour, *Klangfarbenmelodie* and *pointillism*; the asymmetrical shaping of a melodic line; the use of chromaticism to lend meaning to the harmony; the novel treatment of, and preoccupation with, the human voice; the avoidance of exact repetition and sequence; the introduction of irregular rhythms. Underlying his concern with the science of composition was his life-long preoccupation with religion, psychology and metaphysical philosophy. If once we accept that, by turning inwards upon himself, a composer heightens the emotional tension in his music; if once we accept that, in order to achieve intimate and concentrated expression through musical sounds, those sounds must touch the hidden depths of the psyche; then Schoenberg's discoveries appear in a logical light.

In his first and second phases, three works stand out; the *Gurrelieder* (1901), the *Georgelieder* (1908), and *Pierrot Lunaire* (1912). The first of these occupies a position in Schoenberg's development similar to that of the *Rite of Spring* in Stravinsky's; namely it stands at the ultimate point in post-Wagnerian romanticism, while at the same time it contains ideas which are developed in later works. With the *Georgelieder*—15 poems from *Das Buch der Haengenden Gaerten*, by Stefan George—Schoenberg takes up a fresh and decisive artistic stand. It is a foretaste of things to come. He says, in the programme note to the first performance, that he felt he was:

". . . successful in coming near an ideal of expression and form which I had in mind for years . . . now that I have finally embarked on this path, I feel I have broken through all the limitations of a past aesthetic."

What does he mean by "this path"? Chiefly, the use of chords which are unconnected by the functional relationship

Succession of perfect fourths

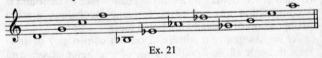

Ex. 21

of a conventional harmonic progression. Instead of using triads built up in thirds, Schoenberg uses chords built up in fourths. By this device he sets course directly for a harmonic style that is totally chromatic; for as Ex. 21 shows, if you proceed up the keyboard in perfect fourths,[1] you encompass

[1] Or perfect fifths, the fifth being the inversion of the fourth. This same principle is applied by Bartok at the opening of his *Music for Strings, Percussion and Celesta*, where successive entries are all a fifth apart.

each of the twelve semitones before repeating any one. The use of chords built up in fourths, already foreshadowed in the Chamber Symphony, Op. 9, was a decisive step in Schoenberg's working out of a style which included all twelve notes of the chromatic scale. The three chords shown in Ex. 22 contain all twelve notes, and chords (b) and (c) are a continuation up the keyboard in fourths from chord (a).

Schoenberg
Das Buch der hängenden gärten
No. 15 (*Introduction*)

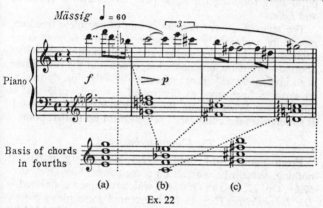

Ex. 22

Schoenberg's freedom, his "breaking through all past aesthetic" was hard-won. It resulted from experiment, which in turn resulted from a deeply-felt psychological necessity. As he was fond of saying, Art comes from necessity (Kunst kommt von Muessen). He did not sever all links with tradition, and there is a strong Symbolist influence in the works of his first phase. Words are used more for their mood than for their meaning. This is particularly true of *Pierrot Lunaire*, the culminating work of the first phase. It is taken from the poems of the Belgian poet Albert Giraud, which are inspired by the late Romantic aesthetic of masochism, perversion and blasphemy. We recall Aubrey Beardsley. Schoenberg's work consists of "Three times seven poems", which are described as a Melodrama. The scoring is for Voice, which has a spoken melody (*Sprechstimme*), Flute (doubling Piccolo), Clarinet (doubling Bass Clarinet), Violin (Doubling Viola), Violoncello and Piano.

The introduction of *Sprechstimme* was an experiment; an extension of song rather than a turning away from it. Schoenberg aimed to arrive at intervals beyond those found within the confines of the equally tempered scale, and at the same time to realise a greater expressive power than comes from pure speech. He had previously experimented in this way in the *Gurrelieder* and in *Die glueckliche Hand*; and his pupil Berg followed the same path in his operas *Wozzeck* and *Lulu*.

The style of *Pierrot Lunaire* is one of complete freedom, metrically, melodically and tonally. The form is more compressed than in earlier works, and contrapuntal ingenuities abound—inversion, augmentation, canon and the rest. There is an immensely wide range of mood, melodic line, dynamics. In short, Schoenberg has discovered a sound-world that is entirely new. What is more, the work was instantly successful. It summarises the composer's achievement up to that point.

The 12-note technique

From about 1914 until 1922/3 Schoenberg published nothing, though he worked on some songs, *Vier Orchesterlieder*, Op. 22; also an Oratorio, which remained unfinished—*Die Jakobsleiter*. Then in 1923 appeared some piano pieces, and a Serenade (Opp. 23 and 24), to be followed in 1924 by his first purely 12-note work, the Piano Suite (Op. 25). His compositions from this point onwards are almost all an exploitation of the paths opened up by this newly-found technique. He first explored its possibilities in Chamber Music, then in some Choral pieces, then in a work for full orchestra, the *Variations for Orchestra* (Op. 31).

For Schoenberg the exclusion of tonality had been a gradual and inevitable process. Several other composers had already felt the need to vary and enrich the tonal scale; for example, Busoni and Richard Strauss. But Schoenberg was moved by a deep, inner compulsion, and his formulation of the 12-note technique was for him a logical step after he had destroyed all valid and functional distinction between consonance and dissonance, harmonically speaking, by giving exactly equal importance to all notes. The idea of 'composition with twelve notes' was not, in fact, Schoenberg's original; it had already been worked out by another Viennese composer, J. M. Hauer, whose approach to it was rather more as a mathematical than as a musical problem.[1] However, the ground had been prepared.

So Schoenberg arrived at his method from his innermost conviction that adherence to tonality was a thing of the past and that "atonality", by itself, was incomplete. He therefore looked for something to take the place of the central seed of tonal music, the thematic phrase or sentence. Hence arose the series, or row, made up of the twelve notes of the chromatic scale. Each note appeared once in the series before any was repeated. The composer could arrange them in any order; rhythm was a separate matter altogether. Thus it will be seen that the notes are related only to each other, and not, as in tonal music, to a single key note, or tonic. The notes of the series can either be sounded in succession, melodically, or simultaneously, as chords. But as these chords do not have a 'root', in the traditional harmonic sense, they do not produce a harmonic progression. The repetition of the series, like the repitition of the thematic *motif* in tonal music, gives coherence to the composition.

The series has four versions, each of equal importance; its Original form (O); the inversion of this (I); the mirror or Retrograde of it, that is to say the notes played backwards, (R); and finally the inversion of this Retrograde (R I). Each of these versions can be transposed eleven times, the equivalent of modulation in tonal composition. No deviation from the note order of the series was normally allowed by Schoenberg, though variation of the *motif* was indispensable. Indeed, the principle of variation was a matter of the greatest importance to him, and a large number of his works are cast in variation form—Variations for Orchestra (Op. 31), Variations on a Recitative for Organ (Op. 40), Variations for Wind Orchestra (Op. 43), and several others.

In the use of the series, a note could appear at any pitch, in the same way as a subject, or theme, could appear at different pitch in the old fugal style of invertible counterpoint. Immediate re-iteration of a note was allowed; for example,

[1] Smith Brindle *Serial Composition*, p. 157–8.

instead of being held for the duration of one minim, it could be separately articulated as four quavers. Enharmonics were interchangeable; for example, C sharp and D flat were thought of as the same note. It is thus apparent that, in one sense, as Schoenberg once said, the 12-note technique was the direct result of equal temperament.

When referring to the use of one of the transpositions of the series, subscript numbers refer to the number of notes (that is to say, semitones)[1] in the interval of downward transposition from the first position. For example:

O_4:   The row in its original form transposed down four semitones, that is to say a minor third.

RI_{10}:   The row in its Retrograde Inversion, transposed down ten semitones, that is to say a major sixth.

The principle of phrase-construction followed by the earlier composers had been to build up a period from two main clauses, the antecedent and the consequent. Ex. 23 is a

Mozart
Eine Kleine Nachtmusik
K.525 (2nd Mov't.)

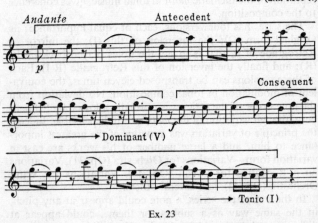

Ex. 23

---

[1] Rufer uses subscript numbers to refer to the tones in the interval of transposition. On the whole, as the 12-note series is one of 12 semitones, it seems preferable to be consistent in this respect when referring to a transposition of it.

straightforward illustration of this construction, from a certain well-known composition. It will be seen that both the antecedent and the consequent contain phrases which are made up of several *motifs*. The same governing principle may be seen in the example from Schoenberg's Serenade, Op. 24 (Ex. 24). Here it will be noticed that the consequent is a

Schoenberg
Serenade Op. 24 (3rd Mov't.)

Ex. 24

retrograde version of the antecedent, the central pivot note being F natural.

On the same principle, the 12-note series may be subdivided into two halves, each of six notes. Notes 1–6 will then be thought of as the antecedent, notes 7–12 as the consequent. Schoenberg tried to work his series in such a way that the inversion of the first six notes (the antecedent) a fifth, or other interval, lower, gave the remaining six notes (the consequent), but in a different order. In this way melodies formed from the antecedent could be accompanied with harmonies made from the consequent without any doubling.[1] It is logical therefore to think of the antecedent of a series as being the equivalent to Schoenberg of a fugue subject to Bach; the

[1] Rufer *op. cit.*, p. 96, illustrates this from the 4th String Quartet.

consequent of a series is then seen as the equivalent of a fugal counter-subject—secondary in nature, and accompanimental.

Two aspects of composition stem directly from the formulation of the original series; one is the character of the thematic material, the other is the way in which that material is to be worked. In a perfectly integrated work the one arises naturally from the other; and none of Schoenberg's 12-note compositions illustrates this better than the *Variations for Orchestra*, Op. 31. The series, Ex. 25, is gradually built up

Schoenberg
Variations for Orchestra Op. 31

Basic Series

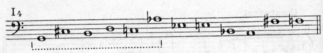

(Same note as consequent of O)

Ex. 25a

Schoenberg
Variations for Orchestra Op. 31
Theme (bars 34–38)

Ex. 25b

note by note, and interval by interval, in the introductory section. In this case, the antecedent is inverted a minor third lower, instead of a fifth, to give the notes of the consequent. In bar 3 of the work the first two notes of the series appear in the clarinet, giving the characteristic interval of the diminished fifth. This is promptly answered and inverted by the bassoon. Thereafter, the series and its inversion gradually appear simultaneously, until the full statement of the theme in bar 34 (Ex. 25b), which comes as the only logical conclusion, towards which the music has been tending up to then.[1]

The basis of Schoenberg's creativity was a search; a search for a way out of the *impasse* that, as he saw it, the traditional harmonic language had reached; a search for deeper, more intense powers of expression; a search for a technique of composition that would meet, and match, a deeply felt spiritual and psychological need. Activity, restlessness were the driving forces of his creative spirit. As he says,[2] the comforts of a pleasure-loving aesthetic were not for him. It is easy to hold a self-satisfied view of the world if you disregard what is unpleasant or disturbing. For him such a view would have been artistically and psychologically dishonest.

Although his search for a way out was successful— atonalism was one solution; the 12-note technique was another —two things made it difficult for him to break with the past in the way he did. The first was a feeling of responsibility for his art. He looked on himself as the guardian certainly of German, if not of Western, musical culture. Just as Moses had been the custodian of God's law against the waywardness and ignorance of the Israelites, so to Schoenberg was his method and attitude to the musical art the one true one that would ensure not just the survival, but the continuing vitality of Western music. Criticism of his work, which was both sustained and bitter during his lifetime, as well as since, has tended to come either from those who have misunderstood his motives, or else from conservatives and amateurs to whom music is primarily pleasure or entertainment.

The second hindrance to his break with the past was his deep love for tradition. Like Busoni, he sprang from the very

---

[1] Schoenberg himself describes his *Variations for Orchestra* in the section on 12-note composition in his book *Style and Idea*.
[2] In the introduction to the *Harmonielehre*.

centre of the European tradition; and so, also like Busoni, if he were to reach beyond the confines of that tradition it could only be through a deliberate and conscious act on his part. Schoenberg's knowledge and love of the traditional musical culture to which he was the heir, which means, in effect, German musical culture from Bach to Brahms, stands out on every page of his theoretical writings. He consistently advised others against the blind adoption of the 12-note technique without a thorough mastery of the methods and styles of Bach, Beethoven, Wagner and Brahms, from which his (Schoenberg's) style was derived. What indeed could be more pointless than an attempt to conduct a revolution by proxy? In general, anyone who does this can hardly avoid appearing more than slightly ridiculous; and a creative artist in particular simply cannot afford to accept the basic tenets of his culture secondhand.

There are certain aspects of Schoenberg's 12-note music which are inherently part of his individual style, and not necessarily the result of his new technique. The use of giant intervals, asymmetry, atonality and ametricality are some examples. But there is no doubt that his progressive development of the 12-note method brought out, and accentuated, trends which were already latent. An example of this is his extreme harmonic sensitivity; he was preoccupied with harmony all his life. Another example is the expressive tension which is so characteristic of his melodic line.

Once Schoenberg had accepted the break-up of the traditional syntax as a *fait accompli*, it is no longer reasonable to consider his music by the traditional standards. Fresh ones are needed. If the musical ideas appear arbitrarily linked, unconnected sections juxtaposed, the harmony illogical, then Schoenberg invites us to reconsider and revise our view of the musical art—and with it, our view of reality. Many are naturally loth to embark on such an undertaking. But for those who do, Schoenberg has indicated certain lines of advance. One of the main principles which guided him, and must therefore be a starting point for the listener, was the principle of variation; variation within the series itself; variation between one appearance of the series and the next; varied phrase length; variation of *motif*; variation from one composition to the next; an absence of repetition, ostinato and sequence. He once observed that "only what has not been said is worth saying."[1]

His pupil Webern has summed it up thus:[2] "Examining the development of variation technique, one has direct access to serial technique. Relationship to theme or row is quite analogous."

"Schoenberg once said: the row is more and less than a variation-theme. More, because the whole is more strictly tied to the row, less, because the row gives fewer possibilities of variation than the theme."

The principles of construction were of secondary importance to him in comparison with the nature and quality of the music. Form should simply give comprehensibility to a composer's musical ideas. He was a composer first, a theorist second; and the least theoretical of composers at that. There is an occasional return to tonality in his later works; for example *Kol Nidre* (Op. 39), a specifically Jewish liturgical work. More interestingly, he attempts to synthesise the principles of serialism with works whose conception is tonal; for example *Variations on a Recitative for Organ* (Op. 40), in which there is a definite tonality of D minor/major. His critics were not slow to hold this against him as an inconsistency, while some of his followers tended to dismiss this tendency as a regrettable lapse from grace. Schoenberg's intentions however become clear from his own words:

"It was not given to me to continue writing in the style of *Verklaerte Nacht* or the *Gurrelieder* or even of *Pelleas und Melisande*. Fate led me along a harder road. But the wish remained constantly within me to return to the earlier style, and from time to time I give in to this desire."[3]

Although the 12-note technique is highly intellectual, Schoenberg was capable of much more than merely intellectualism. He was a man of deep humanity, concerned with the things of the spirit. How else indeed could he have sustained his uncompromising integrity of purpose while surrounded

---

[1] One is inevitably reminded of Beethoven's opposite dictum, that if a thing is worth saying once, it is worth saying twice.

[2] In *The Path to the New Music*, p. 58.

[3] *Stimmen, Monatsblaetter fuer Musik*, Sep. 1949.

by such persistent opposition? He once described his situation as being like falling into an ocean of boiling water. Yet he never compromised his creative purpose.

Certain things moved him deeply; particularly the sufferings of the Jewish people, with whom he unequivocally identified himself. The hell and agony of the Jews in the Warsaw ghetto in August, 1944, epitomise the barbarity and degradation which Nazism brought upon Europe. The impact of this event upon Schoenberg was radical and horrific; *A Survivor from Warsaw* (Op. 46) is his personal testament to the depravity and perversion of the twentieth century. The work is stark, strident, shocking; the 12-note technique is here given a fresh dimension, namely one of deep emotional involvement.

Stern and uncompromising though his 12-note style may be, it has a human as well as a theoretical content. Apart from the emotional element just mentioned, there is also a profound psychological element, which corresponds to the subconscious, the hidden, the irrational in our human make-up. Schoenberg had been concerned with religion and philosophy all his life. The metaphysical poem *Totentanz der Prinzipien* dates from 1919; and his last work, *Modern Psalms*, was of a philosophical nature. Moreover his biggest and most ambitious work, which remained unfinished at his death, and whose text was begun as early as 1925, was in effect a psychological study in the difference between two brothers. The opera *Moses and Aaron* contains a juxtaposition of opposites; the "unutterable truth", represented by Moses, and the expediency represented by Aaron. To offset this, Schoenberg shows us a blend of prophetic, religious belief on the one hand, a pragmatism on the other, marked by a licentious and drunken orgy. We are reminded of William Blake or Hieronymus Bosch.

If *Pierrot Lunaire* sums up his first phase, *Moses and Aaron* sums up Schoenberg's art—a search for a music that would take into account, and satisfy, all the deep, unseeing longings of the human psyche. It is indeed symbolic that Schoenberg allots the chief singing part to the humanist Aaron, while that of Moses is spoken; the Eternal Word. It is also symbolic, and highly significant for us, that the opera is unfinished.

(ii) *Alban Berg* (1885–1935) and *Anton Webern* (1883–1945)

Schoenberg's legacy was immense. As the Italian composer Luigi Dallapiccola says[1]:—

"Schoenberg left his successors an enormous territory to evaluate—a territory which is so large that perhaps only future generations will be able to chart it to its full extent. Every one of the problems which a musician can pose for himself and work out in the future has been anticipated, at least in part, by Schoenberg."

It was one thing to develop the 12-note technique; it was quite another to put it to the test in actual composition, to follow it through, and to meet the myriad of problems, formal, stylistic and technical, posed by its adoption. But Schoenberg's immediate circle were inspired as much by their filial devotion to him as a composer and a teacher as they were by their affection for him as a friend. They were sustained by the example of his idealism, which they shared.

Although in fact Schoenberg outlived both Berg and Webern, we think of these two composers as being his chief 'heirs', since they were the first to take up and exploit the 12-note technique in their own composition.

Broadly speaking there were two possible directions in which Schoenberg's 12-note technique could be developed by subsequent composers; moreover both are apparent in Schoenberg's own work. One direction was for the technique to be adapted to, and integrated with, a traditionally-based style; by this means a sense of tonality, while being made subject to the chromaticism and the organisation of the 12-note system, would nevertheless still be felt, however much it might be kept in the background. Moreover the construction of a movement would still be thematic, the character of the themes being derived from the 12-note series. The series would be so arranged as to contain as many perfect intervals (fourths and fifths) as possible, since these allow for triadic chord-formations if need be. This direction was taken by Alban Berg.

The other direction was to abandon all pretence of tonality,

---

[1] See Rufer *Composition with twelve notes*, p. 179.

and to pursue pure serialism for its own sake, wherever it might lead, unmixed with any sense of obligation to traditional thematic construction. For a composer to follow this direction requires his uncompromising acceptance of the underlying hypothesis that tonality is no longer a positive, structural factor in composition, and that therefore the only logical and honest course is to recognise this as a fact, to abandon it altogether, and to set about developing a substitute for it. According to this hypothesis, the border-territory between consonance and dissonance had become progressively more blurred and ill-defined, until it had virtually disappeared in Schoenberg's atonal works up to *Pierrot Lunaire*. Serialism was the way out of this *impasse*; it must therefore be pursued and developed. This was the direction taken by Anton Webern.

Of these two composers, it has been Webern whose work has proved more of a spur and stimulus to subsequent composers than that of Berg.[1] The main difference between them consists in the fact that whereas Berg bases his music, fundamentally, on the constructional principles of thematic unity that are in direct line with the tradition that stems from Haydn and Mozart, Webern dispenses with themes, in the generally-accepted sense of the word, and uses the 12-note technique to build up sound-formations into self-supporting entities, based on *motifs* of two or three notes. Whereas Berg introduces serialism as a new unifying factor in the time-honoured method of constructing a movement as a whole, Webern is concerned with the discovery of new patterns of sound, which will spontaneously generate their own structure and cohesion; he explores the range, timbre and combination potential of instruments, which the chromatic freedom of the 12-note system makes possible. As far as the listener is concerned, Berg's music becomes a gradual, dynamic unfolding of a musical organism, while Webern's music is a more static pattern of internal relationships, which because of their comparative unfamiliarity require, for their full comprehension, not only an acute and finely-tuned ear, but also an enquiring mind, and one that is susceptible of such

---

[1] Stravinsky describes Webern, in *Memories and Commentaries*, p. 105, as a "perpetual Pentecost". Berg on the other hand was once described by Sibelius as "Schoenberg's best work."

originality. The American composer Gunther Schuller has described the characteristic of Webern's style that is found in a large proportion of recent music, as "intervallic autonomy."[1]

Theodor Adorno, a pupil of Berg, summed it up[2] when he said that Schoenberg composes as though there were no note-rows, Berg casts a spell over them, and Webern forces them to speak.

In other words, Berg looks on the note-row simply as a technical device, a means to an end, and uses it to increase the expressive power of his music, the core of which lies elsewhere; Webern on the other hand looks on the note-row, and its constituent fragments, as the central cell of his music, an end in itself, and the very source of expressive power. To put it metaphysically, Berg sought to subordinate the material to the spiritual world, to use the one as a means to express the other; Webern however sought to make the material world itself speak.

The relationship between the musical personalities of Schoenberg, Berg and Webern has been aptly symbolised by Berg in the motto preceding his Chamber Concerto. The letters in their respective names are played simultaneously by Piano, Horn and Violin; the Piano, the all-embracing instrument, representing Schoenberg; the Horn, the Romantic instrument, representing Berg; the Violin, the lyrical instrument, representing Webern.

Berg

Berg's output, though comparatively small, is remarkably rich and varied. From 1905 his composition was under Schoenberg's tutelage, but even so his early works betray hints and suggestions of what was to come. By 1912, when he was 27, his individuality appeared unmistakeably in the *Altenberg-Songs, Op.* 4 and again three years later in the *Three orchestral pieces, Op.* 6. None of the Viennese composers of Schoenberg's school carried on the symphonic tradition of Mahler;[3] they wrote instead *Pieces for orchestra*, in which

---

[1] In *Perspectives of new music*, Spring 1963, p. 2.

[2] In *Twentieth century music*, p. 126.

[3] Except Egon Wellesz, who has composed six symphonies. See Redlich, *Alban Berg, The man and his music*, p. 66 (note).

they were more concerned with the discovery of new methods of treating orchestral tone-colour than with constructing large-scale symphonies. Nevertheless, Berg's pieces reveal not only the immediate influence of his colleagues, but also that of Mahler; moreover they contain numerous stylistic touches and devices which reappear later in *Wozzeck* and other works.[1]

Berg's creativity reached a climax with the opera *Wozzeck*, which was published in 1923, performed in 1925, when the composer was 40. This is a seminal work, not merely for Berg himself, but also in the history of opera, since it contains features which have left an indelible mark on the music of our century. The opera tells the story of a humble infantryman who is driven to murder, and hounded to death by ruthless and thoughtless superiors. Although the original story referred to the period immediately preceding the 1848 revolution, Berg takes the sufferings of Wozzeck as a symbol for all ages of the effects of tyrannies wherever they occur. As with Beethoven's *Fidelio*, the message of the work is universal, and transcends any one period.

In its construction, the opera is a synthesis of various trends. Stylistically, it contains freely atonal, polytonal and tonal material. The voice part avoids *bel canto* and *recitative*, and exploits the various possibilities of melodramatic declamation, *Sprechgesang* and *Sprechstimme*, that Schoenberg had already introduced. Formally, *Wozzeck* occupies a unique place in the contemporary repertoire, since the scenes are built with such traditional formal structures as the Suite, the Sonata, the Fugue, the Passacaglia; all of which are usually associated with instrumental music of the eighteenth and nineteenth centuries. The overall scheme of the three acts that make up the opera suggests ternary form, A–B–A. There is an unusually large number of orchestral interludes, fourteen in all, and these are organically related to the scenes they separate. They act as bridge-passages, in much the same way as the Development section of a classical symphony acts as a bridge-passage between the Exposition and the Recapitulation.

The musical conception of the work is entirely in keeping with the dramatic; that is to say Berg's vision is of one broad and organic unity. In the manner of true tragedy, the events are inevitable, cumulative, consistent. Moreover despite the

[1] Stravinsky has noted several (in *Conversations*, pp. 72–73).

severity of its theme, with its grim political and moral overtones, to say nothing of the complication of its musical
language, the work has found wide acceptance in the opera
houses of the world.

After *Wozzeck* Berg addressed himself to the problems of
12-note composition as he saw it. Following the *Chamber
Concerto*, the adoption of the 12-note technique led first to
Storm-Lied II, *Schliesse mir die Augen beide* (1925),[1] then to
the *Lyric Suite* for String Quartet (1926). The essence of
Berg is found in this work. Its six movements contain a
strongly programmatic flavour, and their world is derived
from the late quartets of Beethoven, Wagner's *Tristan*, which
is actually quoted in the sixth movement, Mahler's *Lied von
der Erde*, and the *Lyric Symphony* of Alexander Zemlinsky,
from which the title of Berg's work is taken.[2] It is more
lyrical and dramatic than symphonic, and the use of the
12-note style is not strict throughout the work. The movements
are:

I Allegretto gioviale	IV Adagio appassionato
II Andante amoroso	V Presto delirando
III Allegro misterioso	(Trio) Tenebroso
Trio estatico	VI Largo desolato

The series of the *Lyric Suite* (Ex. 26), which is identical
with the series of *Storm-lied* II, contains all the possible

Berg
Lyric Suite. Basic Series

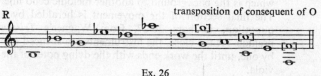

Ex. 26

---

[1] The two *Storm-lieder* are edited with a preface by Hans Redlich
(Universal Edition, 1955).
[2] Zemlinsky had for a short time taught Schoenberg counterpoint.

intervals, and is so constructed that the consequent is a transposition of the retrograde version of the antecedent. The composition as a whole epitomises Berg's concern with the formal problems of working in the 12-note style—that is to say, the reconciling of the new technique with the long-established musical forms that relied for their effect on harmonic contrast. Each of the six movements is differently constructed:

I   Strict 12-note. The form is binary, similar to Sonata form, but without the Development section.

II   Free in style. The form is that of a Scherzo, with Trio-like episodes of varying tempo.

III   Strict 12-note in the Allegro sections, but free in the trio. The form is ternary, with a return to the opening section at bar 93.

IV   Free in style. After a 4-part imitative opening, a long canon at the fifth between violin and viola, starting at bar 24, leads to an intense climax at bar 34. Thereafter the movement is a combination of leading motifs, including a quotation from Zemlinsky's *Lyric symphony* in bars 32/33, and 46/50.

V   Strict 12-note in the Tenebroso sections, but free in the remainder. This Scherzo is a very quick triple time, one-in-a-bar rhythm, with two Trio-like episodes at bar 51 and 211.

VI   Strict 12-note. The form is freely rhapsodic, a fitting epilogue to the action of the previous movements. It starts with a solemn inversion of the series, given out by the cello. The other instruments follow one by one; the note-values gradually reduce, the tempo slackens until a brief outburst (bars 7–8) leads to a *tremolo*, pp, which is the background to another melodic cello line. The final section of the movement is heralded by a quotation, in bars 26/27, from Wagner's *Tristan* prelude. At the close, the instruments are silenced one by one, until the work ends with the dying notes of the viola.

After the *Lyric Suite* just three major works were composed by Berg; the concert aria *Der Wein*, the opera *Lulu*, and finally the Violin concerto. This last work, which the composer never heard played, was first performed under Scherchen in Barcelona in 1936,[1] and has since been the most quoted of all Berg's scores. There is no doubt that it has a strange intensity of feeling informing its every note. The combination of the 12-note technique with the introduction of the traditional chorale from a Bach Cantata[2]—not distorted this time, as the chorale is in *Lulu*, but harmonised (by four clarinets) just as Bach left it—gives the work an additional dimension, and an extra emotional sincerity; joy in living is coupled with the acceptance of death. Berg also quotes Karinthian Folk Song. The circumstance which moved and inspired Berg to compose the work was the death from poliomyelitis of Manon Gropius, Alma Mahler's eighteen-year-old daughter.

Of his remaining two compositions, *Der Wein* was written, to a commission from the singer Ružena Herlinger, when Berg had already embarked on the libretto for his second opera *Lulu*, to which it may be said to form a sort of curtain-raiser. The series on which it is based is scale-like, and as with that of the violin concerto, has pronounced tonal characteristics.

In writing the opera *Lulu*, realism was once again his guiding-line, as it had been with *Wozzeck*. This time Berg's central character is a "female counterpart to Don Giovanni", who is also driven to murder, and whose suffering is brought about by the retribution of men seeking to avenge their own guilt. All illusions are taken from our eyes; we see things as they are. Once again, as with *Wozzeck*, events follow one another with complete inevitability. Lulu's precarious climb to respectability, by her marriage to Dr. Schoen, contains within itself her eventual downfall. The tragedy consists in the fact that beauty can destroy all who succumb to it, until in the end it destroys itself.

As with his other opera, Berg subjects the scenes to a rigid formal discipline. He also continues the exploitation of the

[1] It was to have been conducted by Webern, but Scherchen took over at the last minute.

[2] Cantata No. 60, *O Ewigkeit, du Donnerwort* (O Eternity, thou awful word). This is a Chorale dialogue between Fear and Hope; fear of death is consoled by the assurance of salvation. The cantata ends with the Chorale *Es ist genug* (It is enough), and in choosing this particular hymn Berg was clearly moved by the same thoughts as those which inspired Bach to place it at the end of his Cantata.

human voice, with all the means of expression ranging between speech and *bel canto*. But the music of *Lulu* contains more quasi-symphonic repetition, and more symbolic allusion to character and situation than *Wozzeck*. The series on which the work is based, is used chordally to express Lulu's character (Ex. 27). Other characters are allotted themes. Intervals are

Berg
Lulu. Basic Series

Ex. 27

"Portrait chords" of Lulu

symbolic. For instance the pentatonic scale is used to suggest the Lesbian tendencies of the Countess Geschwitz, while the positive nature of Dr. Schoen is portrayed by a more energetic *motif*, with a strong flavour of major tonality. The use of retrograde movement is introduced to suggest the 'flash-back' of Lulu's life, when it is shown on the film-strip in Act 2. Moral depravity is depicted by the use of jazz instruments.

Although the composition of *Lulu*, which Berg had begun in 1928, was finished, some of the orchestration of Act 3 remained incomplete at his death; and although the *Lulu-Symphony*—an orchestral suite adapted from parts of the opera—was performed in 1934, the composer never lived to see the production of his work on the stage. It was dedicated in its entirety, as was surely most fitting, to Schoenberg, on the latter's sixtieth birthday—September 13th, 1934. Webern also presented his master with a birthday present, his *Konzert*, *Op. 24* (*Concerto for nine instruments*).

Webern

With Webern we stand on the threshold of a new world. His posthumous influence on composers today is one of the most significant factors in contemporary music; we refer to a "post-Webern" style, not so much to a "post-Berg" or "post-Messiaen" one. What is it that singles out Webern's work? What were his aesthetic intentions? How far did he succeed in achieving them?

He did not enjoy during his lifetime the same material success and public recognition that his friend and colleague Berg did after *Wozzeck*; in this respect he much more resembled his teacher Schoenberg, though not one of Webern's works was greeted in the way that *Pierrot Lunaire* had been. Webern was of a retiring disposition and an introspective nature; as well as a composer, he was also a teacher, a conductor and a musicologist, and he took his doctorate at Vienna with a dissertation on the *Choralis Constantinus* of the Renaissance composer H. Isaac; or, more properly, Ysaak (1450–1517). The *Choralis Constantinus* was a cycle of compositions for the Sundays and Feast days of the Church's year, written for the Cathedral of Constanz in Switzerland.

In Webern creative originality was combined with a sense of musical history and tradition. For him newness was necessity. His style—aphoristic, refined, subtle—was directed towards one single goal, namely comprehensibility. He was fond of quoting Schoenberg's dictum that the artist does not do what others find beautiful, but only what he finds necessary. So he expunged from his music everything that he considered superfluous or illogical. He pared it down to the merest essentials, never doubling with a second instrument where one was enough. The enormous orchestra that we associate with the late Romantic period was reduced by Webern to a few individual instruments. His scoring has the clarity of chamber music; and the dimensions of his compositions, particularly the middle-period ones, were similarly attenuated, and their content became correspondingly more concentrated.

Of his thirty two compositions, fifteen (Op. 17 to Op. 31) adopt the 12-note technique. His choice of instruments was entirely conventional, even ordinary; his preference was for the clarinet, which he himself played, and for the human voice, though he did not experiment as Schoenberg and Berg had done with the use of the voice. He wrote altogether 13 song cycles, and his last compositions, the Cantatas Op. 29 and 31[1], are among his most poetic and moving works. His early

---

[1] To words by Hildegard Jone. The last movement of the Cantata Op. 29 must be one of the very few examples of a choral work in which the music was written prior to the words.

compositions, up to the Rilke songs (Op. 8) are naturally much influenced by Schoenberg, particularly in the *klangtecknik*, as shown in Op. 6 and elsewhere, where a melodic line is shared between, and coloured by, various instruments of the orchestra. This technique is also finely illustrated in his orchestration of Bach's 6-part *Ricercare* from the *Musical Offering*, where each *motif* of Bach's theme is brought out with great brilliance.

In the works that follow, leading up to Op. 17, there is a gradual reduction of sound and duration. Erwin Stein referred to him as "the composer of the *pianissimo espressivo*;" this description however is not so applicable to the later works, from 1924 onwards.

The 12-note technique was at a rudimentary stage when Webern first introduced it in his Op. 17 (1924), but it was gradually developed by him according to his own individual style, until by the time of his Op. 20 (the String Trio) and Op. 21 (the Symphony) it had been moulded into something uniquely his own.

Webern's aesthetic intentions, which lend this uniqueness to his work, were the result of his interpretation of historical musical developments. He defined music[1] as natural law related to the sense of hearing; just as Goethe had defined colour as natural law related to the sense of sight. According to Webern the things with which art deals are natural things, subject to the necessity of natural laws; there is nothing illusory or arbitrary about them. So art must not conflict with nature. The 7-note diatonic scale arose from the nature of musical sound itself; it was discovered, not invented. A note is a complex of a fundamental and its overtones; these overtones extend into infinity. So Webern concluded that the only difference between consonance and dissonance is simply that a dissonance is a higher step up on the ladder of overtones than a consonance; otherwise there is no essential difference. The entire range of sound lies in the *materia musica* provided by nature, and thus subject to natural laws.

It follows that in exploiting this material a composer must bring his ideas also within the framework of these universally valid laws. In so far as music is a language—which can be a

---

[1] In *The path to the new music* (Der Weg zur Neuen Musik).

dangerously misleading statement—it must aim above all to be comprehensible; and what chiefly makes for comprehensibility is partly a clear differentiation between what is of primary and what is of secondary importance in its constituent parts, and partly the coherence, or unity, of those related parts.

Webern goes on to say that where music differs from other art-forms is in its need of the time element, as well as the space element, for its unfolding. Starting from the single monodic line of Gregorian chant, two main developments took place; first, the expansion of polyphony, particularly by the Netherland and Flemish school; second, the conquest of tonality. Already by 1600 a climax in the art of polyphony was reached, and we see a return to the single-line melody, this time in the form of melody with accompaniment, which was developed by the Italian composers of the seventeenth century. The idea of a secondary part, or accompaniment, was foreign to the polyphonic technique, which aimed to achieve unity in all the parts, and did this by building a whole piece out of one note-sequence, by means of such contrapuntal devices as inversion, retrograde, and so on.

The accompanied melody, which we associate with the homophonic style of the Classical composers, required some other means to ensure its comprehensibility than the thematic integration of the polyphonic composers; and this was found in the basis of the 8-bar sentence, or period, which became the central core of the Classical symphony and sonata, (see Ex. 23). But the technique of developing a whole musical structure out of one germinating idea, which had been the practice of the Netherland and Flemish school, was not lost; we see numerous examples of it in Bach, particularly the *Art of Fugue*; and in Beethoven; for example the finale of the *Choral Symphony*.

Most developments can be traced back to Bach; and certainly his use of chromaticism is one of his most pronounced features. His Chorale harmonisations stretch tonality by extending the 7-note scale to include all the 12 notes. Later composers added notes and chords to the diatonic scale which did not belong to it, and the influence of which gradually came to supersede the power of the tonic to attract and control the harmonic direction of the music. Chords such as the Neapolitan sixth, the added and augmented sixth, the diminished seventh, all contributed to this progressive erosion of the diatonic scale.

The essence of tonality, Webern said, was the relation of the music to a key-note, or tonic. This relationship naturally became less felt as the use of ambiguous chords was introduced, which made way for all 12 chromatic notes. Soon the necessity to return to the key-note was questioned; Wagner showed the way here. The point where a return to the tonic, if there is to be one, is most strongly felt is at the cadence; the end of a sentence or period. Therefore, it was at the point of cadence that the dissolution of tonality would also be most strongly felt.

The decisive change came in the years preceding 1914, and it was twofold. First the major and minor tonalities, the two genders of music, fused and combined into a single chromatic scale; second the necessity to return to a key-note at the end of a sentence, or the end of a piece, was no longer felt. Moreover, once the return to a key-note, by means of a cadence, was called in question, it was only logical to question also the necessity for a key-note at all. What characterises a key-note is partly its reiteration, partly its cadential resolution. All sense of a key will, therefore, be avoided if, in the cycle of twelve chromatic notes, no one note is repeated, thereby causing it to become prominent. In that case, the unity of the composition as a whole, its formal organisation, which previously had been achieved by tonality, now would need to be assured by imposing some other sort of order and form on the twelve notes of the scale, or series, in a way similar to that in which the old polyphonic composers achieved unity from their use of a scale of seven notes, and from their adherence to a single note-sequence, or *motif*.

Tonality had been the chief means of creating unity and of building a musical structure. Before tonality, this had been achieved by polyphony. Now, to use Webern's words, "just as ripe fruit falls from the tree, music has quite simply given up the formal principle of tonality."

When the form-giving return to the tonic was felt to be no longer valid, some other form had to take its place. 12-note composition was not merely a substitute for tonality; it was felt to be both intuitive and inevitable. The loss of tonality meant the loss of the chief means of constructing long movements; but gradually the natural laws governing the 12-note series were discovered. Composers were led back to the principles of polyphony, in which there was a thematic connection between the main and the subsidiary parts. In serial composition, note repetition is not forbidden *per se*; but what is ruled out is note repetition within the series, or note-sequence, as fixed by the composer. All parts sing the same theme, but varied according to the traditional methods of polyphony. So, concludes Webern, the use of the series ensures unity in a composition; inventiveness in the manipulation and repetition of the series ensures variety.

So much for Webern's aesthetic *apologia*. In his compositions, two factors obsess him; one is an extreme aural sensitivity, a highly concentrated lyrical expression; the other is a desire to achieve an absolute formal purity. In his concern with sound for its own sake, he may be said to stem from Debussy, whose music sometimes resembles not so much an organic growth as a *collage* of sound-impressions. But Webern is unique in his developing of new forms based on his particular serial style; also in his lyricism. The final form a composition took depended entirely on the nature of the particular *motifs* used and the manner of their working.

Traditional harmony, counterpoint and form had followed tonality. Now Webern blended these three elements into a fresh concept, and built from this a new 'tonality', of sounds related only to each other, and not to a key-note. The easiest way, so he said, to make a musical phrase comprehensible is to repeat it; and one of the most exact forms of repetition is the canon. So we find this device, particularly in its mirror form, predominant all through his music. To achieve variety, he concerned himself with grading the pitch, rhythm and duration of notes, and rests; it is this aspect of his technique which led directly, later on, to the more sophisticated methods of serial and electronic composition that we see today.

Webern approached a composition as a new sound-experience in the space-time continuum.[1] Intervals are the chief structural element, which set up frequency-relationships. The primary intervals of the octave, fifth and third—including

---

[1] The unity of musical space had been foreshadowed by Busoni.

their inversions, the fourth and sixth—have a pronounced tonal bias, since they occur comparatively early in the overtones of the harmonic series. For this reason, Webern tends to avoid them and to use instead the second; particularly the minor second,[1] or interval of the semitone, with its inversion the major seventh, and their octave extensions, the minor ninth and major fourteenth.

As far as musical space is concerned, the horizontal and the vertical are not differentiated. Webern is simply concerned with those factors which govern the relationship of notes. Of these the main one is pitch, which is determined by frequencies; other subsidiary factors are timbre, intensity, dynamics, duration, method of attack. As far as musical time is concerned, notes may be sounded simultaneously or successively. The closer they are together in time, and the less the time-interval separating them, the more direct will be their relationship. What is a chord, or density of notes, but a mixing of different frequencies whose separation in terms of time-interval is zero? What is a canon but the replacement of one time-relationship by another? Rhythm is the result of the interaction of the two chief limiting factors[2] in space and time, namely frequency-interval and time-interval. In varying the time-interval, Webern raises the importance of the rest, and makes it an integral part of the structure, of equal importance to the note. A rest, or moment of silence, may also be thought of as zero in the scale of dynamic values.

The relationship between notes determines the structure of the phrase, and hence the overall form of the movement. All the factors governing the relationship are varied by Webern, down to the smallest detail; these include the compass of notes making up chords, the time-interval between chords of different numbers of notes, the grading of note-duration, dynamics, tempo and method of attack to coincide with the symmetrical pattern of various groups of sounds.

[1] For example the 5th of his 6 Bagatelles for String Quartet is made up of simultaneous minor seconds.

[2] These factors are sometimes called by the mathematical term of *parameters*, a generic word which includes pitch, duration, timbre, intensity, attack, tempo. The word was first used in a musical context by Dr. Meyer-Eppler of Bonn University. (See glossary on p. 124).

The notes thus form a sort of chromatic chain, from which the harmony is derived, and of which each link is different. There is a risk that formal chaos could result, but Webern avoids this partly by the adherence to the 12-note series, partly by the use of canon. For example, in his Symphony, Op. 21, not only is the second half of the series the retrograde of the first half (Ex. 28), but also in the second movement

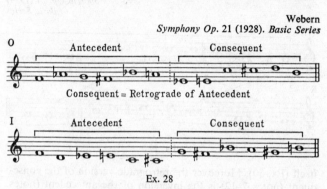

Webern
Symphony Op. 21 (1928). Basic Series

Ex. 28

not merely the theme itself, but the whole movement is in mirror form, a double canon, of which the second half is a retrograde of the first; the pivot occurs in the fourth variation, at bar 50. Also the first movement opens with a double canon in contrary movement, the parts shifting from one instrument to another.

Webern's working unit was the *motif*; the smallest independent musical particle. This he derived from the practice of the Classical composers, whose themes and subjects consisted of such particles. This was where his treatment of the 12-note series differed radically from that of Schoenberg or Berg; whereas Schoenberg would create a theme which contained the twelve notes, Webern would break up the twelve notes into groups of two or three notes each, which contained whatever interval-relationships he required. The series of his Concerto for nine instruments, Op. 24, is a very clear example of four 3-note *motifs*, all interrelated (Ex. 29). The preponderance of semitones will immediately be apparent from the examples given.

Again, the series used in the Variations for Orchestra, Op. 30, is organised into three groups of four notes; the groups are announced at the beginning of the work by double bass, oboe and trombone respectively. The third group mirrors the intervals of the first; the second group mirrors

Webern
Concerto Op. 24 (1934)
Basic Series

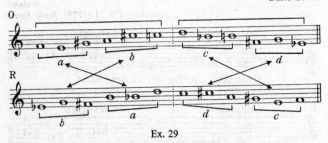

Ex. 29

itself (Ex. 30). Moreover the retrograde version of the consequent (notes 7–12) is the inversion of the antecedent (notes 1–6), and *vice versa*. A consideration of one short section of this composition will serve to indicate some of those features

Webern
Variations for Orchestra Op. 30 (1940)
Basic Series

Ex. 30

in the physical construction of Webern's music that have proved such a spur to composers since 1945.

Variations for Orchestra, Op. 30 (Bars 15–20)

Throughout the work, which lasts for $9\frac{1}{2}$ minutes, the variation principle is grounded in the augmentation and diminution of the three 4-note *motifs* which make up the series. In the example given (Ex. 31) the series occurs twice simultaneously, the first time shared between the violins and the bass-clarinet, (statement of Series I), the second time shared between the brass instruments and the oboe (statement of Series II). The four brass instruments play *motifs* a and c

Webern
Variations for Orchestra Op. 30
(bars 15–20)

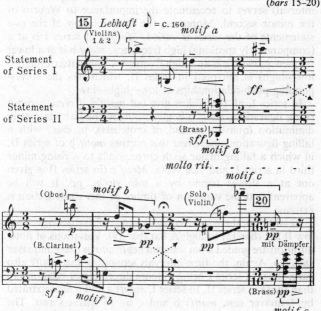

Brass = trumpet, horn, trombone, tuba

Ex. 31

as two 4-note chords; the first chord, of one quaver duration, sff *staccato*; the second chord a fifth higher than the first, also of one quaver duration, but articulated as two semi-quavers, pp and with mutes. The two chords contain the same intervals (except for an octave transposition of the lowest note), but there is a subtle grading of layout and texture. In the first chord (*motif* a), the horn plays the minor third from the top, and the major seventh, which is so characteristic of Webern, occurs between the trumpet and trombone. In the second chord (*motif* c) the trombone plays the corresponding minor third from the top, and the major seventh occurs between the trumpet and horn.

Statement of series I is a semitone higher than statement of series II; this again (like its inversion the major seventh interval) serves to accentuate the importance to Webern of the minor second. Moreover, the pitch-relation of the two statements of the series is varied. *Motif* a of series I is at a (comparatively speaking) high frequency; *motif* b is at a lower frequency; *motif* c is at a high frequency. This pattern (high—low—high) is mirrored in series II, which has the corresponding pitch-relationships of low—high—low.

In series I, all the violins give out *motif* a, f *cresc.*, with a rising figuration; *motif* b is given out by the bass-clarinet in diminution (quavers instead of crotchets), p. *dim.*, with a falling figuration; moreover this mirrors *motif* b of series II, in which a falling major sixth corresponds to a rising minor third in series I, and vice versa. *Motif* c (in series I) is given out at a slower tempo by a solo violin, pp. It will be apparent that the variation of timbre in this short section is extreme.

In addition, there is a frequency-range of five octaves, from low B flat (bar 15) to high A flat (bar 19). Variations of note-duration are graded from the crotchet *tenuto* to the semiquaver *staccato*. Again, the time-intervals separating the *motifs* also vary, those in series I being in more direct, closer relationship than those in series II. In series I, *motifs* a and b are separated by 1 quaver rest, *motifs* b and c by $1\frac{1}{2}$ quavers rest. The corresponding rests in series II are of 4 and $4\frac{1}{2}$ quavers respectively.

The intensity of sound is also varied greatly, ranging from all the violins (f *cresc.*) combined with the brass (sff) in bar 15, to a single violin (pp) in bar 19. Methods of attack vary from *sforzato, tenuto, staccato, legato, sfp, cresc., dim.*, and pp following *cresc.* Changes of time-signature are numerous, and the change of tempo in bar 19 is but one instance of the constant rhythmical ebb and flow that Webern maintains all through the work—in fact, throughout his work as a whole.

To Webern, as to Schoenberg, the principle of variation was the very essence of serial composition; but to him it meant not so much a set of variations on a theme, as variations in the method of presentation of a musical idea. To put it in other words, the process begun by Schoenberg of 12-note composition, which affected only the pitch of notes, was developed by Webern into the serial treatment of other factors as well. This path tended, inevitably, towards total serialisation; more and more pre-determination, less and less 'free' composition. This indeed is how it has turned out to be.

CHAPTER FIVE

POST—WEBERN DEVELOPMENTS

(i) Electronic music

After Webern we enter a period of experiment, of technical and scientific research. Since 1945 there has been a marked change of emphasis by composers of the 'new music'. Hitherto composers have concerned themselves with the relation of notes to each other; and though their answers might be diametrically opposed, at least, the question they asked has been the same. With electronic composition, however, the line of enquiry changes, and the question now asked is not to do with the relation of notes to each other, but with the nature, the physical construction of musical sounds themselves.

Music which is inspired by a wish to exploit the nature of the physical sound-world reflects to a large extent the intellectual and philosophical climate in our West European and American culture today. Webern's aesthetic was derived from the proposition that by following the natural laws of sound a new tonality could be built. This had been foretold earlier by many musicians, such as Alois Haba, Charles Ives, and above all Busoni;[1] but it is only today that the analytical method has been widely accepted; and the exploring of the physical sound-world is the musical counterpart to the exploration by linguistic philosophy into the nature of words.

Innovations since Webern, though at first startling, have followed one of two direct and logical courses; the first is the course of electronic sound-generation, the second is the course of serialism for its own sake. This has led inevitably to an ever-increasing concern, partly with the control over the particles of the sound-spectrum, and partly with the range of that spectrum. Whereas the form and overall structure of traditional music was based on themes, and the contrast of

[1] In *Entwurf einer Neuen Aesthetik der Tonkunst* (1906).

those themes within a movement, the organisation of totally serial music is looked on as an end in itself, and themes become irrelevant. If the ordering of the sound patterns is complete, then the composition may be expected to generate its own mathematical logic, and hence an inevitable formal cohesion and variety. There is a beauty in pure numbers.

Webern's principle of variation in the presentation of musical ideas, if logically followed through, is a never-ending process. It is bound to lead to greater and greater complexity, and ever-evolving sound relationships. It is axiomatic that any sound can also be varied. You can even vary a period of silence. And if human control over the means of sound production is a limitation, an imperfection, you can overcome this by the adoption of mechanical, electronic methods.

The philosophical basis on which the electronic composer works is the belief that the only possible new development of Webern's serialism lies in the further refinement and sophistication of the means of controlling the elements of musical sound. This presupposes increased knowledge of its nature. The justification for electronic music is thus a desire for knowledge, and a belief that knowledge is the source of power and creative energy. It is, of course, a commonplace that now, to a greater extent than ever before in human history, has nature come under the control of man. In all fields of human endeavour in our time, knowledge is looked on as the key, not just to the understanding of past history, but also to future developments; it is looked on, for instance, as the antidote to religious superstitions, and as the insurance against political dictatorships, whose principal weapon is ignorance. What is psychoanalysis but self-knowledge? Without knowledge, it is held, mankind might as well return to the trees; knowledge is the one hope of civilised life. Why should we be surprised therefore if this current thirst for knowledge is found to be reflected in composers' attitude to their art? Moreover it can hardly be said to be a new approach. Did not the great French architect Jean Mignot utter what must surely be the last world on the subject, while overseeing Milan cathedral in 1398?:

Ars sine scientia nihil[1]

---

[1] Quoted by Paul Henry Lang in *Problems of modern music*, p. 7.

A number of musicians today look for an aesthetic justification for the current trend towards the mathematical aspect of composition by referring to the mediaeval scholastic classification of the liberal arts, which placed music as a scientific branch of mathematics, along with arithmetic, geometry and astronomy (called, collectively, *quadrivium*). The other three "liberal arts", which had to do with language, were logic, rhetoric and grammar/poetry. The classifications range from those of Cassiodorus and Boethius (6th century) to Savonarola (15th century); the latter altered the second group so as to include poetry, instead of grammar. We should also bear in mind that during the Middle Ages, the true and only science, that which traced all things to a first cause, was theology.[1]

In electronic music, art and technology meet; the performer is replaced by the tape-recorder. It was developed in the 1950's as a solution to particular musical and technical problems. On the one hand, orchestral instruments were proving a limitation, if not an obstacle, to serially-minded composers; in tonal music the external harmony, what was heard, and the internal harmony, the overtones, were one and the same; but in serial music this was no longer the case. On the other hand, the production of musical tone by artificial means was already, and had been for a long time, a *fait accompli*; for instance the electronic organ, the Ondes Martenot, the Ondioline, and other instruments. Might not this suggest a possible solution for the future? Musically, the only way to proceed along the path indicated by Webern was to seek to grade and to control, to an ever-increasing extent, the elements that constitute musical sound. Technically, it is obvious that, as far as analysis and control of the sound-spectrum are concerned, a much greater thoroughness, precision and efficiency can be achieved by a machine than by any fallible human agency.

But not all electronic music need be serial. It was more or less fortuitous that the introduction of the tape-recorder, and the development of electronic means of sound-generation, as something which was of interest to the composer, as distinct from a laboratory experiment of interest only to the engineer, coincided with the period during the 1950's when the tide of

[1] Hiller and Isaacson *Experimental Music* p. 11 foll.

post-Webern serialism was running at its flood. It was natural therefore that the two should run parallel, particularly as the younger German school of composers, who did the most to promote electronic composition, were also themselves serialists. And so it might be thought that serialism is the *sine qua non* of electronic composition. But this is not the case. Electronic composition may be serially organised (for instance Berio's *Homage to James Joyce*), but this is not necessarily so.

The early, experimental stage began in Paris in 1948, under Pierre Schaeffer, who was working for Radiodiffusion Française. His researches, known as *musique concrète*, led him to make use of sounds which originated in nature, and were not synthetically produced. He abandoned the world of music for the world of noise.[1] According to this aesthetic, anything heard is fit material for a composition. The most characteristic examples of this type of experimental work are *Symphonie pour un homme seul*, by Pierre Schaeffer, and *Le Voile d'Orphée*, by Pierre Henry.

The transition, and evolution, from *musique concrète* to electronic music was inevitable; the distinction being that the latter not only manipulates the sounds by electronic means, but also generates them as well. It is therefore true to say that *musique concrète* has been incorporated into electronic music, and that from now on we can use the latter term to include the former.

Electronic music started in 1951, and the first concert took place on 19th October, 1954, in the studios of Westdeutscher Rundfunk, Cologne.[2] The initial work was done by Herbert Eimert, Karlheinz Stockhausen, Paul Gredinger, Gisheler Klebe; already it has spread to France (Henri Pousseur, Pierre Boulez), Italy (Luciano Berio, Bruno Maderna), America (Ernst Krenek, Vladimir Ussachevsky), and England (Tristram Cary, Daphne Oram).

The electronic composer has at his disposal the means of a very precise and exact mathematical analysis of tones. This

[1] Je décidais de choisir mes éléments initiaux dans un domaine opposé à celui de la musique, celui des bruits. Schaeffer *Op. cit.* (Premier Journal, p. 55).

[2] In America, Luening and Ussachevsky, of Columbia University, presented a public concert of electronic music in October, 1952, at the Museum of Modern Art, New York. The first London concert was presented on 15th January, 1968, by the Redcliffe Concerts (p. 175).

has always been possible to some extent for the traditional composer, but hardly necessary. For normal purposes of composition a general indication of effect (such as mf) has proved adequate, and the exact effect in a performance has been decided by the performer; but in electronic music the manipulation of tones is done with extreme accuracy at the control panel, though there is as yet no standardised notation. The rôle of electronic music is that it should be a unique supplement to music written for instruments; that it should provide a species of sound which can be achieved in no other way. It does not set out to reproduce by electronic means the sort of traditional sounds that belong much more appropriately, and with much greater effectiveness, to the conventional instruments of the orchestra. Nor is it the function of electronic music to synthesise instrumental or orchestral sounds.

The principle on which the electronic composer works is that the apparent shortcomings of instrumental composition are overcome by the breaking up of musical sound into the main elements, or parameters,[1] of pitch, intensity, duration and *timbre*. Each of these is conceived as a continuously graded scale, in a way that can only be obtained electronically. For instance, to take the parameter of pitch, the frequency of g′ is 396 c.p.s.; the frequency of a′, just one tone higher, is 440 c.p.s.; the frequency-interval is thus 44 c.p.s.; but this is reduced by the conventionally-tempered scale to only two semitones. So it becomes apparent that the twelve semitones which make up the octave, give way in electronic music to a much greater range of possibilities.

The elements of pitch, intensity, duration and *timbre* are inseparable, and any modification of one induces a modification of the others. If the composition is serial, then each is made subject to serial permutation. The composer starts with a series of proportions to determine the parameters, and the permutations of this series result in organized sound-complexes.

There are three stages in an electronic composition—the generation of sound, the modification of sound, and the recording of sound on tape. The first is done by oscillators,

[1] See the glossary of terms on p. 124.

which may generate white noise, or sine waves; also square waves, or saw-tooth waves (which are not sinusoidal). When the composer departs from the pure sinus tone, he has available many ready-made harmonic mixtures, which use the natural harmonic series to a greater or lesser extent. But if he wishes to use a note-mixture not based on the natural series he must use sinus-tone mixtures. These tones, once produced, are then passed through various modifying devices, filters, transient generators, which make the required modulation—reverberation and echo effect, or exponential fall-away (like a piano-note). The result is recorded on tape. A central principle of the process of electronic composition is the imposition of one tone upon another, or the beating together of waves, subsonic or supersonic, to make a characteristic tone. In effect, the electronic composer either builds up from sine or square waves, which he combines, or builds down from white noise, which he filters.

His equipment, such as you would expect to find in a broadcasting or recording studio, or university laboratory, consists of a sound-generator, tape-recorders, filters, loud-speakers and control-panel.[1] The equipment available in the electronic laboratory of the University of Michigan, U.S.A., is described by the composer Ross Lee Finney[2]:—

". . . The electronic equipment consists of three two-channel Ampex recorders and one single-channel Ampex. We have twelve sine-square wave oscillators, which is the main sound source, and a battery of equipment for the modification of sound, such as reverberators, band-pass filters, wave form oscillators, etc. etc., and the various mixing panels and switch panels too complicated to give in detail."

With these instruments the composer analyses, differentiates, controls. He controls the parameter of pitch by a continuous gradation of frequencies, and by the manipulation of relative relationships, which he can observe on an oscilloscope: he controls the parameter of intensity by a scale of calculated dynamic levels, measured in decibels, which are logarithmic units, since the ear responds logarithmically. The parameter of duration is measured by centimetres of tape-

[1] Herbert Eimert in *die Reihe*, Vol. 1 (1955).
[2] Writing in *Composer*, No. 15, April 1965.

length. Intricate cross-rhythms are possible as well—they may be obtained, for instance, by running loops out of phase—which are much more elaborate than those which are available to the instrumental composer, who relies on the human performer.

Although the same principles apply to serial composition for instruments as well as for electronic music, there is an essential difference between the two. Whereas instruments sound notes that are made up of overtones, which are related by the harmonic series, electronic music is made up of pure sinus tones, or square tones, related in a way decided entirely by the composer. These tone mixtures, or complexes, are not the same thing as chords played by instruments.

Electronic music is thus an ordered accumulation of tones; and just as the harmonics in instrumental music are graded, the higher ones becoming quieter, so do tones need to be graded. But there is an important new factor implied by electronic music; it spells the end of equal temperament, as established since Bach.[1] The independent manipulation of the parameters produces a new type of sound, not merely an extension of the old. Although the electronic composer may be said to take up where Webern left off—this claim is repeatedly made by the Cologne school—Webern did not, and could not, go farther than instrumentally-produced sound; the pre-determined series of proportions, which is the tool of the serial electronic composer, gives him a quite unprecedented discipline and control over a much wider range of *materia musica*. Only in electronic music is the sinus tone isolated.

The alternation of parameters, which makes up the compositional process, is done by the serial composer with strict regularity, and the permutations of the series rule out the possibility of the recurrence of a complex. The number of possible complexes is infinite, and the temporal (horizontal) structure of electronic music is decided purely and solely by the pre-determined permutations. The overall form of the piece comes, as it always has, from the nature of the material used; and the material in this case, with its texture of sound-complexes, is based on the observed facts of physics—just as

[1] In the *48 Preludes and Fugues* (cf. page 13).

the diatonic system had been, as shown in Rameau's treatise of 250 years ago.

In themselves, the elements of sounds mean nothing; but it is the precise organisation, in time, of the parameters which gives them a specifically musical significance. So the material of a work and its structure are really one and the same thing. Thus it becomes apparent that the centrally important factor in electronic music, the one which decides its very nature, is the precision of the differentiation, and hence the relationship set up, between the parameters.

The composer of electronic music is also its performer, and what has excited at least one composer[1] is not the efficiency of mechanical control that he can exercise, so much as the power to select and to synthesise an enormous range of sound-possibilities; in fact to create the sound itself, from its raw stage to its finished form. The interval (speaking in terms of pitch) has ceased to be; so has the note as such, as we understand the term; so have the boundaries that have hitherto existed between the *timbres* of various orchestral instruments. Instead, there is one unbroken sound-pheno-menon, continuously graded, which the electronic composer seeks to manage and to control by means of unit-values very exactly measured and proportioned. The *timbre* of electronic music is the result of the elaboration of the musical elements of pitch, intensity and duration. If you vary the elements of sound, you thereby vary its colour. The relationship of proportions governs the sound-complexes, and these may be said to correspond to the families of orchestral instruments.

For the serial composer, all aspects of electronic music derive from a single source. The nature of each sound-complex, the permutations of each parameter, the overall form of a composition, in a word its quality as well as its quantity, all have a common basis—the series. The series, and the principle of serialism, is given absolute sovereignty over the kingdom of music. In this sense, electronic music is the logical and inevitable continuation of Webern's adoption of serialism for its own sake.

[1] Pierre Boulez, writing in *die Reihe*, Vol. 1. See also Vladimir Ussachevsky, in *The modern composer and his world*, p. 121 foll.

GLOSSARY OF SOME TERMS USED IN
ELECTRONIC MUSIC

ALEATORIC: (from Latin *alea*, a dice) Dependent on chance. The essence of aleatoricism is that a random, improvisatory element is allowed within fixed and controlled limits. *Aleatoric modulation* (see *Modulation*) is the equivalent of a string player's *vibrato*.

COMPLEX: A combination of tones, whose increments are decided not by the harmonic series but by the composer.

FREQUENCY: The number of cycles per second (c.p.s.), which decide the pitch of a sound (e.g. $a' = 440$ c.p.s.). They are however subject to certain subjective variation, and the wavelength of the same frequency varies in different media.

MODULATION: The expression of one sound in terms of another. *Amplitude modulation* means that the amplitude of one sound is modulated by the frequency of another.

PARAMETER: A limiting, variable factor in musical sound. The main parameters are pitch, duration, intensity, *timbre*.

SERIALISM: The regular permutation of a pre-determined pattern of relationships.

SINUS TONE: Pure tone, unmixed with harmonics; the result of simple harmonic motion; the horizontal projection of a constant rotation; the smallest, purest musical particle, which the composer uses to build up a complex; an ideal limit of which no practical device is really capable.

SQUARE TONE: One of many harmonic mixtures, rougher, more defined, subjectively louder for the same power than sinus tone.

WHITE NOISE: The bringing together of units of sound from the total sound-spectrum; the result of the random generation of pure spectral colour, of which the nearest equivalent is the noise of surf on the sea-shore. It can be suggested by a roll on the side-drum with snares, by a cymbal clash, or by the sound of applause. By filtering it can be reduced to more definite pitch and so be made of use.

(ii) *Later Serialism*

The absence of generally accepted aesthetic standards, and the non-existence of fixed artistic canons, which is the musical situation today, leaves the way wide open to the intellectual snob and the charlatan. It is all too easy to pose as an expert when creative musicians are preoccupied with the organisation of their greatly enlarged material, and when the general listener is too perplexed and uncertain to know what to answer. But we should remember that theory normally follows practice—unless you happen to be a Bach—and as the practice of serialism is even now evolving, it is premature to theorise; still more to legislate.

There are however two important factors which make further investigation into the facts of the case obligatory. One is a certain dogmatism which is noticeable in some *avant-garde* composers and partisans; it could almost be described as an aggressive imperialism, a sort of aesthetic blackmail. According to this group, serialism is the only undoubted musical 'language' of today; it is widely accepted, and becoming more so; it is the way to the musical promised land, which if you do not follow you are a "reactionary", and you condemn yourself to remain in a dead world, colourfully described by one serialist composer, whose ardour somewhat exceeds his assessment of theology, as a "shapeless limbo".[1] It is understandable that, in the present period of

---

[1] For such a criticism of Adorno's *Philosophy of New Music* see *die Reihe*, Vol. 4, p. 63 foll.

flux, there is a tendency to clutch at what appears to be a standard; and the doctrine of "serialism or else" may be seen against this background. It does however violate the one centrally important factor in the creative process, that speculative volition on the part of the composer, which we have already referred to.[1] It is moreover entirely out of keeping with that liberality of spirit which Schoenberg possessed. Dogmatism from any quarter—academic or *avant-garde*—has nothing to do with aesthetics. And in any case, if serialism really is the only way 'forward', there is surely every need, for that reason alone, to investigate it.

The other important factor is the apparently contradictory statement emanating from other experimental quarters, that serialism is already a thing of the past; that it served its purpose for the Schoenberg–Webern school, but that the truly 'advanced' composer today has moved on to fresh pastures. This view, if we accept it, would make serialism a historical event, and would therefore invite our assessment of it as such. What was the nature and purpose of this phenomenon, we ask, which could rise to such heights in the Viennese school, and exert such an influence, only to pass on, when its time came, into a higher phase of evolution?

There is, in fact, very strong evidence that those who would already pronounce the last rites over the corpse, do so out of turn. To one composer at least the mechanics of serialism have opened up exciting possibilities for the enrichment of the musical language; and these possibilities have by no means been worked out. Stravinsky's latest works put his thoughts into practice. One such work, *Movements*, has already been quoted; another is his *Variations*. He puts his view in these words[2]:—

". . . I am becoming not less but more of a serial composer; those younger colleagues who already regard 'serial' as an indecent word, in their claim to have exhausted all that is meant by it and to have gone far beyond, are, I think, greatly in error."

Again for this reason, if for no other, an examination of serialism is imperative.

[1] p. 50.
[2] *Memories and Commentaries*, p. 106.

Webern's 'serialism for its own sake' could only lead eventually to total serialisation of all the musical elements. This principle has been followed up by composers in three ways: in composition for conventional instruments, in electronic composition, and in composition which combines these two. The composers who have done most to develop music in this direction, whom we associate with the Darmstadt *Ferienkurse*, are Boulez, Pousseur, Stockhausen and Berio,[1] who have composed in the three ways mentioned; and their lead has been followed by many composers in many countries, particularly America.

Serialism means the total pre-determination of all the elements of musical sound. It means not just the rejection of tonality, but also the rejection of those things derived from tonality; for instance the use of themes, and of those large-scale forms, such as Symphony, Sonata, Rondo, and so on, whose organisation is thematic. In their place, not merely a new sort of sound is introduced, but a new attitude to the musical experience. In tonal music the harmony, made up of chromatic and diatonic elements, gave to the music a sense of direction, of movement. All parts contributed to the same harmonic purpose and inevitability; and this made it considerably easier for the listener to understand the musical logic. The form arose from the harmony itself.

This homogeneity has been replaced in serial music by the independent and disparate movement of each part. Retrograde and the mirror-canon, were, as we have seen, at the very root of Webern's technique; and these automatically by definition, break up the unity of movement. In later serialism, the direction and movement of the music are entirely replaced by a preoccupation with the static arrangement of the musical material. Tonality had been the source of themes, of harmony, of form; all these contributory factors were therefore consistent and coherent, since they had a common origin. Serialism seeks to achieve a comparable artistic result by making the series replace tonality as the matrix of the entire creative process.

The question of the serial composer's 'inspiration' is one that has been much debated. He works between two poles,

---

[1] *Die Reihe*, Vol. 4, *Young composers.*

whose tendencies, if followed through to their conclusion, will be seen to be mutually exclusive. The first is Schoenberg's conception of the 12-note technique, which was to use the series thematically to decide the pitch and the order of the notes. This amounts to a grafting of a new onto an old tradition; some would call it an impossible attempt to pour new wine into old bottles;[1] nevertheless many composers have been inspired to follow this development, particularly Aaron Copland,[2] Roberto Gerhard, Hans Werner Henze, and many others.

The second is the conception of pure serialism, which substitutes a set of numbers, or proportions, for the 12-note series, and uses this to determine all aspects of composition, not merely the pitch of notes. The recurrence of any sound-complex is avoided by the rotation of this series; and thus the sort of thematic repetition associated with tonal music, which builds a musical structure by calling on the listener's memory, (a very potent factor, incidentally), is quite impossible in pure serial composition. Instead, the musical material is constantly being presented in a fresh guise. For this a new perception is needed, since the music derives its interest not so much from harmonic direction, or movement, or thematic contrast, as from the juxtaposition of sound-blocks.

Serialism of this kind contains within itself not merely dangers, but ambiguities of a profound nature. Total organisation and pre-determination of the musical elements is a denial of creative freedom. The more total the organisation, the more total the denial. Whether this matters or not is, of course, open to question; but composers have attempted to meet this difficulty by admitting into the performance of their otherwise rigidly controlled work an element of chance. This process, known as aleatoricism, may be said to correspond in its purpose to the admission of chromatic notes into a diatonic passage, which will have the effect of colouring it, without betraying its identity. It is not the same thing as improvisation, in the sense in which a jazz musician improvises; nor is it the same as that freedom which a keyboard player of the Baroque period was given when 'realising' the figured bass of a *continuo* part. The chance element in serial

[1] See below, p. 134 foll.
[2] For example, *Connotations*.

composition is a deliberate attempt on the part of the composer to make good a deficiency inherent in the technique itself; it is a part of the process of composition. The performer is invited to improvise, but within defined limits.

There are many examples in the music of Stockhausen. In *Zeitmasse*, which is a study for wind quintet in the relationship between speed and tempo, the movement is constantly quickened up or slowed down. There are directions "as fast as possible", or "as slow as possible", dependent on the nature of the instruments and the capacity of the players. The varying tempo technique is inherently part of serialism; in *Klavierstuck VI*, Stockhausen inserts a 13-line staff to indicate tempi. The top line represents ♪ = 180, the bottom line ♪ = 45; and a continuously variable line, like a graph, indicates to the player the alterations in speed.

In the case of *Klavierstuck XI*, the character of the piece may change with each performance. It consists of nineteen separate episodes which can be played in any order the player wishes. Tempo, dynamics and so on, vary according to the selected order, and the piece ends when any episode has been repeated twice.

Zyclus is a piece for one player and thirteen percussion instruments. The chance element is here so pronounced that no two performances are the same. The score is written on eight two-sided pages, spiral bound. The performer can start at the beginning of any of the pages, and the score may be played either way up. There are nine interlocking scales of density, with varying tempi, so that wherever a player begins, there will be nine moments of climax, each one of a different *timbre*.

In *Refrain*, for piano, celesta and vibraphone, the 'refrains', which occur six times, are written on a transparent plastic ruler, pivoted in the centre of the page. This can be rotated anywhere across the page, but wherever it falls it remains for that performance.

Both Stockhausen in *Momente* and Berio in *Homage to James Joyce* have taken haphazard snippets and fragments from different languages—English, French, German, Italian— as well as random, meaningless noises from anywhere and everywhere; they have combined these noises in a multiplicity of suggestive sounds, a sort of linguistic counterpoint, which

Berio calls an "anamorphosis" of the literary text. This process represents the random element applied also to the source of inspiration.

In the work of other composers also aleatoricism is found. Boulez introduces a certain fantasy into his *Mallarmé improvisation, No. 2.* In the Nonet of the Canadian composer, Otto Joachim (a work which combines instrumental with recorded sound), the five variations which make up the middle section may be played in any order. But far the greatest devotee of the random element is that *enfant terrible* of American music, John Cage. He is much more radical in his approach, and chance decides not just the order of movements and structural organisation of a piece, but the very work itself, and points of details, such as the choice of clef.[1]

Basic to any assessment of serialism is the question of form. The diatonic system led to Sonata form; to what extent has serialism discovered a new one? If you do away with such an essential part of musical structure as the form which resulted from traditional tonality, you must put something in its place.

No composer illustrates the need of serialism to find a new form, as a substitute for the old, better than Stockhausen, each of whose works, whether instrumental or electronic, or both, is a search for a new artistic cohesion, proper to the chosen medium.

His first works, *Kreuzspiel* (1951), *Kontra punkte* (1952), *Punkte* (1953), were written partly under the spell of Messiaen's *Mode de valeurs*, partly as a continuation of Webern's athematic, pointillistic technique. Next, Stockhausen experiments in group form; notes are related to each other in groups, and these groups are then interrelated. His culminating work under this heading is *Gruppen* (1957), which brings into relief the characteristic nature of instrumental serialism and well illustrates its inherent tendency on the one hand to merge rhythm with metre, horizontal with vertical movement, harmony with counterpoint—in a word, to unify the temporal moment of sound, and to make it more immediate; on the other hand to differentiate and diversify the elements of sound,

---

[1] For some further instances, and for a discussion of the effect of aleatoricism on the traditional composer/performer relationship, see Lukas Foss in *Perspectives of New Music*, Spring 1963, p. 45.

to fragmentate them into innumerable particles, and then to synthesise them like a mosaic.[1]

Gruppen fuer drei Orchester (1957).

(References are to the score published by Universal Edition)

The work is played by three orchestral groups, each under a separate conductor,[2] and placed at different positions in the hall. The players total 109. Such a stereophonic effect reminds us of the style of Baroque composers, Gabrieli or Schutz; or of the 19th century Italian composer Pietro Raimondi.[3] Stockhausen's spatial counterpoint adds another dimension—that of physical distance—to the existing musical dimensions of time and space. As in *Zeitmasse*, there are passages of independent movement interspersed between synchronised blocks of sound. The regular, pre-determined organisation of the musical elements, which is the premise from which serialism starts, is here matched by the most thorough organisation of the instruments of the three orchestras; particularly in the percussion sections, which are enormous. This is a trend with important implications.

Each orchestra has four percussion players, and the note-sounding percussion instruments are divided equally between the orchestras. They include marimbaphone, glockenspiel, xylorimba, vibraphone, tubular bells, cowbells. Other instruments are divided into metal, wood and skin sounds. In the metal group, 3 tom-toms and 9 cymbals are arranged in a scale from the largest to the smallest, and divided in fours between the orchestras, so that each orchestra has 1 tam-tam and 3 cymbals whose pitches overlap. The distribution is best illustrated diagrammatically as follows:—

[1] See Stravinsky's *Movements* (p. 55).

[2] At the first performance in Cologne in March 1958, the three conductors were Stockhausen, Maderna and Boulez.

[3] Cecil Gray in *Contingencies*, p. 93 foll., describes the triple oratorio of Raimondi (1786–1853). On one evening in Rome (August 1852) *Putifar* was played; on the second, *Guiseppe*; on the third, *Giacobbe*; and on the fourth all three oratorios were performed simultaneously by 430 performers and 4 conductors. This produced, we are told, "an agitation impossible to describe".

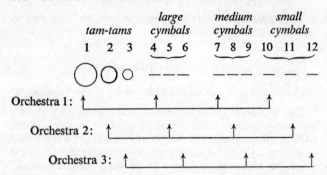

Under the heading of wooden sounds, each orchestra has specially made African wooden drums, each with two pitches. The six drums are tuned to give the twelve notes of the scale, and these are also made to overlap in their distribution between the orchestras.

There are also 12 drums made of skin, tuned to each of the 12 notes, and distributed between the orchestras as shown in Ex. 32. There are 22 bars (between 121 and 122) which

Stockhausen
Distribution of Drums in *Gruppen* (1957)

Skin-drums used are tom-toms, tumbas and bongos in the higher register.

Ex. 32

consist of music for these drums alone. It follows a section (117 to 120) where the brass was correspondingly exploited, and it leads directly to the most shattering climax of the whole work (122–123), when brass and percussion of each orchestra–no strings—synchronise for about 13 bars at a dynamic level of fff. The short example given of the passage for drums (Ex. 33) well illustrates the nature of the work as a whole. There is an interlocking of dynamics, constantly varying tempo, and a rhythmical overlapping, most characteristic of this composer, which is achieved by variously grouping the notes; in fours (Orchestra 1), in sixes (Orchestra 2), and in fives (Orchestra 3).

Karlheinz Stockhausen
Gruppen

Music for 12 drums   12 bars before 122

Ex. 33
for pitch of drums see Ex. 32

The composition, which lasts for 25 minutes, is played without a break. There are no separate movements, in the conventional sense; only a sequence of sound-impressions which exist for the moment only, and rely for their effect solely on the skill of the composer in relating the pre-determined patterns. Ex. 33 is an example of that complexity found throughout the work, indeed throughout all serial composition. It clearly requires inventiveness of a different sort from that required in thematic composition.

What is the nature of this inventiveness? The nature of serial technique bears very little relation to traditional technique; or for that matter to 12-note technique. Serialism is a violent reaction against Schoenberg's innovations on the ground that, according to the *avant-garde*, Schoenberg did not go nearly far enough in pursuing his technical discoveries. Instead, they maintain, he compromised with tradition, with the result that although he admitted serial organisation to decide the pitch of notes, his style remained traditionally based in other respects—rhythm, duration, dynamics, and so on. Serial composers, led by Stockhausen and Boulez, have set themselves the task of removing what they consider to be this inconsistency. This, in fact, is their point of departure.

Boulez has said that, in his opinion, the 12-note technique should not be, as Schoenberg thought, merely an extra discipline in an otherwise conventional style of chromatic composition; it should require also an entirely fresh formal organisation, unrelated to any traditional, outworn style, with which it is inconsistent. Schoenberg's *Klangfarbenmelodie*[1] might have led to a serialisation of *timbre*, if it had been followed through; but Schoenberg was impervious to any rhythmic, dynamic or structural changes. So we can see that the reaction of the serialists against Schoenberg's 12-note technique is far more radical than any reaction Schoenberg himself had (if, indeed, he had any) against the chromatic style of the Romantic period.

Stockhausen, who is more mathematically-minded than Boulez, puts the same point in a different way.[2] The 12 notes of Schoenberg's series are in effect, he maintains, a sequence of 12 fundamental tones, whose "scale of perception" is chromatic, and whose steps are serially composed. But the "scale of perception" of instrumental sounds is harmonic—that is to say the sounds consist of related overtones. The result of this is that, whereas tonal music showed a consistency, an identity between the musical material and the manner of its treatment, this identity ceased with the introduction of the 12-note technique. In effect, Stockhausen is saying, only two courses lie open to the composer: he can either adapt the instruments to serialism, or he can adapt serialism to the instruments. The first course leads directly to electronic music. What are the possibilities of the second?

Serialism means extending the serial principle to other factors than merely pitch. Stockhausen takes duration as his example, and shows what effect the application of serialism would have on it.

It is possible to make a series of 12 durations by starting with the note of smallest duration, and adding one each time:—

In this series the proportion between the first duration (♪) and the last duration (♩.) is in the ratio 1:12, whereas in the equally-tempered octave the ratio between the first and last notes is 1:2 (a' = 440; a'' = 880); and although it is perfectly possible to use this duration-series by ordinary contrapuntal methods—that is to say by distributing it between different parts, and varying its order—the resulting relationships set up would be irregular, and anything but serial. What matters in serialism is the regular proportion of interval-relationships.

It is also possible to build a series by starting with the note of longest duration, which acts as the *fundamental duration* or *phase*, and by progressively increasing the number of constituent notes (or *formants*) making up this fundamental:—

In this series, the duration of any individual note is obtained by dividing the *fundamental* (in this case a semibreve) by the ordinal number of the formant. And just as in pitch the simultaneous sounding of two or more harmonics can suggest the fundamental tone, so in this case the simultaneous sounding of two or more formants can suggest the fundamental phase. In Ex. 33, the *fundamental phase* (♪) is suggested by the formants 4 (𝄢) 5 (𝄢) and 6 (𝄢). Thus it is apparent that the *fundamental phase* corresponds to metre in non-serial composition, and the combination of formants corresponds to rhythm.

Each of the series so far suggested starts out with the note-durations themselves. Serialism, however, is concerned not so much with those as with the regular scale of proportionate relationship; that is its starting-point. It would be illogical to pretend that these non-chromatic series of durations, with their varying intervals of proportions, corresponded at all exactly to the 12-note series of equally spaced semitones. The frequency-ratio of the octave is $2:1$, and each semitone is constant ($\sqrt[12]{2}$) in 12-note composition. To arrive at such a chromatic scale of 12 durations, in which each duration-interval is equal, a similar "equal temperament" of durations would be needed, also based on a logarithmic scale ($\sqrt[12]{2}$).

A metronome would provide the easiest way to measure the duration of each note in such a series. If the longest duration is taken as 60, the shortest (an 'octave' higher) would then be 120. The duration-intervals of the rest of the series would be:—

1	2	3	4	5	6	7	8
(60)	63·6	67·4	71·4	75·6	80·1	84·9	89·9 95·2

9	10	11	12
100·9	106·9	113·3	(120)

Stockhausen sees a very close parallel between pitch and duration. Both are basically made up of proportionate numbers. In the spectrum of pitch, what makes for colour and richness is the relationship between frequency-ratios; in the spectrum of time, what makes for colour and richness is the relationship between duration-proportions. He sees the twelve logarithmic duration-intervals as corresponding with the intervals of the chromatic scale, and each of the durations as a *fundamental phase*, implying its own set of *formants*. Thus the proportion-series (of duration-intervals) may be said to correspond with the harmonic series (of overtones). The 12 durations, as the 12 notes of the pitch-scale, must be treated serially; that is to say, none is repeated before the other 11 have appeared. But what makes a pitch-series interesting is not so much the fact that it consists of 12 notes, all of which occur, as the intervals it uses. Just so with a duration-series. Moreover, just as a pitch series has a range of 7–8 octaves (approximately the compass of a piano) and a note may appear at any pitch, so a duration-series has a similar range of time-registers, and a duration may appear in any one of them. It will be obvious that, as far as instrumental serialism is concerned, the most immediate problem is one of notation.

Stockhausen is primarily influenced by mathematics; Boulez is more influenced by literature—Joyce and Mallarmé, for example. Being French, he could hardly avoid coming under the spell of Debussy to whose example he has never ceased to acknowledge his debt. Like Stockhausen, he was a pupil of Messiaen, and the series of his *Structures for 2 pianos* (1952) was taken from his master's *Mode de valeurs*. Moreover both played together the first performance of *Structures*. Messiaen has said that he in turn was influenced by *Structures* when he wrote his *Messe de la Pentecôte* and *Livre d'Orgue*.

Boulez frequently appears as a conductor as well as a composer, and is particularly sympathetic to Webern and Stravinsky, as well as Debussy. He is greatly respected by orchestral musicians, who usually have a shrewd ability to judge in such matters; the admiration and affection of an orchestra is by no means lightly won, and is the highest qualification a conductor can have.

Starting in 1954, Boulez arranged a series of concerts in Paris of new works. These were called *Domaine Musical*, and reflected the 12-note and serial tendencies of himself and those who think like him: Pousseur, Nono, Philippot, Stockhausen. The former generation were also included: Stravinsky, Messiaen, Varèse, as well as Schoenberg, Berg and Webern.

There is in Boulez a greater sense of creative freedom than in his German colleague. Though he has submitted himself to rigidly controlled serialism (as in the *Second Sonata*, *Polyphonie X*, and *Structures*), the spontaneous musician in him vigorously asserts its independence and freedom in *Le Marteau sans Maître*, with its tempo rubato, its lyricism, its sheer enjoyment of sound; in the *Third Sonata*, and the *Improvisations sur Mallarmé*, with their fantasy and improvisatory element; and in *Pli selon pli*, with its virtuosity. Here is found a true synthesis of the Viennese and French traditions.

Following 1945, the *avant-garde* sought a fresh approach to composition. Starting afresh without roots, *tabula rasa*, it had to be new; it had to be rationally and logically satisfactory. it had to take into account the need for a formal unity. The strongest external influence in Paris at the time was the Existentialism that we associate with Jean Paul Satre, and this we must also take into account.[1] A strong reaction was developing away from the 12-note technique, as it had become traditionally established by this time. The 'rules' of the 12-note school were proving far more oppressive than the traditional academicism which they were supposed to supersede; moreover, the atonalism inherent in Schoenberg's style inevitably tended to destroy all formal unity, without putting anything in its place. To Boulez and his colleagues this was due, as has already been mentioned, to the contradictions inherent in the 12-note technique itself, as developed by Schoenberg; they sought a solution to these contradictions in the integration of serialism. Their preoccupation was with the "how" of composition. For them, serialism was not so much a denial as an extension of the diatonic system. But they maintained that it is illogical and inconsistent to 'extend' tonality in one direction and not in others. Serialism is all or nothing.

Boulez has inherited from Messiaen two main lessons, which he has incorporated into his serial technique; one is the treatment of sophisticated rhythms, the other is the organisation of modes. Rhythmic structures appear in the *Second Sonata* (1948), and have now become one of the hallmarks of Boulez' style. But whereas Messiaen's treatment of modes was fixed, and pitch, duration, attack and intensity

[1] See p. 204.

remained constant, Boulez applied to this the principle of permutation, that is the basis of serialism.

A preoccupation with percussion instruments, as well as with rhythmic syncopation, which is so much a feature of the *avant-garde*, may also be traced to Messiaen; though Stravinsky and Varèse are not very far below the surface. In *Le Marteau sans Maître*, which is a suite of nine movements to poems by René Char, the contralto voice is accompanied by alto flute, viola, vibraphone, xylorimba, guitar, and various oriental and Latin-American percussion instruments. This work is in direct line of descent from *Pierrot Lunaire* and *The Rite of Spring*.

Total serialism has led not only to much greater exploration of the continuum of time and space, but also, inevitably, to an ever-increasing complexity. Boulez' self-expressed aesthetic purpose is to "reconcile conciseness and internal logic of form and structure with the flight of the imagination, of fantasy, of improvisation."

Just as Schoenberg forty years previously had broken away from what to him was a past aesthetic, so did Boulez. He rejected all that appeared to him superfluous—folk song, modalism, neoclassicism—and took what appeared to him vital from the work of his elders—Schoenberg, Webern, Stravinsky, Messiaen. This he re-cast; he called it "gathering up the fascicles of possibilities."

The guiding-lines fundamental to his aesthetic were:

(a) the acceptance of a complexity that is in the very nature of serialism;

(b) the isolation of rhythm and melody as two separate "primordial structure factors";

(c) the replacement of the 12-note row by melodic and rhythmic cells;

(d) an improvisatory, Dionysiac, personal quality;

(e) bold experiments, which he has carried out with an abandoned freedom as rare as it is valuable, for instance with the strings of the orchestra, or with quarter tones (*Le visage nuptial*, 1950), with recorded sounds (*Poésie pour Pouvoir*, 1958), with piano touch and sonority (*Second Sonata*, and other works), or with stereophonic effects (*Doubles*);

(f) the extension of serialism to works of large dimensions, in contrast to Webern's miniatures;

(g) the necessity of logic in composition, and the acceptance of that form which serialism gives to a work (as Sartre said, "existence precedes essence");

(h) the search for nothing less than a complete serial world, which like the world of tonality should meet all requirements of the composer, whether formal, structural, rhythmical, melodic, polyphonic or associative.

The principle of serialism is most fully realised in electronic music; complete serialisation of all the parameters is not possible with orchestral instruments to the same extent as it is with sine-waves. Several composers however have sought to combine both methods: Stockhausen in his *Gesang der Juenglinge* unites the voice with synthetic sound; Berio in his *Homage to James Joyce* manipulates vocal sounds electronically. Many American composers, such as Vladimir Ussachevsky, Ross Lee Finney and Milton Babbitt have combined recorded sound with either vocal or instrumental music. But the most striking work in this medium is *Déserts* by Edgard Varèse, which we shall have reason to refer to again later.

To summarise the aesthetics of serialism,[1] it requires that the composer should first choose a certain number of frequencies; that these should be related; that they should be in a certain order, and graded in certain intervals; that this series should then be applied to all the features of the composition; that from this original series other series can be deduced; and that the proportions of the series constitute the general principles of structure of the composition, to which they will thus give a formal logic.

[1] *Domaine Musicale*, Vol. 1, p. 128.

CHAPTER SIX

NATIONAL TRADITIONS:

THE ENGLISH TRADITION

THOSE English critics who still indulge in the national pastime of decrying the music of their fellow countrymen, usually do so from one of two standpoints; either, simply, that it is regrettably and misguidedly 'English', or that it was composed by, or influenced by, Vaughan Williams, whose work is the first to break away from German domination. The first description would impute to the work an insularity, a lack of acknowledgement or superior continental models, a primitive second-class status, from which there can be no reprieve this side of the English Channel; the second would imply that the work is amateurish, homespun, 'folksy', and therefore beyond the pale of serious consideration.

Although such criticism, if it can be called criticism, is emotive rather than rational, it is for that very reason all the more insidious. It was reflected in the scepticism of critics such as Ernest Newman, whose failure to see the importance and stature of Vaughan Williams, as well as that of several other composers, such as Stravinsky, in no way inhibited his criticism, or prevented it from gaining a considerable currency. Moreover the attitude implied by such criticism proved most crippling and adverse to the emergence of any vital English tradition. That a twentieth century English school could be considered in the same critical breath as the German or the French was regarded as ludicrously unnatural; that criticism itself could make any contribution to such a school was not for a moment contemplated, except by one or two free-thinkers like Edwin Evans and Cecil Gray.

The predominance of the German school extended through all reaches of music in the England of 1900. Teaching in the newly-founded institutions was more or less confined to the nineteenth century, and based on the German model; concerts under conductors like Nikisch or Richter were provincial reproductions of German bourgeois culture. If an Englishman wished to call himself a complete musician he had to go to Leipzig or Vienna in order to become one. As for any spontaneous musicality in England, at the time when Debussy was discovering the new sounds of his *Prélude*, and the German symphony was being developed in new directions by Mahler, the nearest approach to an endemic musical tradition in England was the Mendelssohn-type oratorio, which has always exercised such a hypnotic force over English audiences, or the Victorian music-hall. This is not to say that performances of the European classics were not plentiful in the England of the nineteenth century. Indeed they were. London has always been, and still is, a great cosmopolitan centre of music from all countries; an obligatory port of call for the performer who seeks an international reputation. But this is not a measure of the innate musicality, or of the musical growth, of the man in the street. We must distinguish between the apparent and the real.

It is possible to point to a flourishing and excellent concert life at the very centre of a country, or community, which is musically still at the nursery stage. A tradition, if it is to endure endemically, has to have roots which go considerably deeper than can be measured by concert programmes. Such a tradition cannot, as we have seen,[1] be built overnight. If a start was to be made in England, and the English musical scene was to change from being passively receptive into being actively creative, a two-fold change was necessary; first, on the part of composers, who would have to assert their independence from the continental models on which they based their style; second, on the part of the musical public, and musicians as a whole, who would have to encourage the composers by including their work in concerts.

That such a two-fold change had indeed begun was first announced by two names—Edward Elgar, and Henry Wood. In the music of Elgar a fresh, unexpected sound was heard; in all the *genres* open to him, Concerto, Symphony, Symphonic Poem, Chamber Music, Occasional Music, and of course Oratorio, he achieved both distinction and mastery. The idiom was clearly based on the Romantic school of

[1] See p. 25.

Wagner, Brahms; but the voice that speaks is individual. In the concerts conducted by Henry Wood an exciting break with the past became apparent, and a new trend in programme-building. Strange names, such as Joseph Holbrooke, or Percy Pitt, began to appear alongside the familiar favourites; the English composer was, very gradually, allowed to emerge from the wings, where he had lurked uneasily for well over a century of banishment, and to take his place, however self-consciously, on the platform. His music began to be played, and the ground to be prepared in which a tradition could flourish and an Elgar or a Vaughan Williams could belong naturally. Henry Wood's first Promenade Concert took place in London on 10th August, 1895.

And so any assessment of the contemporary English tradition must start with the fact of its comparatively recent growth. When the English composer of 1900 considered the past periods of his country's music, he would look back to the late seventeenth century, and beyond that to the great Tudor polyphonic school, whose music was only brought to light gradually as the twentieth century progressed.[1] The fact that this is no longer true today is due to the work of a handful of English composers of succeeding generations—Elgar, Vaughan Williams, Holst, Bax, Delius, Warlock, Walton, Rawsthorne, Tippett, Britten. Clearly reflected in the contrasted work of these composers are the characteristics of English society[2] in which they have sought to establish an endemic tradition; and the two composers whose work is most relevant from this point of view are Vaughan Williams and Michael Tippett.

(i) *Vaughan Williams* (1872–1958)

By 1914 the pattern of Vaughan Williams' many-sided career had already been clearly set. He had composed two of his nine symphonies (*Sea Symphony, London Symphony*), the Ballad Opera *Hugh the Drover*, the most characteristic of all his songs (*On Wenlock Edge, Five mystical songs*), the sublimely ecstatic *Fantasia on a theme by Thomas Tallis*, and numerous

---

[1] Particularly by E. H. Fellowes, R. R. Terry and Charles Kennedy Scott.

[2] Admirably analysed by Anthony Sampson in *The anatomy of Britain* (1962).

folk-song settings; he had done his duty by editing the *English Hymnal*; he had seen the foundation of the Leith Hill Festival; he had set out his views and thoughts in several articles and lectures. If his name was already a household word in Cambridge before the first world war, so it was in that university after the second as well. He was *persona grata* to the Establishment, a fact which caused those who were not to view him somewhat askance.

Underlying these multifarious aspects of his work, all of which he pursued consistently and relentlessly throughout his life, was a quite remarkable singleness of aesthetic purpose. Unlike Stravinsky, whose thoughts when composing, so he tells us,[1] were on himself "and the hypothetical other"; and unlike Schoenberg, who saw himself as the guardian of the centuries-old German tradition, Vaughan Williams looked on himself as a public servant, one who placed his craft at the service of his fellow countrymen. This humility, which in his case was entirely genuine, must also be quite fundamental to our assessment of his work. What matters is not so much the technical expertise that he reveals, as the artistic end he sets himself. The priority that he gave to English music, in the England of 1900, was one of ends, not of means.

At one end of the scale his compositions may encompass a wide horizon. This is the case with *Sancta Civitas*, and still more with the *Fantasia* on a theme of Tallis, in which Vaughan Williams the visionary, the mystic, sets his sights afar and finds a vehicle for the modalism to which he was drawn by his predilection for folk-song, in the Elizabethan *Fantasy*, or *Fancy*. Its mood is grave and austere, matched exactly by the solemn, dark-toned Phrygian mode; its structure, like its scoring (for double string orchestra and quartet) is intricate and subtle, while its inspiration draws strength and grandeur from 350 years of ecclesiastical history.

At the other end of the scale, he may set himself an objective of extreme limitation, as in the case of the cantata for women's voices *Folk songs of the four seasons*, of which the very essence is its light-hearted simplicity and naïveté. It is a work which makes no pretence whatever to greatness or significance, but seeks only to give straightforward enjoyment

[1] *Memories and Commentaries*, p. 91.

to amateur singers. It thus stands in complete contrast to Tippett's allegorical and symbolic conception of the four seasons, which he (Tippett) realised in the Ritual Dances in his opera *The Midsummer Marriage*.[1]

Between these two limits, bewilderingly and occasionally with paradoxical results, Vaughan Williams worked. Yet his concern, whatever he wrote, remained constant—to speak to those of his fellow countrymen who wished to listen, in a musical manner that was meaningful and relevant to them. He avoided the continental *avant-garde* not because he did not understand what they were about—on the contrary, few musicians were better informed than he about the latest developments; right to the end of his life he would attend first performances of new works, and keep himself abreast of events—but because their work was irrelevant for his aesthetic purpose. His intention was to create an English tradition.

His clearly defined aims were expressed in lectures and articles from the beginning of his life. A basic tenet of his faith was that an English tradition could start only if English composers were true to themselves. They needed the strength of their own convictions and should only admit influences, whether these came from foreign traditions or from the raw-material of their own folk-songs, if they found them to be consistent with their own nature. As he says:[2]

'There is no form of insincerity more subtle than that which . . . leads us to build up great designs which we cannot fill and to simulate emotions which we can only feel vicariously.'

Music in England, he pointed out in 1902, was not revealed in the musical events and festivals that took place, numerous though these were; it was something latent in the people, as the fine folk-melodies that existed bore witness; it was potential rather than actual, but was cramped and impeded by the false ideals that governed respectable life. A true tradition would only start when English musicians learnt, and were able, to make music for no other reason and with no other

---

[1] See p. 158.
[2] In an article (1912): *Who wants the English composer?*

motive than the joy of doing so. The composer who is sympathetic would find folk-song both beautiful in itself, and a source of richness for his own work.

Vaughan Williams was both a visionary and a realist. He not only wrestled with the problem of his own musical personality, he also fought passionately to discover the musical soul of his country. His genius was lyrical, religious, like that of William Blake; we see in his music both the English Puritan tradition, and the Georgian revival which was epitomised in the poems of A. E. Housman. If he found that the claims of a lyrical style were difficult to reconcile with symphonic construction, there is to be found nevertheless in a work such as the *Pastoral Symphony* a note of sublime fervour, of ecstasy, that is his alone. And it is significant that his music speaks with greater urgency to those whose outlook is idealistic, striving, unfettered by convention, than to those whose ears are sated to overflowing with the sounds of the more sophisticated European traditions; it has more to say to the contemporary American than to the contemporary Englishman. The impact of Vaughan Williams in America has been considerable, while in England, so far, it has been limited.

He not only possessed a wide culture, but he foresaw, realistically, that it would take several generations before an English tradition could take root and flourish in a way at all comparable to the existing French and German schools. He sought to begin by cultivating, instead of the customary philistinism or snobbery that he saw all round him, a sense of musical citizenship, in which the composer should think of his art as belonging to, and enriching, the life of the community. Folk-song was not, as many people wrongly thought, a ready-made national music.[1] It was more a seminal force, a fount of beautiful ideas, which were intelligible to a wide range of people; it was therefore a reasonable starting-point, particularly as in its modalism it shared a common origin with the polyphonic music of the great Elizabethan period. The problems presented to a composer by folk-song material are of a rudimentary nature; after all there is only one thing you can do with such a melody, as Lambert says,[2]

[1] See *National Music and Other Essays* (1963).
[2] *Music Ho!*, p. 117.

and that is to repeat it, this time rather louder. But the indirect influence of folk-song on a composer's imagination is a more subtle matter; the different characteristics of the song of different nationalities produce contrasting artistic results. It is instructive to compare Vaughan Williams' *Pastoral Symphony* with Janacek's Slavonic rhapsody *Taras Bulba* and Bartok's *Rumanian Folk Dances*. All these works use folk material in a symphonic context, and all differ because of the different characteristics of that material.

Thus we see that Vaughan Williams' sense of national tradition was the very opposite of chauvinism or provincialism. It was instead idealistic, historically based, revolutionary.

As he saw it, the essential problem facing the English composer at the beginning of this century was primarily that of the purpose and aim of his art; the means he employed, his technique, was of secondary importance. He suited his composition to the requirements of the moment, as Hindemith did. For instance, *Benedicite* was written as a 'test piece' for amateurs, whereas *Sancta Civitas* was for a more trained choir. Clearly these works must be assessed with this in mind, as it explains why the latter has a mystical grandeur totally lacking in the former. But an apparent paradox is presented by his predilection for opera and ballet. He wrote no fewer than eleven stage works, as well as much incidental music for plays and films. Opera, however, has always been a minority cult in England and, particularly before 1939, a new opera had very little chance of performance. It would appear that in this respect he was going against his declared purpose, which was that music should be broadly based, and truly national in content.

We should remember two factors. The first is that as Vaughan Williams reached back in spirit across the centuries he could hardly fail to be swayed by the great monuments of English literary culture—the works of Shakespeare, Bunyan, William Blake; to say nothing of the Bible. The second factor is that by 1930 the traditional oratorio was becoming defunct, and evolving into something new. Vaughan Williams, being English, could hardly avoid writing choral music; yet he only wrote one oratorio,[1] *Sancta Civitas*, which already (1926)

[1] As distinct from the *Cantata* or the *Choral Suite*.

left the traditional conception of the *genre* far behind, and of which the utterance was a personal statement of his faith, both musical and religious.

The old oratorio had degenerated into musical generalisations at the expense of words; its style was academic; it was a posture, devoid of genuine content; it was comfortable, hybrid, platitudinous. Its dissolution was a gradual process, apparent in many works; for instance, Holst's *Hymn of Jesus* and *Ode to Death*. But the *coup de grâce* was delivered on 8th October, 1931, when William Walton's *Belshazzar's Feast* struck the astonished ears of the audience at a Leeds festival. With this work the days of the old-style oratorio were not merely numbered; they had passed. The fact of their passing was celebrated by Vaughan Williams with his boisterous and extrovert *Five Tudor Portraits*, (1935), a work which shows the clear and positive influence of *Belshazzar's Feast*, and in which the words of the Tudor Poet Laureate, John Skelton, are matched with uncanny fitness by the composer of four centuries later. We may note moreover that archaism, which is so prevalent today, whereby a composer seeks a text from early sources, had begun.[1]

Five Tudor Portraits and *Sancta Civitas* form the twin peaks, which we could describe as the ridiculous and the sublime, of Vaughan Williams' choral output. But another direct and significant result of this basic change which had taken place in English music was that the attention which composers formerly paid to oratorio they now began to pay to opera. Since 1945 there has been a marked increase of interest in, and performances of, opera in England; the first to realise this trend in events was Vaughan Williams, though he was not by any means the only opera composer of his generation.

Another climactic work of 1935 was the *Fourth Symphony* in F minor. This, like the *Five Tudor Portraits*, opens with the germinating idea suggested by the minor second, or semitone; but, strangely, this interval, which is identical in each case, produces a diametrically opposite effect. (Ex. 34 a and 34 b).

This symphony marks the culminating point in Vaughan Williams' output of nine symphonies. Its style is more experimental, more a synthesis of other developments, and its sections are more thematically coordinated and inter-related

[1] See below p. 222.

R. Vaughan Williams
Five Tudor Portraits
No. 1, bars 1–5

(a)

R. Vaughan Williams
Symphony in F Minor (1935)
1st movement, bars 1–6

(b)

Ex. 34

than in any of the other eight symphonies. For instance, the opening of the finale is derived from the flute melody with which the slow movement closes (Ex. 35 a and 35 b). The symphony is representative of, and highly coloured by, the development of the English symphony at this time; other examples are afforded by the Third Symphony of Arnold Bax[1],

R. Vaughan Williams
Symphony in F Minor
2nd Movement, Epilogue, 14

Ex. 35a

R. Vaughan Williams
Symphony in F Minor
Finale, bars 1–4

Ex. 35b

[1] To whom Vaughan Williams gave the manuscript, with its dedication, as a Christmas present in 1935.

and the First Symphony of William Walton, which was first performed in November, 1935.

Vaughan Williams' symphony earned its composer a tumultuous ovation when it was first performed in April, 1935. His famous comment that "I do not know whether I like it, but this is what I meant" exactly summarises this phase of English music, of which he had been the pioneer. Yet he was more than just a pioneer. He not merely saw what was necessary; he showed the way to carry it out. British composers today are in his debt more than anyone else's of his generation. As he said, with reference to Sibelius, with whom he had many points in common, "great music is written, I believe, not by breaking the tradition, but by adding to it."

> Darest thou now O soul,
> Walk out with me toward the unknown region,
> Where neither ground is for the feet nor any path to follow?

(ii) *Michael Tippett* (b. 1905)

The work of Tippett, like that of Stravinsky, is a vital, organic, continuous growth; an astonishingly rich harvest of ideas; a fertile, imaginative synthesis of past tradition and present culture, sustained by a singleness of purpose. His creative thought has a psychological depth which, though it differs from that of Vaughan Williams in many particulars, nevertheless springs from the same source. Both show a firm sense of purpose, a long-term visionary quality, an ecstatic lyricism, which gives their best work a long-term relevance rather than an immediate popularity. Their roots go deep into the English tradition, while their thoughts range beyond the present into a wide view of the future; their tradition is thus nourished. The differences between the two composers are, in one sense, of less importance than their identity of purpose, and are due, in the main, simply to those differences of general outlook that you would expect to occur between one generation and the next. Tippett is post-jazz, post-Schoenberg, post-Jung and post-Vaughan Williams.

His remarkably penetrating insight into the life of our time has, at all phases, coloured his compositions. The human, though all too rare, attributes of compassion, concern, optimism, which form the channel for his creativity, have their counterpart in that complexity and elaboration of rhythm and melody which have always been so fundamental to his technique.

His student days at the Royal College of Music in London were based on the traditional harmonic teaching of the German school, handed down by Charles Wood, and before him by Stanford and Parry. This seemed to Tippett largely unsatisfactory for his purposes; his musicality tended more towards that rhythmic drive and vigour, which is not found in the German harmonic approach to composition, but belongs more to the earlier polyphonic period; he also had a particular interest in word-setting, of which the English Madrigal and the songs of Dowland, provided such shining examples. These however found no place in the course of studies of the College, and it was the work of a Cambridge musician, also a former College student, Boris Ord, who founded the Cambridge University Madrigal Society in 1922, to give such an inspiring lead in rediscovering the nature of the English Madrigal.

And so whereas Vaughan Williams had been drawn more to folk-song on the one hand, and the austere 'one-note-per-syllable' style of the Tudor composers Gibbons and Tallis on the other, Tippett was much more strongly, more instinctively, drawn to the style of Purcell. Moreover he felt much more affinity with the neo-classic tendencies of Stravinsky, (particularly with the additive rhythm technique of a work such as *Les Noces*), than with the neo-expressionism of the Schoenberg school. He could feel nothing but antipathy for the "alphabetical" system of the 12-note technique.

Another strong influence in Tippett's musical make-up is that of jazz. He was attracted to it from the start. It seemed to him remarkable that the Blues, which started as such a simple, primitive folk-art, consisting of only twelve bars and three chords, endlessly repeated, should persist and flourish as it has. Here surely is proof of sheer artistic stamina and vitality; and the composer's problem is not so much to explain this extraordinary fact—any explanation would really be irrelevant—as to decide how he can adapt and use this means of expression in a purposeful way in his own work, so that it will sustain the emotional weight of his thought. In the Blues is a natural melancholy, decorated with an endless Baroque-style variation in the melodic part. Herein is contained a powerful means of expressing that anguish, which is the essence of the musical voice today; here is found a synthesis of musical styles, melodic and rhythmic, syllabic and melismatic, sophisticated and unsophisticated, which gives the art-form a broadly-based appeal.

As far as folk-song was concerned—that remarkable movement which sprang up simultaneously in many different European countries towards the end of the nineteenth century, and reached its climax about 1930—Tippett was never a field collector, as Vaughan Williams had been; nor did he share the purism of a Cecil Sharp, who dismissed the *Beggar's Opera* as spurious folk-song. Folk-song for Tippett is an art-form in embryo, an artistic principle, which may be perfectly legitimately used if the need arises for 'traditional material'. If he wants a folk-song for a particular purpose he will write one; as he did for instance in the *Suite in D* (1948), written for Prince Charles's birthday.

Tippett's most brilliant and colourful student-contemporary was Constant Lambert, and the view expressed in Lambert's *Music Ho!* that "Folk-songs in England are not a vigorous living tradition" was, and is, generally accepted. There is moreover a basic dichotomy between a folk-song style and the requirements of symphonic form; and it is the latter that Tippett has wrestled with.

While Constant Lambert pursued, with characteristic zest, the cosmopolitan world of the Russian Ballet, Tippett was drawn instinctively to the less glittering, more humdrum, yet more relevant and peculiarly English world of amateur music-making. If his work is to have a lasting life, a composer needs to have roots, secure and deep; and Tippett, like Vaughan Williams, has always recognised the importance of amateur music-making to the growth of the nation's musicality. His concern with this has covered his whole career and ranges from early operatic ventures, such as *Love in a village* (1929) which he wrote for the local choral society at Oxted in Surrey, and *Robin Hood*, a one-act Ballad Opera, which he wrote for the miners of Cleveland in Yorkshire at a time (1931) of industrial depression; it includes his work at

Morley College in London, where he remained as Music Director until 1951; it extends finally to his work with the Leicestershire County Youth Orchestra, whom he took on a tour of Belgium in 1966 and conducted in programmes of music by English composers of this century.

By his fortieth year the basic pattern of his work had begun to take shape in a way that was remarkably parallel to that of Vaughan Williams thirty years previously. The three most characteristic works by which Vaughan Williams was known by 1914 were the *Tallis Fantasia*, the *Sea Symphony*, and the settings of Housman poems for Tenor, Piano and String Quartet, *On Wenlock Edge*; the three most characteristic works by which Tippett was known by 1945 were the *Concerto for Double String Orchestra*, the oratorio *A child of our time*, and the cantata for Tenor and piano, on a prose-text by W. H. Hudson, *Boyhood's End*. A large number of compositions before 1935 were later withdrawn.

The mainstream of his output has been marked by one or two climactic works, whose gestation and creation has cost great labour over a long period and which have proved to be the source from which subsequent works have flowed. Thus the second symphony flows directly from *The Midsummer Marriage*; the *Concerto for Orchestra* flows directly from the opera *King Priam*. The fact that the seminal compositions tend to be in the form of opera or oratorio, and are not so much settings of words as settings of thoughts, ideas, dreams, is due partly to the fact that he is English, partly to his bent of mind. These mainstream works are the *Concerto for Double String Orchestra* (1939), the oratorio *A child of our time* (1941), the operas *The Midsummer Marriage* (1952) and *King Priam* (1962), and *The Vision of Saint Augustine* (1965). The first of these, the *Concerto*, has obvious affinities with Vaughan Williams's *Tallis Fantasia*; both composers were inspired by the medium of the String Orchestra which, in this century at least, is chiefly confined to England;[1] both composers derived from a common source, the old English *Fancy*. *King Priam* also marks a turning point in Tippett's style, as its idiom is different from before, bolder and fresher. There is a vigour, what Tippett has called a 'toughness', in

[1] There are a few notable works for String Orchestra by American composers, for instance Barber's *Adagio*, Copland's *Nonet*.

King Priam, which, once found, is not then lost sight of in the ensuing works.

Tippett's imagination is acute, his thought revolutionary. An artist who can in the way he does,[1] concern himself with the evanescent and incorporeal world of ideas beyond the confines of time or the senses, to the extent of setting the products of the spiritual imagination on equal terms with those of the world of technics, is both in the worldly sense, unrealistic and, in the true sense, revolutionary—completing the cycle, and circle, of human life that today is so divided. He seeks with his art to heal that rift between material and technical progress on the one hand, and the things of the spirit on the other. Material abundance, he says, should encourage, not exclude, artistic growth. What better way is there of demonstrating this coming together, this oneness, of different people, or of people who have been driven apart by wars, racial tensions, or other human failings, than by means of an opera or oratorio, which, if anything, is the artist's vision of a collective experience?

Tippett is a keen student of Greek literature and ideas; and indeed what better source of material is there than the legends, the mythology of old, which draw on the universal experience of mankind over an untold period of time, and which we know, by Jung's definition, as the 'collective unconscious'? Music's power to unify has already been noted[2] as one of its underlying characteristics; Tippett's interpretation of this in the contemporary situation is his unique contribution to contemporary music; and just as Stravinsky's aesthetic finds some expression in the words of Picasso, so that of Tippett is found to be paralleled in T. S. Eliot and W. B. Yeats.

The influence of T. S. Eliot is mainly seen in Tippett's attitude towards the problem of music in the theatre.[3] To be able to achieve stage effects is an essential part of an opera composer's technique; nothing can be left to chance; otherwise there is the greatest risk of slipping into the sort of operatic *cliché* which is very commonly found among less experienced composers. The composer needs to treat his

[1] As he described in *Moving into Aquarius*.
[2] See p. 24.
[3] See *Moving into Aquarius*.

libretto as the poet would if it were to become a poem or a play. If the poet asserts his poetry too strongly, the composer's work is to some extent superfluous. A libretto, therefore, needs short lines, simple sentences, which the composer—not the poet—then completes. In order that the experience of an opera should be an immediate one, the material and the language need to be everyday, even ordinary. Eliot's play *The Cocktail Party* is an excellent example of this, and Tippett's own libretti are invariably of this nature.

Whereas Eliot interpreted Christianity, Yeats "wrestled with mythology." For him, as for Goethe, mythology was reality; the contemporary and the mythological were one. Tippett was most influenced by Yeats at the time of *King Priam*. Helen's song in Act III is pure Yeats; particularly the words:

"For I am Zeus's daughter, conceived when the great wings beat above Leda."

At about the same time as *King Priam*, other settings of Yeats also appear, such as the *Lullaby for six voices*, and *Music for words, perhaps*.

The influence of Jung belongs to an earlier stage of Tippett's work. Apart from Jungian concepts, which he found congruent with his own at a particular period of his life, the metaphysical language seemed to him a way to express religious truths.

"I would know my shadow and my light, so shall I at last be whole"

is the Jungian philosophy which provides the closing moment in *A child of our time*; and the motto which heads this work, taken from T. S. Eliot's *Murder in the Cathedral*, sums up the underlying theme of division and wholeness:

". . . the darkness declares the glory of light."

If generalisations about most composers are unsatisfactory, they are even more unsatisfactory in the case of Tippett. He has avoided self-repetition; each work is re-thought *de novo*; and the works written since *King Priam*, for instance the *Concerto for Orchestra* and *The Vision of Saint Augustine*, are in a starker, bolder idiom than those written before; they

are still centred round a tonality, but it is a tonality built in
fourths rather than thirds. Since therefore a bird's-eye view
of his whole output would be valueless, let us consider just
one single work in rather more detail; the work which is the
central pivot of his output so far, *King Priam*.

King Priam   An Opera in three Acts
(references are to the vocal score published by Schott & Co.)

Introductory

Opera, as we have seen, has developed steadily in England
since 1945. The year 1955 was a particularly important one,
with no fewer than four new productions by prominent
composers. These were Lennox Berkeley's *Nelson*, Benjamin
Britten's *The Turn of the Screw*, William Walton's *Troilus
and Cressida*, and Michael Tippett's *The Midsummer Marriage*.
It was the last work which held out the most promise for the
future, not just of Tippett's creative career, but of English
music in a wider context. Not that the opera was flawless
by any means; indeed, if one merely wishes to point out its
shortcomings, one will be disconcerted to find that the
composer himself has already done so. Certainly it lacks the
sense of theatre that Walton's work has in abundance;
certainly Britten shows greater fluency and sheer technical
adroitness; all this may be conceded; yet to weigh against
these shortcomings, if they are shortcomings, Tippett brought
nothing less than a totally fresh sense of purpose into opera;
namely, dramatic unity through the fusion of opposing
principles; the confrontation and the relationship of opposites.
He thus sought to make common, age-old, timeless experiences
relevant to us today. His music is magical.

Such a creative vision is of a basically different order from
that of the composer who sees opera either as a play with
music or as a structure of related songs and choral ensembles.
Any competent hack composer—to say nothing of the not-so-
competent ones—can add musical icing to a ready-made
dramatic cake. But Tippett's art is on an altogether different
plane; he approaches the problem of opera from the other
end. His concern is to express the eternal in terms of the
temporal.[1] The universal, archetypal experience of humanity,

[1] "A timeless music played in time", as Hermes says at the end of
Priam.

which may be found symbolically expressed in mythological legends and folklore, is sought out and discovered by the receptive imagination of the artist, and re-interpreted for his contemporaries. In this respect Tippett is the successor of Berg, though very little influenced by him, if at all.

If in *The Midsummer Marriage*, whose theme is love, he did not quite succeed in projecting the somewhat static situation and nature of his characters with the dynamic of structural unity and dramatic urgency, no such qualification applies to *King Priam*, whose theme is war. In *The Midsummer Marriage* he sought to compose a sort of twentieth century *Magic Flute*; but the symbolism and imagery are difficult to comprehend to anyone not acquainted with Hindu mythology or Fraser's *Golden Bough*. Moreover the opera consists in a sequence of symbolic ideas rather than a succession of inevitable events; as a result, the conclusion towards which we are drawn, the union of the lovers, does not provide the work with that psychological centre of gravity that it needs if it is to be presented convincingly on the stage. The action may be symbolically meaningful, but that does not necessarily make it relevant to us. But for anyone who can overcome this initial challenge, the spark of true inspiration is there, and Tippett reveals a totally fresh world of artistic experience. When he pursued this in another opera, whose theme and events were of very direct concern to Europeans in the 1960's, the result could hardly fail to be an explosive challenge of the greatest importance to the history of opera and of contemporary music generally.

In *King Priam* Tippett took the traditional story of the sack of Troy by the Greeks, and told it from the Trojan (i.e. the defeated enemy) point of view. Here was a theme that all understood; war, with its pity and its terror. Priam is made a tragic hero. Love is certainly a timeless theme, if ever there was one; but the main advantage of his choosing the Trojan war as the subject for his second opera was that he found not only a great theme, with other subsidiary themes, love included, deriving from it, but also a traditional and well-known story, which would act as a framework for the theme. Imagery there certainly is in *King Priam*, but it is immediately recognisable, relevant and dramatic because we relate it without doubt or difficulty to the events. Moreover the second opera has a realism not found in the first. If we need points of reference they are to be found in Wagner, Stravinsky, Brecht, T. S. Eliot.

In *King Priam* Tippett does not confine the action to a single time or place; the duration of the opera is the life-span of Priam's son Paris. Scenes also shift. As with his first opera, and *A child of our time*, Tippett wrote his own libretto. A starting-point from which to study the construction and the composition of the work is provided by the four principles which he himself laid down,[1] and which form a sort of aesthetic philosophy of his work as an opera composer:

1 Opera is ultimately dependent on the contemporary theatre.
2 The more collective an artistic imaginative experience is going to be, the more the discovery of suitable material is involuntary.
3 While the collective, mythological material is always traditional, the specific twentieth-century quality is the power to transmute such material into an immediate experience of our day.
4 In opera the musical schemes are always dictated by the situations.

Let us first lay out the opera, in a scene-by-scene analysis; then see how Tippett has drawn up a corresponding 'musical scheme', in accordance with these principles.

ACT I

Scene 1   A chorus of lament is heard off-stage; a baby cries, and a point of light falls on a cradle. The child's mother, Hecuba, wife of Priam, King of Troy, is disturbed by a dream which she cannot understand. This is interpreted by an old man to mean that the child, Paris, will be the cause of his father's death. Priam, therefore, decides that the child must be killed, and orders a guard to do this.

  Interlude 1—The old man, a nurse, and the guard reflect on this dilemma; child-murder is a crime, but what if it is your duty?

[1] In *The birth of an opera* (from *Moving into Aquarius*).

Scene 2   Some years later Priam's eldest son, Hector, while out hunting, meets his brother Paris, who has been brought up secretly all this time by a shepherd.[1] Paris chooses to go to Troy, and when asked outright, gives his name. Priam reflects on this trick of fate. Will the old prophecy come true? He nevertheless accepts his son's choice.

    Interlude 2—The old man, nurse, and guard see life as a 'bitter charade'. Hector meanwhile has found a perfect wife in Andromache, while Paris leaves Troy in disgust, and sails to Greece, where the King of Sparta, Menelaus, and his wife Helen "keep open house".

Scene 3   Paris is enamoured of and captivated by Helen. He persuades her to leave Menelaus and go to Troy with him as his wife. Hermes, the messenger of the gods, comes to him in a dream, and tells him to choose between the three goddesses, Athene, Hera and Aphrodite. Athene appears to him as Hecuba, representing prudence; Hera as Andromache, representing faithfulness; and Aphrodite as Helen, representing the "eternal feminine" principle.[2] In spite of warnings of the inevitable vengeance that will follow, he chooses Aphrodite.

ACT II

Scene 1   The 10-year Trojan war is now approaching its terrible climax. Hector the soldier chides Paris the adulterer and expresses more respect for the Greek Menelaus than for his own brother. Priam tries to mediate, and urges them to fight the enemy, not each other.

    Interlude 1—Hermes takes the old man (thereby also the audience) over to the Greek camp, to Achilles' tent.

Scene 2   Achilles and his friend Patroclus look back nostalgically to their childhood in Greece. Now, however, Achilles has quarrelled with Agamemnon, the Greek Commander-in-chief, over the ownership of a

[1] A common feature of legends; cf. the story of Oedipus.
[2] The 3-fold nature of woman is a Freudian conception.

captive girl Briseïs, and has refused to fight. But a plan is worked out, whereby Patroclus, wearing Achilles' armour, shall pretend to be Achilles, and go into battle against the Trojans.

Interlude 2—A threat to Troy is foreseen.

Scene 3   Back in Troy, we hear that Patroclus, in Achilles' armour, led the Greeks up to the walls, only to be killed by Hector in single combat. Priam, Hector and Paris sing a hymn of thanks to Zeus. At that moment, from the Greek side, Achilles utters his war-cry of vengeance for Patroclus.

ACT III

Scene 1   Hecuba, Andromache and Helen express their different loves and loyalties; to the city, to the home, to love itself. Hecuba tries to mediate when the other two quarrel. Andromache has an intuitive premonition of Hector's death.

Interlude 1—News of Hector's death spreads. All but King Priam have heard. Who will tell him?

Scene 2   It falls to Paris to tell his father the news of Hector's death and mutilation at the hands of Achilles. He vows to kill Achilles in return; whereupon Priam contemplates the unbreakable cycle of vengeance. Hector killed Patroclus, and Achilles in revenge killed Hector; Paris will in turn seek revenge by killing Achilles; who will then kill Paris? Why was he not killed as a baby? It was the fatal flaw of pity. Yet why should one son (Hector) be allowed to live only if it meant the death of the other (Paris)? Life is a trick, without meaning.

Interlude 2—Instrumental music, to suggest the passage of time; the past leading to the present, and both making up the future.

Scene 3   Hermes brings Priam, unarmed, to Achilles' tent to ransom his son Hector's body. Achilles is moved by pity for the old man—(that 'fatal flaw' again?)—and grants his request. They drink, and their deaths are foretold, Achilles at the hands of Paris, Priam at the hands of Achilles' son, Neoptolemus.

Interlude 3—Hermes prepares the audience for Priam's death and transformation; "He already breathes an air as from another planet."[1]

Scene 4 Paris kills Achilles, but too late, since Troy is being sacked by the Greeks and is already burning. Once more the three women come, this time to care for Priam; once more Hecuba and Andromache give place to Helen, who is tenderly addressed by Priam, after he has sent out Paris to a hero's death in the flames of Troy. Priam kisses Helen, who he knows now will return to Greece. He himself then sinks before the altar, where Achilles's son Neoptolemus, as had been foretold, runs him through with a sword.

In telling the story from the Trojan point of view, thus making the old king the central character of his opera, Tippett deliberately challenges us to look at the theme of war through the eyes of compassion and understanding. Priam loved his son Hector just as much as Achilles loved his friend Patroclus; more if anything, as he was older; therefore he suffered just as much when he was killed. Yet if we try to find the answer to this human riddle we will not succeed, since human conduct has no satisfactory rational explanation. Priam may curse; he may invoke all the gods he knows; he may turn this way or that; but it is not given to him to understand. War has no meaning. Yet, paradoxically, he does not need to understand in order to provide the solution. He goes to Achilles himself, using only the weapon of pity for an old man. This not only achieves its purpose, but it is a course of action which brings no retribution in its train. On the contrary; the two drink together.

Another thing Priam does. He first of all dismisses Paris; and by doing this, he shows that wars are fought by the young, not by the old, and that his function is not on the field of battle. Then he forgives Helen. This is entirely in keeping with the end of Homer's *Iliad*, and lends a truly noble air to the end of the opera. Helen had been the ostensible cause of the whole war, as a result of which Priam's city

[1] For this idea of transformation, compare the myth of the journey of the soul in Plato's *Phaedrus* (247 foll.).

was destroyed; yet he forgives her. He might well have asked her "why?"; but such a question, as we know, can have no answer. The opera ends with the chords depicting the theme of war, sounding, very quietly this time, for Priam himself. His death at the close of the opera is simply the final stage of that transformation, which had already begun.

The fusion of opposing principles is everywhere apparent in *King Priam*; life and death, friend and foe, heaven and hell, choice and destiny. Tippett's artistry is a receptiveness to the inner as well as the outer meaning of events. He is concerned with the mysterious nature of human choice; and the character whose choice is most central to the whole story is Paris. Paris is much more than a sort of epic Casanova; he represents that archetypal principle of search, inspiration, passion. But because his search is directed towards a fantasy, an unreal phantom,[1] it can never be fulfilled. His cry

Is there a choice at all?

might well be the motto of the whole opera.

In Act I Priam chooses to have his son killed; later Paris chooses to go to Troy, and Priam chooses to accept this decision. Most important of all, Helen chooses Paris, Paris chooses Helen. It seems they are driven by a force stronger than themselves; yet the choice is theirs. In Act II Achilles chooses not to fight, Patroclus chooses to take his place; whereupon Achilles chooses to avenge Patroclus' death. In Act III each of the three women chooses her loyalty; Paris chooses to avenge Hector his brother; finally, Priam makes the two culminating choices of the opera, to confront Achilles and to forgive Helen. In every case, the choice was freely taken, freely followed by the deed; in no case could the result of the deed be foreseen.

The opera moves forward to its appointed end with an irresistable sweep of inevitability. In Act I the events and the premonitions surrounding Paris, all the more ominous for being vague and unspecified, pile up and accumulate a dramatic tension that erupts, starkly and violently, in Act II, the "war act". The resolution occurs in Act III, in which the implications of what has gone before are seen in their true

[1] For the idea of Helen as a phantom, cf. Plato's *Republic* (IX,585); also Euripides' *Helena*.

light. This dramatic inevitability is matched by a remarkable structural cohesion and balance. The number three is used as a unifying factor. There are three acts, two of them with three scenes. Three male characters (Priam, Hector, Paris) balance three female characters (Hecuba, Andromache, Helen), and they each have trios. The Chorus consists of three people (Old man, nurse, guard). At the opening, the introductory chorus occurs three times; at the close of the opera, the "war" chord is sounded three times; at the centre of the most violent part of the opera Achilles' war cry rings out three times.

There are also several points of cross-reference and symbolism in the opera, which serve to unite the parts into a single compelling whole. For instance, Priam's attempt to mediate between his sons' quarrel is balanced by Hecuba's attempt to keep Andromache and Helen apart. Again, on the psychological level, the flames that consume Troy symbolise the burning flame of love that consumes Helen and Paris, that ecstasy that brings tragedy in its wake.

But far the greatest unifying factor is the music itself. That fusion of opposites in the personalities of the story is matched by the fusion of words and music, consonance and dissonance, present and past time, that makes up Tippett's score. The characters are contrasted by means of *motif* and instrumentation. The theme of war and killing is given to the brass, woodwind, and timpani. This feature of the orchestration reaches its climax in Act II, the war act, when Tippett leaves out the strings altogether, except the piano and guitar. The latter is used for Achilles' sentimental and nostalgic song. The idea of the home on the other hand, and the domestic love of women, is expressed by the strings. Hecuba's *motif* is given out by the violins, in agitated sextuplets, while that of Andromache is a more intensely lyrical melody for cellos alone. The love of Helen and Paris is expressed by flutes, the instrument with traditional erotic associations. The harp is used to suggest the imagery of dreams, and the world of the unconscious. Flute and harp are used together, in Interlude 3 of Act III, for the music of the transformation of Priam.

Tippett's instinct for instrumental *timbre* is nowhere more apparent than in the score of *King Priam* generally, and in his use of the piano in particular. The opera almost amounts to a compendium of writing for the piano, which curiously chameleon-like tends to vary its nature according to its surroundings. The use of piano and xylophone is especially remarkable, and reminds us of Yeats's "drum, flute and zither"[1]—or rhythm, melody and accompaniment; the rhythm in this case being provided by the somewhat hard and percussive sound of the xylophone.

The underlying *motif* of the entire opera is made up of two fourths, a perfect fourth with an augmented fourth super-imposed (Ex. 36). This is used either melodically or chordally to express the theme of war, violence, killing. If its appearance is gradual in Act I, in Act II, as we would expect, it is the main formative element. It opens the act, played ff on the timpani (Ex. 37), and it brings the act to a blood-curdling close, when it is used to form Achilles' war-cry (Ex. 38).

Michael Tippett
King Priam (1962)

Act II Scene 1, opening

Ex. 36 & 37

But in addition to this the augmented fourth is also used to express the love between Helen and Paris (which takes place off-stage, as this is not a Romantic opera). The love-scene at the end of Act I begins with it (Ex. 39); Paris's lyrical outburst later in the same scene is built round it (Ex. 40). The implication of this is quite clear, namely that the addition of the augmented fourth to the perfect fourth produced the *motif* of war in just as direct a way as the love of Helen and Paris led to war.

In Act I, as we have already said, the *motif* is introduced subtly; only later do we recall its use, and realise its full implication. It is present in Scene I in the violin music which accompanies Hecuba's outburst. In Scene 3, it appears when the identical passage is played on the timpani to introduce

---

[1] See *Moving into Aquarius*.

Ex. 38

each of the three goddesses: and again when Helen is on the point of committing herself to Paris. This reminds us of the opening of the opera, when a solo oboe had played over the crib where the infant Paris lay. Now an oboe again plays, at the words "how can I choose?", but this time a more menacing phrase (Ex. 41). Once the fateful choice has been made, the *motif* appears more blatantly, boldly stated by the violins.

Michael Tippett
King Priam

Act I Scene 3, opening

Ex. 39

Michael Tippett
King Priam

Act I Scene 3

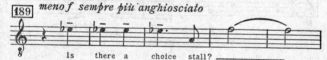

Ex. 40

The *motif* insistently dominates Act II. It forms a biting, chordal accompaniment to Paris's defence of himself against Hector in Scene 1 (Ex. 42); it gives lyrical shape to Achilles' song in Scene 2; it is used with overwhelming effect, both horizontally in the melody and vertically in the harmony, to build up the three-part texture of the hymn to Zeus, which consists of 36 bars of imitative counterpoint, to a brilliant accompaniment of brass and woodwind.

Michael Tippett
King Priam

Act I Scene 3

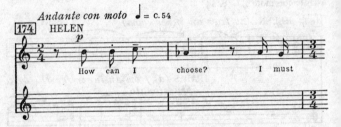

Ex. 41

Michael Tippett
King Priam

Act II Scene 1

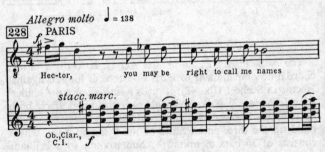

Ex. 42

In Act III Tippett uses the *motif* retrospectively, to remind us of the theme of war, which is the cause from which the remaining events in the opera stem. In Scene I, when Helen says to Hecuba (referring to Andromache) "let her rave", the *motif*, played very quietly, just once, as a chord, is enough to remind us that Andromache at least has cause to rave, as her husband Hector is about to be killed. A little later, when Helen sings:

"women like you cannot know what men may feel with me",

again the *motif* sounds out, to remind us what the consequences were of her adultery. The trio of the three women, like that of the men in the previous act, is also built horizontally and vertically round the *motif*. This trio however has a delicate, filigree accompaniment of strings and harp. The notes of the *motif* are such as to lead to an effect of bitonality —E flat major and D major—and Tippett makes magical use of this tendency (Ex. 43). The juxtaposition of two keys a semitone apart also explains the prevalent use of the interval of the second, which is apparent throughout the opera; for instance, at the very opening of the work, in the trumpet fanfare.

Michael Tippett
King Priam

Act III Scene 1

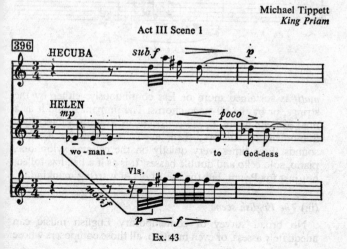

Ex. 43

At the close of Scene 3, in which Achilles and Priam look ahead to their own deaths, the *motif* appears again on the timpani, but with an important alteration, a diminuendo. Thus is the final transformation foreshadowed. This occurs during the third interlude, in which the *motif* is played on the harp as an accompaniment.

When it appears as a sudden brief outburst by the brass, at the beginning of Scene 4, it comes as a shock. The chords introduce Paris the soldier, who has killed Achilles. Thereafter, the *motif* appears metamorphosed. The three women appear one by one, and each one is introduced, as she had been in Act I, by an identical statement of the *motif*, made up of three parts each in diminution, (Ex. 44). From then on the

Michael Tippett
King Priam

Act III Scene 4

Ex. 44

motif is sustained more or less continuously, either by the strings, or by the off-stage chorus. The timpani sound it as a final *ostinato* figure, ff, *marcatissimo*, as Priam is killed; then a moment of stillness; then, as if from eternity itself, it sounds three times, very quietly on the celesta, xylophone, piano, solo cello and double basses. It is as if a bell has tolled, not just for Priam, but for the whole of warring mankind.

(iii) *The English scene*

No broad survey of contemporary English music can adequately assess, or even mention, all those composers whose active work has covered the span of some sixty years. The Composers' Guild today includes among its living members over 350 names; and even allowing for that considerable proportion who do not primarily base their musical citizenship on composition, there is still a formidable number who do.

Every shade of allegiance is represented, from the conservative-academic, who cling to what they conceive to be the established tradition of the past, to the ruthlessly iconoclastic, who pursue what they conceive to be the trends of the future. Between these two extremes—both equally passive, both equally derivative—there labour, and have laboured, the truly creative musicians, who seek a more lasting goal.

Those composers whose formative years occurred before 1939, and whose main precedent was therefore provided by Elgar, Vaughan Williams or Holst, have tended to write substantial symphonies, concertos and orchestral works; we think of Arnold Bax, Arthur Bliss, Edmund Rubbra, Alan Rawsthorne, William Walton, to name only some. In recent years, the symphony orchestra has claimed the attention of musicians of a later generation as well, whose styles differ greatly; notably Maxwell Davies, Malcolm Lipkin, Robin Orr.

But if there is one aspect of musical composition which is in the very fibre of the English tradition, a thread of pure gold which we can point to as being peculiarly indigenous—more comparable for instance with the French school of organ music than with the German school of the *lied*—that is the song, whether solo or choral. It is when treating the human voice that the English composer is truest to himself, and is most likely to strike a responsive chord in his audience. He reaches back to Purcell, Dowland, the Elizabethan Madrigalists; he has at his disposal the whole immense wealth of English literature; moreover, he is able in song to establish a point of contact with that tradition of amateurism, which is one of the hallmarks of the English character.

The song may be given simply an accompaniment of piano, or of a group of instruments, or of full orchestra. Songs with piano accompaniment are far too numerous to mention; the list is endless. Songs with chamber music accompaniment include chiefly Vaughan Williams's *On Wenlock Edge*, Warlock's *Curlew*; more recently Britten's *Serenade* and *Les*

Illuminations, Tippett's *Songs for Ariel* (from Shakespeare's *Tempest*); also there are several of an experimental nature such as Birtwhistle's *Ring a dumb carillon*. Songs with orchestral accompaniment have been a continuous source of inspiration to composers throughout the contemporary period. Chief examples are Constant Lambert's *Summer's last will and Testament*, Rubbra's *Four Mediaeval Lyrics*; Berkeley's *Four poems of St. Teresa*, Britten's *War Requiem*.

In style and content the range is immense. Poems of every age have been used by composers, ranging from the mediaeval poets, particularly Chaucer, to the complex works of Yeats or James Joyce. Among the composers of the early years of the twentieth century, Elgar was subject to German influences —he even called his songs 'lieder'—whereas Delius set the words of Scandinavian and French poets, such as Ibsen, Munck and Verlaine, as well as Nietzsche and Shelley. Holst was drawn to Humbert Wolfe and mediaeval sources. Chinese texts have attracted composers of all generations, including Bernard van Dieren, Arthur Oldham, Robin Orr, Robert Sherlaw Johnson. Those composers most immediately affected by Vaughan Williams, such as George Butterworth, Ivor Gurney and C. W. Orr, were drawn to A. E. Housman's *A Shropshire Lad*.

As far as style is concerned, Vaughan Williams's successors predictably adopted a model style; for instance Stanley Bate's *Five songs of James Joyce*, or Rubbra's Christmas songs, *Hymn to the Virgin* and *Jesukin*. In the case of Rubbra, the modal style has led to a certain religious serenity and ecstasy; for instance in the *Two Sonnets by William Alabaster*. Warlock's style is also modal, though allied to a chromaticism derived from Delius and van Dieren. Frank Bridge's style, however, is more diatonic, while that of his pupil Benjamin Britten is characterised by the technique of an illustrative *ostinato* accompaniment. The poets whose words he has set cover a very wide range and include Hardy, Keats, Blake, Donne; those poets who have inspired Lennox Berkeley include W. H. Auden, Walter de la Mare, and French authors. Another composer strongly moved by religious feelings is Anthony Milner, as he shows in *Our Lady's hours*. If these composers' styles may all be said to be recognisably conventional, 12-note song-composers include Elisabeth Lutyens, with her setting of Rimbaud's *O saisons, O châteaux*, and Humphrey Searle, with his *Three songs of Jocelyn Brooke*.

The song-cycle as an extended form has been used by many composers, but by none more successfully than Tippett. His two song-cycles, *Boyhood's End* and *The Heart's Assurance*, are among the most notable examples in the contemporary repertoire. The piano is used on equal terms with the voice, and forms not so much an accompaniment as a duo.

Choral songs for unaccompanied voices are also a central feature of contemporary British music. The eclipse of the traditional oratorio from the 1930's onwards, has meant that the large chorus has given place to the choir of smaller size, which is better able to achieve rhythmic flexibility, and variety of tone. Even before 1930 some composers wrote choral works which were the forerunners of the pattern that we see today; for instance Arnold Bax's *Mater Ora Filium*, and Holst's *Tomorrow shall be my dancing day*. Since 1945 the interest in the unaccompanied choir on the part of composers of both the middle and younger generations has shown a marked increase.

And so the long list can be continued. There is also a debit side; the number of boring and dull songs is formidable. Particularly is this apparent in the work of church composers. If we are to take it that those twentieth century compositions included in *The Treasury of English Church Music*[1] are as representative of the contemporary situation as they are purported to be, then the picture is indeed a dismal one. It is a sad reflection on the non-acceptance of the contemporary composer by his society, that the English Church should accept as suitable for the worship of the Almighty such lugubrious and miserable music as appears to be the case

A satisfactory overall picture is almost impossible to achieve for another reason; only a small fraction of contemporary works is published or performed. There is no equivalent in England to the Viennese publishing firm of Universal Edition, who have made it their business, as a matter of principle, to print the works of contemporary composers, however commercially unprofitable this may prove. On the continent, particularly in Germany, a new work will be performed unless

---

[1] Vol. 5, published by Blandford (1965).

there is a very good reason why not; in England a new work will not be performed unless there is a very good reason why it should be. The composer, more than most artists, is subject to that crippling tide of fashion which is so prevalent in England, and which ebbs and flows with such relentless caprice, aided and abetted no doubt by those whose concern it is to anticipate and respond to such things. Those who manipulate the media of publicity are doubly cautious before promoting a new composer whose publicity-value is doubtful.

By far the majority of works performed in a London concert season are of the Classical and Romantic repertory. The contemporary composer is allotted a very small share, while the share allotted to the living English contemporary composer is minuscule.[1] London is an international musical forum; a meeting-place of performers (not so much composers) from the four quarters of the globe. It seeks primarily not to cultivate its own musical culture, but to listen with avid curiosity to that of others.

The influence of broadcasting on contemporary music in Great Britain has been, in one sense, enormous, in another sense negligible. It is enormous in that one centralised authority extends its influence up and down the land. All musicians, concert organisations, orchestras have to allow for a proportion of their work to be broadcast; and so perforce they must listen to the dictates of the broadcasters. Unfortunately this enormous potential for good has not been realised. Government by committee is not always compatible with artistic achievement. It is the nature of committees to become bureaucratic, and for monopolies to tend towards secrecy and corrupt practices; and as far as the performance of contemporary English music is concerned, and the sponsoring of new works, there never was a clearer illustration of that 'reserve' which we are always told is a part of the English character. In the case of 'popular music' (see Appendix II) it amounts to self-administered asphyxiation.

The performance and sponsoring of new works, which is not done by the main concert promoters, is left in the hands of a small number of private societies, whose shoe-string financial resources are as small as their enthusiasm is great. Many of these societies formed an association in London,

[1] See Appendix II.

known as Contemporary Concerts Coordination, for the purpose of avoiding date clashes, and of publishing jointly a leaflet announcing their concerts. Among the member societies are the Institute of Contemporary Arts, Macnaghten Concerts, Park Lane Group, and the Redcliffe Concerts of British Music. Though their appeal is to a minority, and their influence is peripheral, the growth of these small, privately-sponsored societies is the most positive development in the presentation of contemporary music on the concert platform.

It is a curious fact which can hardly escape the notice of the student of English contemporary music that the current wave of fashion has all but engulfed an entire generation of composers. From the period 1920–1939 very little is heard today; scarcely a name appears in performances. Vaughan Williams chiefly stands out, and even he has long since been disowned by today's *avant-garde*. As far as they are concerned he also might as well join that twilight company of English musicians who are fast receding into the mists of the history books; if indeed they have not already reached that blessed, if questionable, state.

Some younger composers decided to start afresh in the 1950's, and by so doing to consign to the past the period of the much-vaunted English 'renaissance'. But you cannot have it both ways; the composer, like other mortals, needs to be true to himself. Other European composers also started afresh after 1945; Boulez for example. But whereas he recast the traditions of Debussy, Stravinsky and Webern, and sought to refashion them according to his serialist principles, the English avant-gardists have blithely and unthinkingly rejected their own tradition, and attached themselves to whatever trend appeared to be the thing of the moment— whether that of Webern, Messiaen, Stockhausen, or indeed of Boulez himself. But there is the world of difference between a creative synthesis and a derivative one; and by following the course they chose their idiom ceased to be a continuation of their nascent endemic tradition, and became instead parasitic on another. By this reckoning the English musical 'renaissance' would be a figment, an illusion, since you cannot claim credit for something you reject. But it is only out of an active tradition, over a period of years, that a composer rises who overreaches his immediate age and country.

If, taken as a whole, the environment in which the British composer works today is highly unfavourable, and severely handicaps the emergence of a vital contemporary tradition of British music, there seems to be a compensatory importance laid on the work of the executive musician. Numerous openings exist for the performer. And what is perhaps more important, the teaching and training of children, which is not something for which this country has been particularly noted in the past, has received most welcome attention. A particularly noteworthy example of this is provided by the Junior Department of the Royal College of Music in London, who arrange for schoolchildren to be given full facilities for professional musical instruction, in a way that will not conflict with their normal education. Orchestral training is available in one of four orchestras, and many of the children who are competent enough to be placed in the first of these orchestras, also belong to the National Youth Orchestra, and appear in concerts.

Such experience for the student performer is difficult to overrate. Something of this enthusiasm is needed to bring about the vitalisation of the British musical scene as a whole.

CHAPTER SEVEN

NATIONAL TRADITIONS:

THE AMERICAN TRADITION

(i) *Charles Ives* (1874–1954)

Although parallels between composers are notoriously dangerous, the student of contemporary music can hardly fail to notice a remarkable similarity of outlook and artistic purpose between the Englishman Vaughan Williams and the American Charles Ives. Their dates coincide; both took the musical situation of their respective countries as they found it, and sought to establish an endemic tradition; both pioneers, they shared a love of their country; both possessed a visionary, mystical quality, tempered with realism; both had a deep understanding of their country's literary and religious culture; both were misunderstood and accused of 'amateurism'.

Two basic points of difference however must be noted. Whereas Vaughan Williams was *persona grata* to the Establishment (both musical and academic) of his day, and was recognised by all the right people, Charles Ives most decidedly was not. His was a life of isolation, and for the greater part of it his music was neither performed nor understood by his professional colleagues, except for a significant handful, including Webern who presented his work in Vienna, and Copland.[1] So it was that his *Concord Sonata* (1908–1915) had to wait until 1939 for a performance; after this his symphonies began gradually to be played; the *Third Symphony* in 1947 (when it was awarded a Pulitzer prize); the *Second Symphony* in 1951, 50 years after its completion, the *Fourth Symphony* in 1964, under the 82-year-old Leopold Stokowski, when it created a profound impression. In his seventies Charles Ives suddenly became famous. But by then the years of neglect had taken their toll, and for the last thirty years of his life he wrote nothing. This is in direct contrast to Vaughan Williams.

[1] See below, p. 188.

Charles Ives was rooted in the heritage of New England—
that peculiarly American blend of innocence and audacity,
simplicity of emotion and fearlessness of intellect. This
duality is plain throughout his music, and particularly in his
best known work, the Concord Sonata, which we shall
consider soon. He was born in Danbury, Connecticut, and
from an early age his musical originality was encouraged by
his father, who had been a bandmaster since the days of the
Civil War. An appointment as church organist at the age of
13 gave him a love of simple hymn tunes which he never lost
in later life.

After four years' study at Yale he made a decision which
was to have far-reaching effects on his work as a composer;
one might almost say on the whole course of twentieth
century American music. He decided against the life of a
professional musician, and went instead into an insurance
business. He later became head of a large agency, and worked
at composition only at night and at weekends.

Underlying his work was a sense of purpose, an attitude
to life. He saw no contradiction between the world of com-
merce and the world of art. The two for him were complementary. The material and the spiritual worlds, or, to use his
terms, the real and the transcendental, were interdependent,
the one feeding the other. His idealism was matched by
realism. Not for him was the derivative style of a European
culture; rather, like Walt Whitman, he wrestled with his own.
Whereas Vaughan Williams could invoke the English Elizabethan period of 300 years previously, Charles Ives could make
no such appeal to a past tradition. Behind him were the open
spaces; the New World of the spirit had yet to be discovered.
It could only come from American culture.

He had no doubt which of the two, the conventional or the
original, his contemporaries would prefer. In describing his
decision to earn his living from something other than music,
he says:

"Assuming that a man lives by himself and with no depen-
dents, he might write music that no one would play prettily,
listen to or buy. But—but if he has a nice wife and some
nice children, how can he let the children starve on his
dissonances? So he has to weaken (and if he is a man

he *should* weaken for his children); but his music more than weakens—it goes 'ta-ta' for money! Bad for him, bad for music!"

He experimented freely in style; cluster chords, absence of barlines, polytonality, atonality, ametricality, and all the devices of counterpoint, which he might place in the same context as a hymn tune or popular song. Whereas the 'atonalism' of Schoenberg and other European composers was arrived at only after a considerable intellectual process, Ives did no more than listen to the sounds of life around him; an out-of-tune fiddler at a country dance; different bands playing simultaneously in different parts of his home town; a congregation of inadequate vocal resource singing together conflicting versions of the same hymn, with yet another version provided by an asthmatic harmonium accompaniment. Such inexpert music-making roused the artist in him. How could the very background of life be "wrong"? It would indeed be unnatural to turn the sounds of reality into an unreal convention. What was it, Ives asked, that gave that piquancy to the sound of bells? Where were the notes "in the cracks between the keys"?

The nature of his large output is best seen in three major compositions which occupied him more or less for the first two decades of this century. These are the second piano Sonata, or *Concord Sonata*; the orchestral work *Three places in New England* (1903–1911); and the *Fourth Symphony* (1910–1916).

(a) *Sonata No. 2—"Concord, Mass., 1845"*

The composer's intentions in this work are fully described in his *Essays before a Sonata*—prescribed reading for any who would understand the genesis of American contemporary music.

The small town of Concord, Massachusetts, in 1845 was the home of the Transcendentalists; the writer and philosopher Ralph Waldo Emerson, the novelist Nathaniel Hawthorne, the Alcott family, whose daughter Louisa wrote *Little Women*, and Henry Thoreau, author of *Walden*. In this flowering of American literature Ives saw just those roots that he sought, and this sonata, which was the first work of his to achieve public, though belated, acclamation, consists of four impressionistic pictures of these citizens of Concord.

J. B. Priestley has pointed out[1] the direct influence of the German Romantic movement on these Transcendental New Englanders, particularly on Emerson, the intellectual leader. Indeed the impressionistic depiction of ideas or personalities is a central theme of Romantic composers. We recall Schumann's *Carnaval*, or Elgar's *Enigma* Variations, to mention only two. But this is by no means to be confused simply with 'programme music'; in the *Prologue* of his *Essays before a Sonata*, Ives discusses in a few succinct pages, the whole immeasurable range of artistic inspiration, as it appeared to him.

This work is called 'Sonata' for want of a better word, and the title should not be taken to imply the thematic development and the harmonic connection of a conventional scheme such as sonata form. Right from the opening the harmony is without a tonal centre.

(i) Emerson

Emerson was a philosopher after Ives' own heart. He calls him "America's deepest explorer of the spiritual immensities." His message was "spiritual hopefulness", and "courageous universalism that gives conviction to his prophecy and that makes his symphonies of revelation begin and end with nothing but strength and beauty of innate goodness in Man, in Nature and in God, the greatest and most inspiring theme of Concord Transcendental Philosophy."

So the first movement is the longest and the most difficult. The artist seeks to impose unity on the chaos of intractable material. Barless, keyless and apparently formless, the music falls into two main categories, "prose" and "verse"; the first free in form and complex; the second more orthodox and formal. Ives also introduces the 4-note *motif* from Beethoven's fifth symphony, which appears in many different guises; "the soul of humanity knocking at the door of the Divine mysteries, radiant in the faith that it will be opened—and the human become the Divine!"

The music cannot be identified with any specific passage in

[1] In *Literature and Western Man*, pp. 197–8.

Emerson's writings, though there is a correspondence of mood. At one point the player is instructed to sound a particularly violent chord "in as strong and hard a way as possible, almost as though the Mountains of the Universe were shouting, as all of humanity rises to behold the 'Massive Eternities' and the 'Spiritual Immensities'."

At another point, high notes played pp, "reflect the overtones of the soul of humanity as they rise away almost inaudibly to the Ultimate Destiny."

(ii) Hawthorne

If Emerson represents the positive side of the Transcendental group, Hawthorne represents the darker world of "phantasmal realms"; guilt-ridden desires, and childhood longings. As Priestley says, if psychoanalysis had been invented at this time, surely Hawthorne would have provided the ideal study-material. Most of the characters in *The Scarlet Letter* symbolise some part of the unconscious. Like Emerson, he had Calvinism in the blood, though Ives does not stress this aspect. Instead he suggests the background sensibility of the unconscious with a whirling, metre-less glittering texture, against which, in relief, fragments of melody stand out. Free rein is given to the artist's fancy, to which Ives has given us this clue:

"It may have something to do with the children's excitement on that frosty Berkshire morning, and the frost imagery on the enchanted hall window, or something to do with "Feathertop" the Scarecrow, and his Looking Glass, and the little demons dancing around his pipe bowl; or something to do with the old hymn tune that haunts the church and sings only to those in the churchyard, to protect them from secular noises, as when the circus parade comes down Main Street. . . ."

And Ives's circus parade is true to life, vulgarity and all. The brass band blares away in competition with the Drum Corps; at one point the Drum Corps "gets the best of the Band—for a moment". Certain notes are hit hard with the left hand, like a trombone setting the pace "for the old Cornet Band to march off to."

7

(iii) *The Alcotts*

The Alcotts conjure up a picture of healthy New England childhood; the sort of wholesome and homely innocence that middle-aged children like to turn back to later with ease and affection, not to say nostalgic sentiment; the "richness of not having", as Ives calls it; the good fortune of being without ready-made entertainment; spiritual sturdiness and Puritan severity; the family hymns that were sung at the end of each day; the "Orchard House" beneath the old elms, where "sits the little old spinet-piano Sophia Thoreau gave to the Alcott children, on which Beth played the old Scotch airs, and played at the *Fifth Symphony*."

The lyrical simplicity of the movement is marked by off-beat rhythms and bitonality. Beethoven's Fifth Symphony motto is used this time to set off an improvisatory train of thought.

(iv) *Thoreau*

Henry James said that "Thoreau is more than provincial—he is parochial". But is it not by 'contracting out' of day to day affairs that original and solitary contemplation is possible? Is not that the story of Ives himself? Priestley[1] calls Thoreau "in many respect the more considerable writer" (than Emerson), precisely because of his originality; Ives would have added, also because of his universality. In Nature Thoreau saw an analogy to the "innate goodness" of Transcendentalism.

If the Sonata has a conclusion at all it is in this last movement. If we need a programme for it, as Ives says,

"Let it follow his thought on an Autumn day of Indian summer at Walden—a shadow of a thought at first, colored by the mist and haze over the pond:

> Low anchored cloud,
> Fountain head and
> Source of rivers . . .
> Dew cloth, dream drapery—
> Drifting meadow of the air . . . (Ex. 45)

[1] *Op. cit.*, p. 198.

". . . the beauty of the day moves him to a certain restlessness; as he stands on the side of the pleasant hill of pines and hickories in front of his cabin, he is still disturbed by a restlessness and goes down the white-pebbled and sandy eastern shore . . ."

So the day passes, and the music gradually assumes an endlessly melodic character, for which the composer calls for a flute if possible; the most evocative of instruments, as

Charles Ives
"Concord" Sonata

IV Thoreau

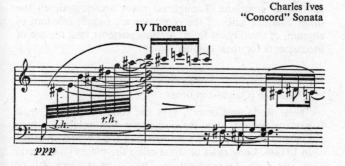

Ex. 45

Debussy found in his *Prélude*. Then the evening comes, "when the whole body is one sense"; and "as candles are lit on earth, stars are lit in heaven."

(b) *Three places in New England* (Orchestral Suite)

Place-names rich in associations for a New Englander are evoked.

(i) *The "St. Gaudens" in Boston Common: Col. Shaw and his Colored Regiment. Very slowly.*

> Moving,—Marching—Faces of Souls!
> Marked with generations of pain,
> Part-freers of a Destiny,
> Slowly, restlessly—swaying us on with you
> Towards other Freedom! . . .

Beginning and ending ppp, this solemn movement evokes Civil War emotions. Though no tunes are quoted, all the other characteristics of the composer are found; freedom of rhythm, of tonality, of form; *ostinato* patterns, and the use of instruments for their colour.

(ii) *General Putnam's Camp, Redding, Connecticut.*

> *Allegro* (Quick-step time)

"Near Redding Center", says the composer, "is a small park preserved as a Revolutionary Memorial; for here General Israel Putnam's soldiers had their winter quarters in 1778/9. Long rows of stone camp fire-places still remain to stir a child's imagination. During an outdoor 4th of July celebration, the child wanders into the woods and dreams of the far-off days of the war; when he wakes, he hears the children's songs, and runs back to listen to the two bands, and join in the games and dances."

Amid general hubbub and excitement, the two bands are heard; their march rhythms clash, four bars of one are equal to three bars of the other. Many other tunes and ideas, including Ragtime, build up to a shattering conclusion (ffff).

(iii) *The Housatonic at Stockbridge*

> *Adagio molto* (Very slowly)

Those who recognise composers on the strength of one work only—Handel on the strength of his *Messiah*, Beethoven of his *Fifth Symphony*—would probably recognise Charles Ives by this piece. Its movement is steady, yet with the customary rhythmical freedom; it starts quietly, builds up to fff, then subsides to a serene pp. Ives has described the origin of the piece in these words:

". . . a Sunday morning walk that Mrs. Ives and I took near Stockbridge. We walked in the meadows along the river and heard the distant singing from the church across the river. The mist had not entirely left the river bed, and the colour, the running water, the banks and the trees were something that one would always remember."[1]

Against a hazy ripple of strings a horn melody sounds out, richly and subtly accompanied, yet four-square like a hymn. Gradually other elements and sounds swell up, the texture and the groupings of instruments becomes more complex, until the peaceful melody is lost. Ives quotes the poem of the same name by Robert Underwood Johnson:

> Contented river! in thy dreamy realm—
> The cloudy willow and the plumy elm . . .
> Thou hast grown human laboring with men
> At wheel and spindle; sorrow thou dost ken . . .
> . . . Wouldst thou away!
> I also of much resting have a fear;
> Let me thy companion be
> By fall and shallow to the adventurous sea!

(c) The *Fourth Symphony*

Of his *Fourth Symphony* Charles Ives said:

"The aesthetic programme of the work is that of the searching questions of 'What?' and 'Why?' which the spirit of man asks of life. This is particularly the sense of the *Prelude*. The three succeeding movements are the diverse answers in which existence replies."

(i) *Prelude: Maestoso*. The first movement uses two orchestral groups. The main orchestra, which is huge and includes a Theremin,[2] two pianos, organ and large percussion section, builds up the *Prelude* boldly, atonally; against this a phrase from the hymn *Nearer, my God, to Thee* is given to a distant chamber-music group of violins and harp. Then, against a

---

[1] Quoted by Mellers in *Music in a new found land*, p. 45.
[2] An electronic instrument, named after its Russian inventor.

richly suggestive background, the chorus sing this hymn, solemnly, quietly:

> Watchman, tell us of the night,
> What the signs of promise are:
> Traveller, o'er yon mountain's height,
> See that Glory-beaming star.
> Watchman, aught of joy or hope?
> Traveller, yes; it brings the day,
> Promised day of Israel.
> Dost thou see its beauteous ray?

Suddenly, inconclusively, the short introductory movement ends.

(ii) *Allegretto*. The second movement, which attempts an answer to the 'What?' and the 'Why?' of the first, is not a scherzo in an accepted sense of the word. It is rather, says Ives,

> "a comedy—in which an exciting, easy and worldly progress through life is contrasted with the trials of the Pilgrims in their journey through the swamps and rough country. The occasional slow episodes—Pilgrims' hymns —are constantly crowded out and overwhelmed by the former. The dream, or fantasy, ends with an interruption of reality—the Fourth of July in Concord—brass bands, drum corps, etc."

The complexity is polytonal and polyrhythmic; numerous melodies and popular tunes sound together, each with its own characteristic colour and tonality; also many rhythmical patterns are contrasted, and the *tempo* is constantly varied.

(iii) *Fuge: Andante moderato*. The third movement is diatonic, and rhythmically simple. There could hardly be a greater contrast with the preceding movement. It is a double fugue on the hymns *From Greenland's icy mountains* and *All hail the power*; the second tune, played by trombones and horns, appears as a counterpoint to the first, played by the strings. Much of the movement is scored for strings only, and is in fact a transcription of an earlier String Quartet (1896). The composer described this movement as "an expression of the reaction of life into formalism and ritualism."

(iv) *Largo maestoso*. The final movement is conceived on three orchestral levels, which need three conductors; these are the percussion (which begins and ends the movement, very quietly, and which maintains its separate rhythm throughout), the main orchestra, and, as in the first movement, the distant chamber-music group. At the close the chorus are added, this time without words. The movement is thus a synthesis of the preceding ideas, and, like the *Prelude*, uses the tune of *Nearer, my God, to Thee*. The composer describes the intention of the finale as "an apotheosis of the preceding content, in terms that have something to do with the reality of existence and its religious experience."

Gradually a huge, complex climax is built up, of multi-linear counterpoint on a grand scale; the placing together not just of one part with another, but of one orchestra with another, one rhythm with another, one tonality with another. And instead of the harmonic development of sonata form, Ives constructs centres of tonal and rhythmic climax, with varying degrees of complexity.

Charles Ives achieved in music what the Transcendentalists of Concord had achieved fifty years earlier in literature and thought. Music for him, like philosophy for the Greeks, began in wonder; later, something that was local, 'parochial', as Henry James called it, became gradually national, international, universal.

(ii) *Aaron Copland* (*b.* 1900)

The generation that succeeded Ives has included Elliott Carter, Howard Hanson, Roy Harris, Quincy Porter, Roger Sessions, Randall Thompson and many others. Gradually during the thirties the work of these composers unfolded; the wide range of their idioms emerged, from the elegant classicism of Quincy Porter to the more deliberate expressionism of Roger Sessions; from the melodic style of Randall Thompson to the more rhythmical style of Elliott Carter. But the composer whose work encompasses most features, and is most typical of the newly-emerging American tradition, is Aaron Copland. He has sought nothing less than to express "the deepest reactions of the American consciousness to the American scene". As composer, teacher, conductor, pianist, writer, concert organiser, and general musical protagonist, he represents in his work the focal point of the American achievement.

Born in Brooklyn, he spent his childhood in "a street that could only be described as drab". He received little musical encouragement from his parents, and it was not until he went to France in 1921 that his latent musicality began to flourish. He went, he heard, he was conquered by the musical vistas that opened up before him, as well as by Nadia Boulanger, that remarkable teacher whose list of pupils reads like a roll-call of the most noteworthy composers of Europe and America.

Copland has been consistently active in ventures which had to do with the furtherance of American music. He organised the "Copland-Sessions Concerts", 1928–1931; he was responsible for arranging the Yaddo Festivals, at Saratoga Springs, New York, which started on 30th April, 1932, and were devoted entirely to American contemporary music. He has lectured at many universities, taught at Harvard and at the Berkshire Music Center; he has written numerous books and articles; he has received many awards, including the Pulitzer Prize (for *Appalachian Spring*), an Academy award (for *The Heiress*), and—what would be inconceivable in England—an award by the New York Critics' Circle (for his *Third Symphony*).

His first compositions included the *Organ Symphony*, the trio *Vitebsk* (a study on a Jewish theme), and many other works. It was after the first performance of the Organ Symphony in 1925 in New York, with Mlle Boulanger playing the solo part, that the conductor, Walter Damrosch,[1] earned immortality with the remark that ". . . when the gifted young American who wrote this Symphony can compose, at the age of 23, a work like this one, it seems evident that in five years he will be ready to commit murder." The 'murder' five years later turned out to be the *Piano Variations* (1930). Moreover two other works for piano, the *Piano Sonata* (1941) and the *Piano Fantasy* (1957), mark out the course of his instrumental, and orchestral, style. These three compositions

[1] Whose father Leopold founded the N.Y. Symphony in 1878.

contain the essence of his development in one direction, that of 'absolute' music. It was the first that marked his emergence as a mature composer with an individual style.

Piano Variations

This work, which was later orchestrated, and performed as a ballet, was first played by the composer himself, in January 1931. In style, it is partly a continuation of earlier works, particularly of *Music for the Theatre* and of *Two pieces for Strings*, partly the result of contributory factors, such as the ambiguous tonality, and rhythmic syncopation, of Blues, and the contrapuntal discipline of serialism. The theme is treated like a 4-note row, with the texture of each variation derived directly from it. There is no harmonic modulation. All the contributory influences are subservient to the overall musical structure, which is thus consistent and coherent. Copland has assimilated influences, not merely reflected them.

The theme is triadic, based on the tonality of C, and curiously reminiscent of B–A–C–H (Ex. 46); the twenty

Theme   Opening

Aaron Copland
Piano Variations (1930)

Ex. 46

continuous variations treat intervals, texture, rhythm, tempo, method of attack, in a quasi-serial way. Each variation is self-consistent, built round a characteristic feature or turn of phrase, which is repeated like an *ostinato*. The variations differ in bar-length, and the metre is frequently varied, particularly from Var. 14 onwards, when the metrical unit, hitherto the crotchet, becomes the quaver.

Instead of introducing harmonic modulations, Copland transposes the tonal centre—to E flat (Var. 6–7), to D flat (Var. 10), to D (Var. 11–13); the return to C at Var. 14 coincides with the change of metre and thus represents an important structural join (Ex. 47). Thereafter the tonality remains fixed, and the interest becomes mainly rhythmic, as in Var. 16 (Ex. 48). At Var. 19 the tonality changes to G; Var. 20 is the longest, and combines a Retrograde Inversion of the theme in the right hand, with a G major transposition in the left. A coda brings back the tonality of C.

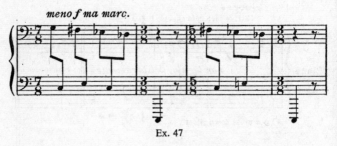

Ex. 47

The strength of this most characteristic work lies in the assimilation of so many factors. The use of counterpoint after the manner of serialism is anything but a device, but is the chief means whereby that clarity of texture is obtained which becomes such a marked feature of his work from now on;

Ex. 48

the element of harmony is treated originally and successfully, and the polytonality which characterises his mature style is here evident. It appears again soon, in *Statements* for orchestra (1933–35), and numerous other works.

Those features which mark the *Variations* also appear in the Sonata. Again, the opening is triadic (Ex. 49a); the texture is wide-spreading, the metre frequently varied. The vigour of the second, Scherzo, movement, which is a brilliant $\frac{5}{8}$ metre, marked *delicate*, *restless*, and later *with suppressed excitement*, is completely balanced by the third movement, which is free in form and tonality, and opens with harmonically ambiguous chords, played starkly, ff. A tender, modal melody, with a metrical unit of a crotchet, is treated in 3 imitative parts; a climax is worked over a characteristic, dotted-rhythm *ostinato*. The music however then becomes more and more remote, and dies away to nothingness. The conclusion, infinitely peaceful, is marked with a transposition of the opening triadic theme of the first movement (Ex. 49b).

Aaron Copland
Piano Sonata (1939–41)

(a) Beginning of first movement

(b) End of third movement

Ex. 49

Arising directly out of the Piano Sonata, and owing a lot to it in form and style, is the orchestral work that typifies Copland's symphonic composition, the *Third Symphony* (1944–46).

Third Symphony

(References are to the Hawkes Pocket Score).

The effect achieved in this symphony is of a powerful *cantabile*. The hallmarks of his style, as shown in this work, are the extension of tonality into polytonality and other ambiguous harmonic relationships; double phrases extended or shortened; dotted and syncopated rhythms; varied metre. The work is characteristically American, but as Copland says, it contains:

"no folk or popular material. During the late twenties it was customary to pigeon-hole me as a composer of symphonic jazz, with emphasis on the jazz. More recently I have been catalogued as a folk-lorist and purveyor of Americana. Any reference to jazz or folk material in this work is purely unconscious."

Nevertheless it would be surprising if something of the mood of *Appalachian Spring*, which had been composed just previously, were not to be found also in this score.

I. The opening of the first movement, which is E major, spelt out in even crotchets, recalls New England hymnody. There are three themes; the first starts the work, with falling fourths in the violins; the second occurs at $\boxed{4}$, with rising fifths; the third is given to the trombones and horns at $\boxed{6}$.

"The general form is that of an arch, in which the central portion is more animated, and the final section, and extended coda, presenting a broadened version of the opening material. Both first and third themes are referred to again in later movements."

II. As with the Piano Sonata, the second movement follows the normal symphonic procedure of Scherzo and Trio. The texture has a French lightness, also found in the work of other good Boulanger pupils.[1] The metre changes for the Trio at $\boxed{37}$, which, like the second subject of the Sonata, is a *legato*, sequential theme, in thirds. The woodwind have imitative counterpoint. Later, when the Trio theme returns towards the end of the movement, at $\boxed{49}$, it is treated in canon.

III. Except for a short passage for solo trumpet and horn, no brass is used in this movement. The formal scheme is free.

"The various sections are intended to emerge one from the other in continuous flow, somewhat in the manner of a closely-knit series of variations. The opening section however plays no rôle other than that of introducing the main body of the movement. High up in the unaccompanied first violins is heard a rhythmically transformed version of the third theme of the 1st movement. . . . A new and more tonal

---

[1] Compare, for instance, the scoring of Lennox Berkeley's *Divertimento* in B flat.

theme is introduced in the solo flute. This is the melody that
supplies the thematic substance for the sectional metamorphoses that follow. . . ."

Aaron Copland
Third Symphony (1944–46)

Ex. 50

Aaron Copland
Third Symphony (1944–46)

Ex. 51

The theme occurs at 61 , (Ex. 50), and the 'metamorphoses'
involve changes of tonality to F, A, G, back to A (Ex. 51).
The variations unfold "at first with quiet singing nostalgia;
then faster and heavier—almost dance-like; then more
childlike and naïve, finally vigorous and forthright."

As with the end of the Piano Sonata, the movement gradually becomes more remote, a distant background from which "floats the single line of the beginning," sung by a solo violin and piccolo, accompanied by two harps and celesta.

IV. This movement comes closest to sonata form, and is introduced by a fanfare, based on *Fanfare for the Common Man* (1942). The first theme moves with an "animated sixteenth-note[1] motion." The second theme, "broader and more songlike in character" is found unexpectedly in the development section. In the concluding coda, the opening theme of the first movement is restated.

The division of Copland's output into two broad categories —absolute, instrumental music, and popular music, mainly for the theatre or cinema, is not only a natural one, but one that reflects the composer's underlying aesthetic intention. That he was well versed in the developments brought to music by Stravinsky or the Viennese School has already been demonstrated; but he wished to address a wider American audience.

Of his two operas and five ballets, none could be more representative of his theatrical style than *Appalachian Spring*. This was commissioned by the Elizabeth Sprague Coolidge Foundation, and composed in 1943/4 as a ballet for Martha Graham, whose individual approach to dancing and choreography has had a marked influence on many other composers as well as Copland. For instance Wallingford Riegger has acknowledged[2] that he was drawn, through Martha Graham and her remarkable company, towards the modern dance as if "into a new sphere of creative activity."

Appalachian Spring

The title is from a poem by Hart Crane, and both this and the story were submitted to Copland by Miss Graham. The original scoring was for 13 instruments; later (1945) the composer made an abridged version of the ballet score into an orchestral Suite, using the customary Symphony orchestra.

The action of the ballet is a "pioneer celebration in spring around a newly built farmhouse in the Pennsylvania hills in the early part of the last century. The bride-to-be and her

---

[1] i.e. semiquaver.
[2] Quoted in Mellers, *Op. Cit.*, p. 123.

young farmer-husband enact the emotions, joyful and apprehensive, their new domestic partnership invites. An older neighbor suggests now and then the rocky confidence of experience. A revivalist and his followers remind the new householders of the strange and terrible aspects of human fate. At the end the couple are left quiet and strong in their new house."

The introduction is a leisurely unfolding of the tonality of A major, suggesting the arrival of spring in the world as well as the awakening of love. During this music the characters

Aaron Copland
Appalachian Spring (1943–44)

Ex. 52 and 53

are introduced, in a suffused light. Soon an *Allegro* section
is built up round an unashamedly diatonic theme (Ex. 52).
Later, as the revivalist appears, there are echoes of square
dancing and country fiddlers; also numerous and characteristically rhythmical developments of the *Allegro* theme
(Ex. 53). To depict "scenes of daily activity for the bride
and her farmer-husband", Copland introduces a theme and
5 variations. The theme he chooses is an old Shaker tune.

The Shakers were originally a sect of the Quakers, who
made free use of singing and dancing to express their religious
emotions, and produced a large collection of hymns and
songs, many of which were of the sort used at Revivalist and
Camp Meetings in the early nineteenth century. They quite
deliberately took folk-songs, or tunes from some other such
worldly source, and added their own words. One Shaker
hymn of 1813[1] is a colourful defence of their plagiarism:

> "Let justice seize old Adam's crew,
> And all the whore's production;
> We'll take the choicest of their songs,
> Which to the Church of God belongs,
> And recompense them for their wrongs,
> In singing their destruction."

If the tune called 'Simple Gifts', which dates from 1848,
was acquired in this way, then Aaron Copland acquired it
back again, just 100 years later. And in choosing this particular song, which expresses the Shaker spirit exactly, he clearly
recognised that they had one quality which was an important
factor in the American scene; the 'gift to be simple'. The
Revivalist movement reached its height in the early nineteenth
century—the very period of *Appalachian Spring*. The tune,
with its repeated notes in the 3rd and 8th bars, recalls Celtic
folk-melody (Ex. 54).

Copland's later work is a consistent exploitation of his
many-sided technique. Just as the American scene itself is
compounded of many cultures, a cosmopolitan and polyglot
society, so is Copland's musical style a synthesis of many
factors. His technique of evolving a movement from a single
thematic idea, which is stated at the opening, is entirely in

[1] Quoted in Chase, *America's Music*, p. 224.

Aaron Copland
Appalachian Spring

Ex. 54

keeping with the serial principle of using a series, or note-row, as the germ from which the composition derives. But serialism for Copland is not an act of faith; simply an extra contrapuntal discipline, an additional source of variety, in a style that is predominantly lyrical. Although such practice is heresy to the doctrinaire serialist, the adoption of serialism by Copland involves no marked change of idiom, since his style has, ever since the *Piano Variations*, been grounded in counterpoint. This is particularly noticeable in *Connotations* (1962/2), a 20-minute orchestral work, written for the opening season of the Lincoln Center for the Performing Arts in New York. The customary fanfare-like opening this time announces a 12-note work, since the composer is here addressing himself to an international concert audience, to whom he shows not so much his Americanism, as the European context from which his Americanism evolved.

Throughout all phases of his work, he has taken the symphony orchestra as he found it; he has had no recourse to tricks or gimmicks of any kind. Unlike the *avant-garde*, he uses ordinary instruments to play ordinary notes; his means are therefore simply the effects of sonorities, and the sheer vigour and variety of his musical utterance. He has shown the very opposite of musical isolationism, and has never sought to solve a problem by the convenient sophism of pretending that it does not exist. His originality and importance consist not in his invention of new musical means, but in the very much more difficult task of applying the existing musical means that lay to hand, in a fresher and wider context.

(iii) *Edgard Varèse* (1885–1965)

The American tradition that began with Charles Ives received a transfusion of great potency and originality in the work of Edgard Varèse. His potency derives from the fact that his fearless experiments were invariably disciplined and tempered by human, practical and formal considerations, which thus distinguishes his music from irresponsible experiment for its own sake; his originality derives from the fact that he saw the direction in which the European traditions were leading, and the trends of which Debussy and Busoni were the forerunners, and pursued and developed his ideas within the context of the newly-emerging American tradition.

He was born in Paris of Italian-French origin and received his initial training in science and mathematics. His early years were shared between Paris and Berlin. In addition to a conventional musical education at the Schola Cantorum and Paris Conservatoire, he made the acquaintance of Debussy as well as younger composers, such as Jolivet. He was active as a conductor, particularly of new music and early polyphonic music, and after moving to Berlin in 1909 he was associated with Busoni, whose pupil he became, and who exercised great influence over him at this formative stage. It is reasonable to guess that Busoni's influence helped him decide to emigrate to America during the first world war. The violent criticism to which Busoni, Schoenberg and others were subjected can hardly have escaped the notice of Varèse; and we know that Busoni considered America to be less bound by convention, more open to innovations than Europe. He held the view[1] that:

"in Europe inventions had been made to meet wants, whereas in America the inventions came first and the wants found for them; in Europe railways were built to join towns, while in America the railways were built first and the towns afterwards."

So in 1915 Varèse went to America and became an American citizen, as many leading European composers were later to do.

[1] Quoted in Dent *Ferruccio Busoni*, p. 191.

He lost no time in getting on with his work, and conducted orchestral concerts in New York and other cities. He consistently championed new developments in music, and introduced American audiences to the music of Webern and Berg, as well as to the works of their fellow-countrymen. But the public were not yet ready to receive what they heard, and he attempted to meet this difficulty by forming, in 1921, in collaboration with Carlos Salzedo, the International Composers' Guild, whose purpose was to perform the music of living composers. During the six years of its life, this Guild fulfilled much the same function as Schoenberg's Society for Private Musical Performances,[1] which had been formed in Vienna a few years earlier.

Varèse rejected most of his early compositions, with the result that we have today very few published works; only thirteen. These fall into two groups. The first group of works are based, generally speaking, on orchestral instruments—however unconventional some of these may be—and were composed in the 20's and early 30's. The second group date from the 50's, and are separated from the first group by a silence of about twenty years; they introduce the use of electronic instruments. The gap between the two groups is explained partly by the indifference and the opposition which he encountered, partly by his preoccupation with research into electronic instruments and their use by the composer. In fact, it fell to Varèse to realise practically what his teacher Busoni had foreseen theoretically, namely the breaking down of the artificial barriers in music (tones, scales, bar-lines and the rest), and the creation of an uninterrupted sound-source.

But not all his life was one of frustration. He found an early advocate in Leopold Stokowski, who has also championed other American composers, including Ives. Several of Varèse's compositions have been recorded. Later in his life, in the 1950's at Darmstadt, he found a new spirit of adventure in Europe, and less complacency. By that time electronic music too was beginning to appear, at Cologne and elsewhere,[2] and his was no longer a lone voice in the wilderness.

Varèse respected tradition but abhorred convention. He found the American life both faster and more concentrated

[1] See p. 83.
[2] See p. 119.

than the European, and matched his musical aesthetic to that fact. As he said[1]:

"Speed and synthesis are characteristic of our epoch. We need 20th century instruments to help us realise those in music."

These instruments he found by paying heed to the sounds of urban, industrial life; motors, whistles, factory hooters, all the restless noise of a machine civilization, which he sought to realise in his composition by means of the comparative freedom and primitivism of non-tonal percussion instruments. This characteristic of his work underlines his style, which is compounded from a negation of melody and harmony, and a correspondingly greater insistence and emphasis on rhythm. Rhythm for Varèse was the throbbing hum of a great metropolis, a counterpoint of city-sounds.

The most immediate and pressing problem which such an aesthetic presents is that of form. If you do away with the cohesion and unity that come from a harmonically-based structure, what do you put in their place? The answer that Varèse gives to this question[2] is central to an appreciation of his work:

"Form is the result of process. I have never tried to make my compositions fit into a known container. Musical form, considered as the result of a process, suggests an analogy with the phenomenon of crystallization. The clearest answer I can give to people who ask how I compose is to say: 'by crystallization.' The crystal is characterised by a definite external form and a definite internal structure. The internal structure is built on the unit of crystal, the smallest grouping having the order and composition of the substance. The extension of the unit into space forms the whole crystal. In spite of the limited variety of internal structures, the external forms of crystals are almost limitless. I believe that this suggests, better than any explanation I can give, the way my works are formed. One has an idea, the basis of internal structure; it is expanded or split into

[1] Quoted by Machlis, *Introduction to contemporary music*, p. 624.
[2] Quoted by Mellers, *Music in a new found land*, p. 158.

different shapes or groups of sounds that constantly change
in shape, direction and speed, attracted or repulsed by
various forces. The form is the consequence of this interaction. Possible musical forms are as limitless as the exterior
forms of crystals."

Is not this a remarkably lucid exposition of an elusive and
almost indefinable process? The old harmonically derived
structures, such as Sonata form, may be considered as the
finite assertion of the superiority of the creative human mind
over the infinite, intractable world of nature; to Beethoven in
particular they were a visible, actual expression of that in-
visible, psychological struggle that makes up the spirit of man.
Varèse however seeks not to overcome, but to imitate nature.
There is in his scores no harmonic integration of one part
with another, no thematic development; simply the placing
together of sound-blocks.

In seeking freedom from the established norms, the 'arbitrary restrictions', as he calls them, of musical expression,
Varèse found himself in a sort of aesthetic no-man's land,
where the frontiers that separate music from the other arts
are ill-defined. Clearly, if you reject, as a basis of composition,
all the conventional devices of your craft, you must look
elsewhere for something to take their place. Varèse looked
to the visual arts, to sculpture and architecture. It is interesting and significant that it was Le Corbusier who, when
he had designed a pavilion for the Brussels fair in 1958, which
he called "a poem of the electronic age", asked Varèse to
compose a piece to match it, that would put the audience
"in the presence of the genesis of the world". So Varèse
wrote the *Poème electronique*.

Varèse blurs the distinction between time and space; his
pieces are given geometrical titles, for instance *Hyperprism*,
Octandre, and his sound-patterns are the musical equivalent
of that Futurism, Cubism, Primitivism that we associate in
painting and sculpture with the work of Braque, Picasso,
Giacometti, Moore. A hint of the philosophy underlying such
developments in art is provided in the writings of André
Masson,[1] the French painter:

---

[1] See J. P. Hodin, *The dilemma of being modern*, p. 150.

"Je ne suis pas devant la nature, j'en fais partie."
(I am no longer confronted by nature, I am part of it).
"Qui'il ne soit plus question d'object dans l'espace. C'est l'object qui deviendra espace."
(It is no longer a question of an object in space. It is the object which will become space).

In the same way Varèse rejected the impressionistic use of sound; instead, he made sounds intrinsic to the structure. Apart from percussion instruments he had a marked preference for wind and brass, and used strings only in those compositions which had traditional leanings; for instance in *Offrandes* (Offerings, 1921), which is a setting for Soprano and Chamber Orchestra of two surrealist poems, *Chanson de Là-haut*, (Song from on high), and *La croix du Sud* (The Southern Cross). This work has direct affiliations with Debussy.

In *Octandre* (1924) he uses only the double bass to provide the foundation; the other seven instruments are wind and brass. Even in his comparatively unexperimental works, such as *Amériques* (1922) or *Arcana* (1927), his characteristic voice is present. But each of the two groups of his compositions is marked by a work of culminating importance; the first group by *Ionisation* (1931), the second group by *Déserts* (1954).

Ionisation, which earned an accolade from Stravinsky,[1] is a one-movement piece for 35 percussion instruments. These include some unusual ones, from Chinese and Latin-American sources, as well as anvils, high and low sirens, and a 'lion's roar'. The instruments are graded both in tone-quality and in pitch. The composer thus constructs a balanced orchestra and proceeds to manipulate his rhythmic sonorities with great virtuosity. The protracted wail of the sirens acts as a sort of accompaniment, or *continuo*, to the polyphony of the other instruments. The work has been analysed by Nicolas Slonimsky, to whom it is dedicated, into 'first subject' and 'second subject', though we must treat these terms with a certain flexibility. At the end the composer introduces three instruments of definite pitch, tubular bells, glockenspiel and piano, and the work dies away to its close.

[1] In *Ricordiana*, April 1962 (published by Ricordi & Co. Ltd.).

Déserts consists of an orchestral score with three interpolations of electronic sound. The orchestra is made up of 14 wind and brass instruments (no strings), 47 percussion instruments shared between 5 players, and a piano as an "element of resonance". The composition comes after the 20-year gap in his output; yet his technique has, if anything, gained in force. The raw material for the interpolations of 'organised sound' partly comes from industrial noises—"friction, percussion, hissing, grinding, puffing"—which were first recorded in factories and then processed by electronic means; partly also from the use of percussion instruments. Varèse clearly implies a synthesis of the non-human and the human aspects of life.

The deserts of the title are both the empty places of the world, and those of the mind.

"Not only those stripped aspects of nature that suggest bareness, aloofness, timelessness, but also that remote inner space no telescope can reach, where man is alone, a world of mystery and essential loneliness."

The four instrumental sections, of which the second is the longest, are so constructed as to build up to a structural climax, which then dies away before the next interpolation begins. As in *Ionisation*, we find that detailed preoccupation with *timbre*, dynamic, method of attack, particularly of the percussion instruments which is such a pronounced characteristic of later *avant-garde* composers.

The cataclysmal sound-structures of *Déserts* are not so much a representation of certain aspects of urban life, as "an identification of a man with his inner nature, as well as with his outward environment." This idea finds it parallel in the philosophy of existentialism, which we associate with Jean-Paul Satre, and which was particularly prevalent after 1945. It found a considerable response in American literature. According to this a man can, by his own choice, shape his own existence. To quote from the *Oxford Companion to French Literature*:

"Circumstances are a void (*néant*) from which man can emerge if he is intelligent enough . . . he can by gratuitous choice give a shape to human existence, and confer meaning and purpose on the universe . . . liberty is overwhelming."

This is remarkably close to Varèse's compositional process, particularly in *Déserts*, and the later *Poème electronique*. He does not seek to assert the human will so much as to submit it to the timeless void that is nature. We move through a waste-land of sound; this or that feature is made prominent. Does Varèse succeed in impressing us with his "meaning and purpose"? There is no doubt of the disturbing relevance of his work, nor of its influence on later composers of the *avant-garde*, both because of the finer points of his technique, and because of the broad scope of his quest.

(iv) *The American Scene*

Charles Ives stands in the same relationship to the American tradition as Vaughan Williams does to the English. There are however differences between the two environments which mainly explain the disparity between the subsequent development of the two traditions. The range of musical endeavour in America is as varied and vast as the country itself; in England the scale and scope is much reduced, and centred on London. More importantly, a fundamental difference of intention and attitude towards the contemporary composer prevails in the institutions and universities of America from what is normally the case in England. In England, academic music is one thing, practical music-making very much another; rarely do the twain meet. In America the function of the university has always been seen not merely as the furtherance of academic learning, important though this is, but as the focussing and the directing of talent. Composers and performers are able to develop their art within the precincts of the campus; composition and instrumental performance form part of the student's syllabus.

The American Society of University Composers, which was founded in 1966, underlines this approach to music at university level. It declares that "a university is an appropriate place to pursue serious composition and the whole range of professional activity necessary to it. The University, with its tradition of respect for serious intellectual activity, professionally established standards, and rational discourse, can be more than a convenient economic haven for composers; it is at present, for better or for worse, the American institution best suited to the development of an adequate environment for our profession."

This statement gives formal expression to a practice which has existed for a long time; and the direct benefits to the contemporary American musical scene—to say nothing of the indirect benefits—are incalculable. Two chiefly may be mentioned. In 1931 an annual festival of American music was started at the Eastman School, University of Rochester. Under its director, Howard Hanson, it has directly and positively fostered a long line of composers, including Peter Mennin, Robert Palmer, Burrill Phillips, Gardner Read, Bernard Rogers, Robert Ward, and many others.

Louisville, Kentucky, provides another example of direct sponsoring; since 1948 a new work has been commissioned for every subscription concert by the Louisville orchestra. Thus a further asset is added to the already acknowledged list of the city's attractions: "beautiful women, fast horses, and good Bourbon whiskey".

Another far-reaching result of this broad, positive approach to the accommodation of the composer is seen in the countless number of musicians from Europe, particularly composers, who have made their home in America over the past forty years, largely after 1933. Schoenberg and Stravinsky are just two of the long list, which includes chiefly Bartok, Bloch, Hindemith, Krenek and Milhaud. As composers and teachers, the pervasive influence on the American scene today of these European composers, each with his own idiom, style and aesthetic intention, is quite impossible to calculate. The musical voice of the New World has been formed out of the experience of the Old. This factor is also in marked contrast with the English environment, which has had no such cross-fertilisation.

As far as past tradition is concerned, a New Englander born in 1876, Carl Ruggles would compare the centuries-old European tradition with that of his own country, which was just awakening to creative consciousness. No-one illustrates the spirit of individualism better than Ruggles, who sought out of the mountains, prairies, deserts and rivers of America; out of its growing, insatiable industrialism; out of its simplicity and idealism; in a word out of its New Englandism, to carve something of grandeur and sublimity. *Men and Mountains* (1924) and *The Sun-Treader* (1932) are typical of his works.

Extreme aural sensitivity and thorough workmanship were his hallmarks—as they were Webern's, though Ruggles never adopted serialism. He used a 21-note scale, which he conceived as being made up of the 7 diatonic notes, each with its own sharp and flat inflection. In the shaping of a melody, he considered that note repetition was a source of weakness; and though he allowed the reiteration of a note, he avoided repeating a note in a melodic line if there were fewer than nine or ten notes intervening. In addition to his rejection of academicism in all its forms, he also, surprisingly, rejected jazz, which perhaps explains why his work has had comparatively small success. He aimed instead at a polyphonic texture. His mentors were Bach and Handel. But behind Bach he saw there were centuries of tradition-makers, such as Ysaak, Monteverdi, Gabrieli, Schutz, Buxtehude, and many more. There was no time to be lost.

A story told by Henry Cowell[1] epitomises the restless spirit of Carl Ruggles. True or false, it can well bear repetition:

"One morning when I arrived at the abandoned schoolhouse in Arlington where he now lives, he was sitting at the old piano, singing a single tone at the top of his raucous composer's voice, and banging a single chord at intervals over and over. He refused to be interrupted in this pursuit, and after an hour or so, I insisted on knowing what the idea was."

"I'm trying over this damned chord," said he, "to see whether it still sounds superb after so many hearings."

"Oh," I said tritely, "time will tell whether the chord has lasting value."

"The hell with time!" Carl replied. "I'll give this chord the test of time right now. If I find I still like it after trying it over several thousand times, it'll stand the test of time all right!' "

The desire for a distinctively American musical speech was basic among the first twentieth century American composers. "A new art . . . everything new and everything American," said the Cuban composer Amadeo Roldan, which reminds us

---

[1] Quoted by Gilbert Chase in *America's Music*, p. 576.

that a distinctive voice was found by the Latin-American Villa-Lobos, and Chavez. The latter's *Toccata* (1942) for percussion only, evokes the Aztec civilisation prior to the Spanish occupation of Mexico. And referring to his early years, Copland says "I was anxious to write a work that would immediately be recognised as American in character."

The most original, entirely American development in music was jazz; yet Copland's acceptance of jazz was qualified. He saw it as an "easy way to be American"; yet he considered that, since it was confined to the Blues and the "snappy number," it had a "limited emotional range." The piano concerto (1926), the "Jazz Concerto", was his last attempt at the direct use of jazz, though he admitted the strongest effect of jazz was felt in the development of rhythm, and in certain techniques.

In the 20's, the 'jazz age', it was used by composers of widely differing idioms; for instance, by the eminently unexceptionable Randall Thompson, as well as by the not-quite-so-unexceptionable George Antheil. But the con-summation of this trend was realised by Copland's contemporary—also from Brooklyn—George Gershwin. Jazz for him represented the "energy stored up in America". As he put it:

"The great music of the past in other countries has always been built on folk-music . . . America is no exception. Jazz, ragtime, Negro spiritual and Blues, Southern mountain songs, country fiddling and cowboy songs can all be employed in the creation of American art-music . . . Jazz I regard as an American folk-music; not the only one, but a very powerful one which is probably in the blood and feeling of the American people more than any other style of folk music. I believe that it can be made the basis of serious symphonic works of lasting value, in the hands of a composer with talent for both jazz and symphonic music."

His *Rhapsody in Blue* (1924), *Piano Concerto* (1925), and *An American in Paris* (1928) are testaments to this. But the climax of his work was *Porgy and Bess* (1935), the first distinctively all-American opera, which has held its own on the international stage. The plot is about Negroes, and Gershwin therefore not only uses Negro folk-music, but also draws a positive influence from those all-too-American institutions, Broadway and Hollywood. The result is a totally new form.

Other composers of Gershwin's generation were Charles Griffes, who died in 1920 at the early age of 36; Henry Cowell, whose experimental work brought him into association with Varèse and Ruggles, and who, apart from his compositions, has been the constant champion of the American composer, largely by means of his periodical *New Music*; and Roy Harris, whose aim has been to "capture and communicate feeling"; and specifically to create the idea of an American symphony. This he does with a judicious mixture of originality and a basically traditional idiom. Harris himself has said:

> "The moods which seem particularly American to me are the noisy ribaldry, the sadness, a groping earnestness . . . an asymmetrical balancing of rhythmic phrases is in our blood."

His best-known work, and the one that is most typical of his times, is the third Symphony, which was first performed by Koussevitzky in 1939, to wide acclaim. This was followed by the Folksong Symphony (1940). Copland has said of Roy Harris that "his music comes nearest to a distinctively American melos of anything yet done in the more ambitious forms." His pupil and successor William Schuman has continued in this direction; his output consists of concertos, symphonies, string quartets, and choral works of a highly nationalist flavour. Poets who have attracted him are Walt Whitman and Genevieve Taggard.

Schuman's contemporary Elliott Carter is more cosmopolitan in outlook. He has developed a basically traditional idiom along highly personal lines, with different influences at work in different compositions; Copland in the piano Sonata (1946), Bartok in the String Quartet (1951), Schoenberg in the Orchestral Variations (1955), though this is not a 12-note work. Carter tells us "Its quality of harmony is derived from the theme and is arrived at by ear and not by a system." Each variation contains changes of character within itself. A certain individual complexity of style is also apparent in the highly original first String Quartet; particularly in the flexibility of metre.

Composers of the next generation whose Americanism is also compounded from different sources are Billy Jim Layton from Texas, whose starting point is Bartok and Elliott Carter, for instance in his *String Quartet in two movements* (1956); and Berlin-born Lukas Foss, whose cantata *The Prairie* (1944) suggests the influence of Hindemith and Copland. He is also a pianist with a strong flair for improvisation, and a teacher; he was Schoenberg's successor in 1953 at the University of California. His later works, such as *A parable of Death* (1953), and *Time cycle* (1960) develop greater complexity; the latter work consists of four songs, each based on the same chord, and varied by means of serial devices; the former is a setting for narrator and orchestra of *Geschichten vom lieben Gott* by Rainer Maria Rilke. In seeking to avoid melodrama, and the suffocation of the drama by the music, Foss has drawn direct inspiration from Bach's Passions.

Many composers of Copland's generation have built their style on a traditional idiom. They include Walter Piston, Howard Hanson, Virgil Thomson, Randall Thompson. If Piston's best-known work is his ballet *The incredible Flutist*, he has also written many conventional instrumental works. His aesthetic intention is a simple one: "to make music to be played and listened to." Though he was referring specifically to his sixth Symphony, this could well apply to his work as a whole. Hanson is a self-proclaimed Romantic. The statement accompanying his second symphony (1930) has been called the 'Romantic Manifesto'. He tried to interest a generation brought up on Brahms, Franck, Sibelius, by the use of a similar idiom. His opera, *Merry Mount*, though indeed mounted with all the panoply of the Metropolitan Opera House, did not achieve the impact or the success that his contemporary Virgil Thomson did, when his opera *Four Saints in three acts*, with a libretto by Gertrude Stein and an all-Negro cast, was produced the same year (1934). Thomson's diatonic idiom is simple, not naïve; and deceptively simple, as the composer's seven years among the Parisian *avant-garde* (1925–32) have given his music a certain *chic* naughtiness, which is an excellent foil for the often unintelligible text. Other compositions with words by Gertrude Stein were *Capital, Capitals* (1927), and a second opera *The mother of us all* (1946). The wit of his critical faculties enlivened the pages of the *New York Herald Tribune* for fifteen years, up to 1955.

Instead of the Parisian *finesse* of his namesake, Randall Thompson has infused his traditionalism with a combination of folk-song and patriotism. *The Testament of Freedom*, with words by Thomas Jefferson, is entirely straight-forward; entirely, and exclusively, American.

Traditional composers of a younger generation include the highly successful Samuel Barber and Alan Hovhaness. Apart from the *Essay* for Orchestra, and the *Adagio for Strings*—the popularity of the *Adagio* is largely due to its being recorded by Toscanini—Barber has also composed much symphonic ballet and chamber music, in a predominantly lyrical style, enriched in later works by rhythmic and harmonic innovations. His music owes little to folk idiom, except in small pieces such as *Four excursions* for piano (1944). Hovhaness's romanticism, on the other hand, has been tempered by Armenian folk-and church-music, as he is of mixed Armenian and Scottish descent. His *Magnificat* goes to early Greek and Jewish music "to suggest the mystery, inspiration and mysticism of early Christianity."

The 12-note technique, and serialism, have made a limited though real impact on American composers. It is clear that a thrusting, formative culture, such as the American, cannot be expected to take kindly to dogmatism, from whatever quarter. Some composers have taken certain aspects of serialism, but not the whole; Copland, for instance; also Walter Piston and Samuel Barber have used the 12-note technique in some of their works, though always retaining tonality. The *doyen* of serialists, however, is Wallingford Riegger. His early works were romantic; Henry Cowell referred to him as a "Romantic who admires strict forms". Then, like Schoenberg, he gradually moved away from tonality towards 'atonality', in works such as *Rhapsody* (1925) and *Study in sonority* (1929). His adoption of serialism was gradual, his use of it highly personal, until in 1948 his third symphony was awarded a prize by the ever-vigilant *New York Music Critics' Circle*.

Eleven years Riegger's junior, Roger Sessions is in spirit, if not by birth, a New Englander. He is also widely-travelled, and has been active and very influential as a teacher as well as a composer. His cooperation with Copland in the encouragement of American music has already been mentioned. As in the case of Riegger, his first compositions, for instance *Symphony No.* 1 (1928), were tonal, and he adopted serialism later. The key-work in the transition is his *2nd Symphony* (1946). Like Schoenberg, he conceives the 12-note row thematically, though he is not committed to the 12-note technique as an article of faith. His style has been aptly described as "intensely serious". His *Idyll of Theocritus* (1954) is a setting for dramatic soprano of the "intense and passionate" second Idyll. Its four sections, each depicting different emotions, correspond to the four movements of a symphony. Sessions has aimed at a "big line", lyrical in nature.

His pupil Milton Babbitt on the other hand has never shown any doubt about where his allegiance lay. He has always been a committed and dogmatic serialist, whose declared belief in cerebral music, perhaps the result of his training in mathematics, was entirely consistent with his point of departure as a composer, which was the aesthetic of Webern. He has been led, like Stockhausen, to the development of electronic sounds, which is a course also followed by another serial composer Ross Lee Finney, for instance in his cantata *Still are new worlds*. Finney however was a pupil of Berg, and his adoption of the 12-note style was a later development in his career, beginning with his *6th String Quartet* (1950). As with Berg, he never loses sight of tonality, even in such a late work as the *2nd Symphony* (1959). His early works are traditional, and some employ folk material. His studio at Ann Arbor, Michigan, has already been mentioned.

Experimentalists

The 12-note technique, and serialism, derived from European models, through such teachers as Schoenberg, Krenek, and (later) Sessions. The course followed by the experimentalists has been more original, and underivative, though the aesthetic justification for their work may be said to have originated in Europe, with the *Futurist Manifesto* (1913) of an Italian, Luigi Russolo, who urged composers to "break out of the narrow circle of musical sounds, and conquer the infinite variety of noise-sounds"; also in Dadaism, which originated in Zurich (1916).

Musical experimentalism started with a bang in America on 10th April, 1927, when the 'noise-sounds' of George Antheil's *Ballet Mécanique*, which had already been performed in Paris, disturbed the decorous atmosphere of Carnegie Hall. Its reception was mixed, though when the work was repeated in 1954 at a Composers' Forum in New York, it earned the composer an ovation. Antheil's aim was a new approach to "musical engineering"; time, not tonality, was his basic "canvas". The work combines the sound of 10 pianos and assorted items of hardware—anvils, bells, horns, buzzsaws and an airplane propeller. (In 1954 this was replaced by a recording of a more up-to-date jet engine). Antheil has also written conventional works, as well as a number of scores for Hollywood films. This he shares in common with Harry Partch, whose aesthetic ideas and experiments with new sounds were integrated into a system of composition to a greater extent than Antheil's were. Partch has devised a tonality made up of 43 tones to the octave instead of 12. This in turn necessitated the invention by him of new instruments capable of playing these microtonal intervals— Kitharas, Marimbas, glass bowls, and reed-organs with a special keyboard, which he called "chromelodeon".

Most of Partch's work has been in the theatre or cinema, and he conceives his music as integrated with Drama and Dance, not self-subsistent. This is in accordance with the Greek practice, and indeed he has a strong interest in classical drama, as his score for Yeat's translation of Sophocles' *Oedipus Rex* shows. Partch draws a sharp distinction between his conception of 'monophony', and the traditional Western harmony; in this score the actors intone with an inflected speech clearly derived from Schoenbergian *sprechstimme*. He has said of this score, which dates from 1952:

"The music is conceived as an emotional saturation that it is the particular province of dramatic music to achieve. My idea has been to present the drama expressed by language, not to obscure it, either by operatic aria or symphonic instrumentation. Hence in critical dialogue music enters almost insidiously as tensions enter."

As Gilbert Chase points out,[1] Partch's conception of

---

[1] In *America's Music*, p. 591.

music's function for drama is very similar to T. S. Eliot's conception of the function of poetry for drama; namely not to draw too much attention to itself, thus obscuring the drama, but to "intensify the dramatic situation."

Partch's classical leaning is also shown in *Revelation in Courthouse Park*, which is a modern parallel to Euripides' *Bacchae*; also in his trilogy of Satyr-plays, *Ring around the moon*, *Castor and Pollux*, and *Even wild horses*. These are a medley of music, words and mime, with no plot. They are derived from the old Roman *satura* (*satur* meaning 'full').

Like Partch, John Cage also came from California, where he was born in Los Angeles in 1912. His mentors included Henry Cowell, from whom he gained an interest in Oriental music, and Schoenberg. It became apparent in the late 30's that Cage's work was not to follow any preconceived pattern. His first works are mainly for percussion (*Constructions*), and in the 40's he introduced his 'prepared piano' pieces. Virgil Thomson has called their effect "a ping qualified by a thud". *Imaginary Landscape* followed in 1951, in which 12 radio receivers are tuned and adjusted simultaneously. The chance element in this depends on what happens to be 'on the air' when the operation takes place.

The chance element in *Concert* (1957/8) is even more radical, since each player is instructed to play all, any or none of his notes. Theoretically therefore this could result in absolute silence; a novel conception, even for Cage.

John Cage represents the point of no return; nothingness, zero. We are bidden to leave the world of reality as if in a trance. The sound has no beginning, middle or end; disembodiment is the ideal; the music is not to be "listened to" so much as "experienced", which is not easy for a Westerner. Anyone who listens to Cage's music as sound is liable to register the same effect as Virgil Thomson. But, Cage says, forget all you have ever heard, all traditions, musical associations, everything; forget life.

The flaw in this is unmistakable; if the listener is to enter such a state of nihilism, he will also forget John Cage. Moreover, has not King Lear already told us what can 'come of nothing'? And in denying its past, the Cage aesthetic inevitably denies any possible future. This is best summed up by Cage himself, in a lecture given at the Juilliard School of Music, in March 1952[1]:

(the blank spaces represent musical interludes)

from *Words for Prepared Discourse*

"I have nothing to say   and I am saying it   and that is poetry as I need it   contemporary music is changing.

But since everything's changing   we could simply decide to drink a glass of water   To have something to be a masterpiece you   have to have enough time to talk when you have nothing to say.

In other words   there is no split   between spirit and matter. And to realise this   we have only suddenly   to awake to the fact."

[1] Quoted in *Bulletin of the American Composers Alliance*, June 1952.

ANTITHESIS

ANTITHESIS

CHAPTER EIGHT

GENERAL FACTORS IN CONTEMPORARY MUSIC

THE wide spectrum of contemporary music, some of which we have examined, presents the listener with a formidable challenge. There are several ways of meeting it. Composers may be classified in categories—Nationalist; 12-note; neo-Romantic; post-Webern. Or they may be grouped country by country. Probably no two people would agree on the best approach, except that all attempts to categorize a composer are to some extent unsatisfactory. It helps not at all towards a true understanding of his music to be told that Mr. X is a serialist with neo-Romantic leanings, that he was born in Argentina, that he lives in Clapham Junction. Such classification is little more than a substitute for true critical appraisal; it fails to take into account the composer's aesthetic purpose, his personal intent and motivation. Environment certainly may affect a composer's work, though even this is questionable. Environment affects the way a work is received more than it affects the work itself. In any case it is, if not irrelevant, certainly of secondary importance to the artistic decisions a composer takes, the direction of his thoughts, the way in which he interprets those musical developments of today to which he is the heir.

A composer's interpretation of contemporary musical history, and the priorities he sets himself, are the basis for an assessment of his work. There are several basic forces which bear on him and Siren-like seek to influence his course and tempt his loyalty. Unless he asserts his will, they will engulf him in their swirling cross-currents, dashing him against the rocks of compromise on the one hand, or the subservience of a derivative style on the other.

The brief survey we have made suggests that there are, in the main, six such forces, or trends of artistic thought, that have chiefly characterised the work of composers of this century. These are the forces of nationalism, of historical research, of psychology, of experimentalism, of scientific or quasi-scientific investigation, and, last but by no means least, of conservatism. Each can be shown to have a positive and a negative side; each is strongly active and exerts a gravitational pull over the composers we have considered; each is of prime concern to the listener if that critical rethinking is to take place, which will bridge the gulf between the composer and his audience that has already been mentioned.[1]

(i) *Nationalism*

Nationalism is the strongest positive force in music. It always has been. Every composer whose work is international derives strength and inspiration from a national tradition. Apart from the specifically nationalist schools of the last century, such as the Bohemian or the Russian, it has been the chief motivating influence in many periods of musical history; for instance in Elizabethan England. As far as this century is concerned the strongest nationalist of all has been Schoenberg, whose avowed aim was to sustain the hegemony of German music; but in addition to him, the work of all the important contemporary composers—Stravinsky, Tippett, Copland, Boulez—has been coloured by their nationality.

The negative effect of nationalism is comparatively slight, though real. It has to do more with the reception of a composition by the listener than with the merit of that composition itself. The question of a composer's nationality may appear to the listener a limiting factor; it may cause a work to be judged by political rather than artistic standards. Jingoism, provincialism may creep in. For instance in Russia the Communist Party frown heavily on the use, by Soviet composers, of serialist or experimental techniques; not, in the first instance, for any musical or technical reasons, but because these developments derive from "Western, bourgeois, capitalist" countries. Conversely in England the trend is precisely the reverse, and the reasoning, as in the case of Soviet Russia, equally has nothing to do with music. It is, and always has been, the English habit to extend the warmest welcome to any composer or musician provided only that his

[1] See p. 6.

nationality is not English. As Sir Thomas Beecham once so shrewdly remarked, it is indeed odd that the English should prefer to listen to third-rate musicians from other countries, when they already have so many second-rate ones of their own.

(ii) *Historical research*

An awareness of musical history and a curiosity about past periods of music, are marked characteristics of the twentieth century. They are Alexandrian features which, very patently, have a positive and a negative side. The more the century advances, the more marked these features become. This is the age of the musicologist, and the fruits of his work have had great influence over composers. Some composers are themselves musicologists; Wellesz and Malipiero, for example. After all, if you are going to introduce changes, it is as well to know what it is you are changing from, and the direction of your change; also whether there is a precedent for your innovations. Many hopeful revolutionaries have raised the banner of fourteenth century *Ars Nova* or seventeenth century *Nuove Musiche*, as if to give themselves courage on their somewhat lonely march.

Inspiration from the past has been a contributory factor in the technique of most of the composers we have considered. Stravinsky, Webern, Tippett have all in their several ways been concerned with the mediaeval, renaissance and polyphonic periods. Schoenberg in particular, being concerned with harmony, traced the development of the diatonic system from the eighteenth century onwards. He wished to discover the true nature and the origin of the *impasse* in which he saw himself, and he looked to history to provide the answer.

The negative influence of the force of history on the contemporary composer is subtle and insidious. It has already been hinted at, in that the composer may hoodwink the listener by means of irrelevant considerations, and divert his attention from the music itself. "If you think that what I write is new", he seems to say, "you might care to know that it has all been done before." It is all too easy to dress up an innovation or an experiment in plausible historical clothes, to give it a respectable mediaeval pedigree, and to present it as being a present result, following on inevitably from a past cause. Unfortunately, as we all know, history is open to various interpretations. It all depends on your point of view. Schoenberg was criticised by those who did not share his feeling for harmony. Stravinsky, however, had a stronger instinctive feeling for rhythm, and in his turn received his share of criticism from those who were more concerned with harmony. Historical antecedence is not a true substitute for the intrinsic worth of a composition.

There is a further aspect of the negative force of history over the composer today. Contemporary music provides many examples of composers imitating the technical practices of earlier periods; for instance Maxwell Davies, Anthony Milner and several others, who have introduced the mediaeval devices of hocket and isorhythm, and made use of the technical procedures of mensural notation, and certain mediaeval forms, such as the carol. Moreover the setting of the words of mediaeval authors, complete with their unintelligible meaning and archaic spelling, is today a commonplace. It is a weakness inherent in an Alexandrian period, such as ours, that it tends to be imitative. And although archaism can, in certain circumstances, be an inspiration, it has in many cases led merely to sterility of invention—if indeed it is not a cover for it.

(iii) *Psychology*

As far as psychology is concerned, two considerations have particularly concerned the contemporary composer. First, the development of depth psychology, and the discoveries of Freud, Jung and others into the nature of the unconscious and the *psyche* generally; second, the impact from outside, and the psychological effect on each individual, of the tragic and violent catastrophes that have marked the history of the twentieth century—its ugliness, cruelty, torture and war. It is hard to see how composers could avoid in some way seeking to represent such violence in their work. If you do not, are you not being unrealistic, out of touch? It was often said, with reference to the great war of 1914–1918, that after it was over "things could never be the same again". This was certainly true politically; but for the composer it was true psychologically.

An awareness of the force of the unconscious has both

helped and hindered composers of this century. Some have sought directly to reflect in their art the psychological stresses and strains of the age. Occasionally, for instance in Berg's *Wozzeck* or Tippett's *King Priam*, a composer has by his artistry transformed the ugly into the beautiful.

But for the composer the negative result of the psychological factor is that it may lead him to confuse the actual with the imaginary, the objective with the subjective. The result, as frequently happens, is that he seeks to represent the ugly by means of ugliness. But the force that is peculiar to music, as Debussy so well shows us, is one of association; not of direct representation.

(iv) *Experimentalism*

There is something of the experimentalist in every important composer. It is part of his fibre; and the twentieth century has certainly been no exception. Experiments which have achieved positive, though not necessarily permanent, results have been numerous; that is to say experiments in which composers have attempted to vary or enlarge an existing idiom. We call to mind the comparatively harmless experiment by Sibelius of telescoping a symphony into one movement; or again the more radical experiments carried out by numerous composers, notably Alóis Haba and Harry Partch in the thirties, into the microtonal division of the scale.

More recently, Iannis Xenakis has experimented with a computer, introducing composition on "stochastic" principles —that is to say, based on probability theory.[1] *Pithoprakta* for instance is a study in texture and density for 46 solo strings, 2 trombones and percussion; an ordered confusion of effects.

The positive value and necessity of experiments is obvious; but so is their negative aspect. An experiment is just that; it is not a finished composition. Moreover, experimentalism may develop as a thing in itself and for its own sake. Contemporary

---

[1] From the Greek στοχαζομαι, meaning

    (a) to aim or shoot at.

    (b) to make a guess or conjecture.

Another computer-composer is Peter Zinovieff.

music can show many cases of this. There is a world of difference between an experiment which seeks to enlarge an existing idiom, and one which seeks to deny it. An experiment that is, in essence, a denial of an existing method or idiom will, almost by definition, lack the cultural soil in which to grow and become fruitful. The twentieth century shows us that if you wish your revolutionary new style to take root and become a lasting form, the very last thing you will do is to dissociate yourself from your predecessors. On the contrary, you will seek to establish direct links with them and stress the closeness of your connection.

Nihilistic experiments may well have a momentary interest; but no more. This is clearly shown in Dadaism. Though novelty might appear to be an artistic necessity, it is, taken by itself, an illusion. Nothing deadens the effect of a protest more than its repetition; what is fresh today is stale tomorrow. What is there that is more dated than yesterday's newspaper?

(v) *Scientific developments*

The inroads made by science into the realm of music have been considerable; and since 1945 the pace has quickened. The basis of electronic music lies not only in the means of electronic sound-generation, but also in the refinement of the tape-recorder as a reliable means of sound-reproduction. The positive value of this technological advance has been most noticeable, both directly and indirectly. Directly, it has made possible a new type of sound whose use is still a matter of experiment and speculation. For instance, it is gradually being assimilated for use as background music for radio and television. Indirectly, the value of this advance is that it is now apparent whither all the experimental thought and work of earlier years by composers in many countries was tending. In the early 1900's the question was asked: "What happens if the sound-source of music is freed from the trappings and limitations of instruments and notation?"; in the 1950's the answer was given: "Electronic music". No one can deny the importance or the positive nature of this event.

Its negative aspect has to do with the possible effect of the scientific method on the aesthetic approach of the composer, and on the aesthetic judgement of the listener. There is a danger that the separate and distinct functions of science and art will be confused; that the one will be mistaken for the other.

Science is a method of correlating facts; art is an association of ideas. The function of science is to analyse, to question, to deduce; that of art to synthesise, to communicate, to inspire. The primary purpose of science is to discover truth; the primary purpose of art is to discover and to reveal beauty. Whereas the work of the scientist comes to an end when once he has established on a basis of proven fact that new-born theory or image which was originally an unproven hypothesis, this is the very point from which the artist sets out. So the two processes, the scientific and the artistic, are not so much contradictory as complementary.

The danger inherent in the composer's calling on the assistance of the scientist is clear. Unless he is particularly watchful and self-critical he may confuse the result of a scientific process with a work of art; he may identify something that is scientifically true with something that is artistically beautiful. The creative compositional process may be short-circuited, and the scientific or electronic means of sound-generation may be mistaken for the artistic end to which his creativity is directed. It is not. Science and technology can provide the composer with new sources and species of sound; they can in no way prescribe the artistic use he makes of them, nor can they exempt him at all from that speculative volition which lies at the root of the creative process.

If the means of electronic sound-generation concerns only the scientist, the completion of a composition, when he takes an overall view of the work as a whole, concerns only the composer. This creative vision has nothing in common with the scientific method. This moment of recognition comes after the completion of every work, large or small, when the composer sees fully for the first time the uniqueness of his composition in its totality. It is the culmination of the creative process.

(vi) Conservatism

Conservatism is very prevalent among twentieth century composers. Not only are there many whose style and outlook are conservative, and to whom any adventure or experiment is plainly abhorrent, but also some comparatively conservative works appear occasionally in the output of otherwise more 'advanced' composers. On the whole the negative effect of conservatism outweighs the positive. Conservatism is not merely caution; it means retaining what already exists and a reluctance to attempt anything new. Since with each composition a composer enters a new world, it is difficult to see how conservatism can be reconciled with the qualities that make a work lasting and important.

Conservatism means retaining what already exists. A conservative composer will either retain, or repeat, a style he has developed, or repeat and copy someone else's style. In either case, the chief negative effect is the same, namely that it produces boredom. A composer can be just as boring when he attempts to conserve someone else's *avant-garde* style, as when he prefers to conserve one that is most pedantically academic. The conservative composer may well be easy to listen to, because he knows, and everybody else knows, that it has all been heard before. This may well earn him an immediate hearing; a Telemann is always much less demanding than a Bach; a Meyerbeer than a Berlioz; but sooner or later boredom will inevitably ensue. The compositional process is partly one of discovery; there are few things more pointless than discovering what has already been discovered.

The tendency towards conservatism in a century of change such as ours is easy to understand. A non-acceptance of, or a reaction against, the direction taken by more experimental composers may easily lead to a mistrust of innovations *per se*. But if the direction indicated by the innovations of one school appear to someone else to be artistically in error, the solution lies not in the rejection of all innovation, and a return to the *status quo ante*—that would indeed spell the end of music as a living art form—but in the pursuance of a different kind of innovation. The true creator is never afraid of innovation. He may well mistrust novelty; but imitative and derivative work, or self-repetition, which are the hall-mark of conservatism, are really the very reverse of creativity.

The lack of a "powerful academic art", to which Picasso refers,[1] and which today is just as true of music as of painting,

[1] See p. 48.

underlines the negative aspect of conservatism. In so far as 'academic' means a style that can be taught by rules, it is only possible for an academic style to be 'powerful' in a period when there is a common musical language, in general currency, which all can understand. It is impossible today, since this is not the case. It is true that certain styles and techniques can be taught—dodecaphony for example; but this is not a generally accepted idiom, if indeed it ever was one. In so far as 'academic' means conservative it is really a contradiction in terms to refer to a 'powerful conservative art'. Conservative art can never be powerful, since it sets out, by definition, to conserve; not to "synthesise, communicate and inspire"; and what you attempt to conserve depends on an interpretation of history; it is essentially retrospective, and selective.

Twentieth century composers have been affected by these six forces of influence in varying ways; but one thing applies in common: the work of those composers has proved of lasting value who have achieved an artistic independence from convention and formalised academicism. And though independence by itself does not necessarily make a composer's work noteworthy, a society that encourages independence of this sort will be more likely to foster a true tradition than one which does not.[2]

[2] See Appendix II.

CHAPTER NINE

DODECAPHONY AND SERIALISM

A CRITICAL challenge of the first magnitude is presented to
the listener by the dodecaphonic and serialist techniques. It is
a challenge which has not been met, with the result that
conclusions based on unproven hypotheses are accepted as
finalities, false arguments are allowed to pass by default.
Music can only first be apprehended by the listener as an
aural experience; and the challenge consists in the fact that
the sound of dodecaphonic and serial music is radically
different from that of music which uses the diatonic-chromatic
idiom. The implications of this are far-reaching.

It is logical to treat dodecaphony and serialism together
since the latter is an extension of the former; the serialists
carried forward the process begun by Schoenberg, continued
by Webern. Therefore any assessment must start with
Schoenberg.

If a composer's greatness is measured by the influence he
exerts over his contemporaries and successors, then assuredly
Schoenberg was one of the greatest who ever lived. Directly
or indirectly he has exerted an influence in every Western
country where the art of music is seriously practised; his
followers and converts include many German composers, as
you would expect; Blacher, Fortner, Henze; the Italians,
Dallapiccola and Nono; the Spaniard, Roberto Gerhard;
the Austrian, Ernst Krenek; the Greek, Nikos Skalkottas;
the Englishman, Humphrey Searle, the Hungarian, Matyas
Seiber; the Americans, Milton Babbitt and Ross Lee Finney;
the most spectacular conversion of all was that of Stravinsky;
there have been several lesser ones. So the serial technique
has exercised, and is exercising still, a potent and widespread
force; for this reason alone it is not to be dismissed out of
hand. Even if we wished to, it would be impossible for us to
revert to the world of Victorianism.

Dodecaphony has however been subjected to much wrong

criticism and misunderstanding. For instance, the fact that a large quantity of boring and derivative music has been written in the 12-note style is not necessarily a valid reason for dismissing the system in its entirety. Boredom has been known to occur at other periods and in other styles; if a composer is bent on writing boring music, he will do so, you may be sure, whatever the idiom he uses. It is also sometimes said that, because the style is so difficult to understand, and so patently lacking in anything resembling popular appeal, it can never become really established as something of permanent worth or even interest. But to the listener who protests his dislike of the style, Schoenberg would reply that what must be, must be; it is a question not of likes or dislikes, but of artistic and historical necessity.

But the essential criticism of dodecaphony is not of this sort. The nature and origin of the system were philosophical. That is to say, it arose from a logical speculation, by Schoenberg and others, into the whole process and structure of musical composition. Any assessment, therefore, to be valid, must be also on a logical or philosophical level. We need to ask whether the hypotheses on which he based his thoughts were true or false; and if they were true, whether he drew correct and valid conclusions from them.

The diatonic-chromatic system was not permanently and immutably fixed, and the belief that it would need to be changed and modified to suit the requirements of composers can be traced back well into the nineteenth century.[1] The 7-note diatonic scale, and the two modes, major and minor, which were established by 1722, were a limitation that was necessary at that period of musical history. By the beginning of the twentieth century, however, the musical situation was markedly different.

Up to this point all musicians are in agreement; the hypothesis is universally acceptable. But the next question concerns the form that the modifications are to take. By about the second decade of the twentieth century, two possible solutions were put forward. One was to modify the tonal divisions of the scale. Many musicians apart from Alóis Haba concerned themselves with microtones; the Swiss composer

[1] See Helmholtz *On the sensations of tone* (1877).

Hans Barth, for instance, and the Mexican Julian Carrillo. Theirs was the basically simple, pragmatic approach; namely that, if the division of the octave into 12 semitones is not enough, then the obvious solution is to make units of division smaller than the semitone, and to have more of them. At the end of this road, as we have seen lies electronic music.

The other solution, put forward by Schoenberg, was to retain the existing division of the octave into 12 semitones, but to reassess the relationship of the constituent notes to each other. Whereas the diatonic system had relegated 5 of the 12 notes to a subservient, chromatic status, Schoenberg gave all 12 notes exactly equal importance. The former tonal hierarchy of Tonic-Dominant-Subdominant gave place to a system of relating notes only to each other, according to interval, dynamics, instrumentation and so on.

Underlying Schoenberg's thought-process (as distinct from his composition-process) are two characteristically twentieth century ideas; one is that of Relativity, the other is that of Logical Philosophy.

Relativity is a basic principle of thought today; a fundamental questioning of the absolute, whether of physics, or of human behaviour,[1] or of such basic data as (in art) perspective, and (in music) tonality. Once admit the principle of Relativity, and it acts as a flood-tide, ever-rising, irresistible. Whereas previously composers worked from the necessity of a common musical currency, Schoenberg substituted the necessity of the individual composer's own choosing. Much more important than the conclusions to which Schoenberg's own particular choice led him, whether to 'atonalism' or to the 12-note technique, were the basic changes in perspective that he introduced to the musical art. Relativity is a self-perpetuating and continuous process; and the questioning that started with Schoenberg has continued and grown ever since. It has inevitably been directed against him by those who, following his example, and taking the advantage of his lead, pursue the goal of personal rather than collective artistic fulfilment. Just as serialism superseded Schoenberg's 12-note technique, so will it in turn be superseded; the principle which underlies the system is far stronger than the system itself.

[1] Russell *History of Western Philosophy*, p. 786.

Schoenberg is, in a word, the Prometheus of contemporary music, who driven by his own will, asserted the contemporary composer's right to decide his own means of expression, against the collective tradition and power of the established system. Let the composer, said Schoenberg, be his own arbiter. Many evidently agree; but how many have the wisdom and the insight that enabled him to make the choice originally? How many are as aware, as he was, of what the cost is of making a choice? The more you seek to extend the range of musical expression, the more insight you need to understand what you are achieving. A gain in one direction may well be a loss in another. For instance, the substitution of space-time for space and time means that each loses something of its former nature. Thus a gain in music's expressivity is only made at the price of something of its former power.

Composition, say the serialists, has to do with imposing order on the elements of music. This has a dual implication: first, that each individual composer must reach back *de novo* to the elements of music, the raw material, if he is to avoid the predetermined *cliché*; second, that the ordering of the material is entirely external; that the expressive force of a composition comes not from any tonally inherent quality in the notes themselves, but is decided purely by the composer's arrangement of them. Both these implications contain partly truth, partly falsehood. Their fallacy is primarily due to the Logical-Philosophical nature of the thought-process with which the serialists, starting with Schoenberg, have approached the *materia musica*.

Logical Philosophy

There is a remarkable identity of method between Schoenberg's 12-note technique, leading to later serialism, and the method of linguistic analysis adopted by the logical philosophers. Linguistic philosophy appeared first as Logical Atomism, put forward by Russell, Whitehead and others; later as Logical Positivism, put forward by the Vienna Circle, under the influence of Wittgenstein. The serialists' approach to the structure and function of music was parallel to the philosophers' approach to the structure and function of language. Both represent a radical re-examination of the technical means of expression; both have affinities with mathematics; both occur at about the same time; both are centred round Vienna. It is no real surprise to learn that Wittgenstein himself was highly musical; that his brother Paul was the left-handed pianist for whom Strauss, Ravel and Benjamin Britten wrote works; that his parents' house in Vienna was the scene of many musical gatherings; that Brahms had been a close family friend; and that apart from philosophy, his interests extended to architecture, sculpture and engineering. Schoenberg's concern with philosophy has already been mentioned.

Logical Philosophy derived its impetus from Russell's *Principia Mathematica* (1903) and Wittgenstein's *Tractatus Logico-Philosophicus* (1921). Russell had been led by his success in mathematical logic to put forward Logical Atomism as the form of the one perfect language. The function of philosophy was accepted as being linguistic analysis; the world itself, the total sum of atomic facts, can be perfectly represented by an ideal language. Atomic statements correspond to atomic facts. Wittgenstein saw them as pictures of reality. Statements are either single atomic propositions, or truth-functions of such propositions. Non-atomic, or molecular propositions are simply a group of atomic propositions. Language is an indefinitely large collection of such atomic facts.

Variables (p, q, r, etc.) are used in the place of statements, and these variables can be placed in any logical relationship; e.g. p *and* q; p *or* q; *if* p *then* q; *not*-p and *not*-q;

$$not\text{-}p \; without \; q; \quad \text{and so on.}$$

Russell conceived language like a calculus. Truth-functional logic was a mathematical concept. Wittgenstein was aware of certain weaknesses in Logical Atomism, and under the influence of his *Tractatus* the Vienna Circle developed Logical Positivism as a justification of reductive analysis. The function of philosophy was the logical clarification of thought, the avoidance of linguistic abuse. The results of philosophy were therefore not so much a set of propositions as the clear presentation of propositions, free from metaphysical or general weaknesses. We note that later (1929) Wittgenstein came to reject reductive analysis as the way to reveal the structure of the world.

Our concern is the similarity between this method and the method of serial or 12-note technique. Both were logical systems; both employed means which were abstracted and derived from the traditional language; both declined to continue the treatment of traditional problems with the traditional means of their respective disciplines, but instead tried to find a new way round the apparent intractability of those problems. In both cases the radical novelty of their respective approaches has been subsequently called in question.

The interval-relationship between the notes of Schoenberg's row is exactly defined and rationally based, and is analogous to the truth-functional relationship between the variables of Logical Atomism. Schoenberg stripped the notes of his series of all prior associations, and gave them instead a preselected order, in just the same way as the philosophers stripped everyday words of their traditional, associative meaning, and substituted a logically-based symbolism.

The aim of Schoenberg was to relate every note to the final structure of a composition, according to its original position in the series; the aim of the philosophers was to make every atomic statement an adequate picture of the reality it referred to. Schoenberg had observed the properties of the diatonic system, the construction of phrases and periods, the harmonic-structural relationship of sections of a composition. His aim was that the 12-note technique should equally be capable of such overall construction, but without any of the associations with the older method. Similarly the Logical Atomists sought to reproduce the perfect *rationale* of language, without any of the non-logical associations of words.

* * *

The nature of the 12-note technique, and later serialism, can be further seen by setting them against the diatonic system, and comparing the two. It is sometimes said, somewhat loosely, and usually by way of apology, that the 12-note system arose *via* atonalism, out of the "break-up" of the "old" diatonic system, in much the same way as the diatonic system itself arose out of the "break-up" of the "old" polyphonic technique. The comparison is inaccurate. 'Atonalism' had been the result of a free empirical approach; serialism was the logical formulation of it, which would enable the composer to construct large forms, such as had been possible previously by means of tonality. It is incorrect to refer to the "break-up" of the old polyphony, as polyphony is still a very active force. Tonal harmony was inherent in the contrapuntal style; it only required formulation for it to proceed

Ex. 55

and develop in its own right. A remarkable instance is shown in Ex. 55 of a polyphonic composition of the sixteenth century whose harmonic groundwork is so pronounced that the identical sequence (of rising fourths) can be used by Beethoven 250 years later. After the formulation of tonal harmony in 1722, it took only 50 years for the first Viennese school, of Haydn and Mozart, to appear. The formulation of the diatonic system was simply the acknowledgement of something which already existed. It was in no sense of the word a revolutionary change of direction. The new harmony was a crystallisation of the old counterpoint, and arose from it, logically and inevitably.

The 12-note and serialist techniques differ from this in every particular. They are based on the hypothesis that the diatonic system has ceased to be structurally valid. Serialism can in no way be said to rise out of tonal composition; on the contrary, it is the negation of it; if it "rises out of" anything, it is the "old" polyphony. Since the formulation of the 12-note technique by 1920, it has by no means found that universal acceptance by musicians that the diatonic system did 200 years earlier. Where it has been accepted, it has been as the starting-point for further experiment. But then all rules for art, like all commandments for living, are only a starting-point; they are made to be broken, and they are certainly not an end in themselves. Now that it is almost 50 years since Schoenberg put forward his system, it is possible to assess its nature in the light of events. There appear to be six basic weaknesses in it.

The first weakness in serialism is that it does not take fully into account the nature of the material of which most music is made; that is to say, notes. As long as you use notes of definite pitch, you must take account of both their physical properties, and the characteristics of the human ear. The two are connected. The harmonic series of a note is a logarithmic progression of intervals; moreover, as Ansermet points out,[1] the ear of the listener relates notes logarithmically. A note is a complex, not a single sound; louder or quieter, both the fundamental and its overtones sound proportionately louder or quieter. The ear registers them all. If the harmony of the chords of a passage moves in parallel to the overtones of the notes that make them up, the listener's ear will register the concordance; if the harmony moves counter to the overtones, the listener's ear will register the discordance. In either case the ear, by a process of unconscious association, registers not merely the pitch of notes but their tonally inherent properties. In other words, notes imply tonality. A composer may realise this implication; he may deliberately play on it, even

---

[1] In *Les fondements de la musique.*

frustrate it; but to deny its existence, to seek to eliminate it from the process of composition altogether, is to deny both the nature of musical sound, and the ability of the ear to associate and combine sounds.

Curiously enough, the recent marked tendency towards the use and development of percussion instruments, particularly those of indefinite pitch, strongly suggests an instinctive desire on the part of serial composers to break loose from note-sounding instruments into a world of sound free from all associations of tonality. But this can only come about if no sound is allowed with definite pitch. It is true that later serialists have carried the process far further then Schoenberg, who never lost sight of the pitch of notes, visualised; yet already in his music can be detected that latent contradiction, which was to emerge fully later; namely that notes, as long as they sound at a definite pitch, are related straight away to the ear and mind of the listener, by association, by memory; they, therefore, cannot be used by the composer as if they were "related only to each other", without this resulting in an impediment to understanding.

Next, there is a certain monotony of sound, a sameness about both dodecaphonic and serial music. Even the technique of endless variation itself becomes monotonous. The emotional range is thus limited. The grimness, the intensity of style are plain for all to hear. Where is the corresponding gaiety or lightness to match this? A dodecaphonic rondo or waltz or a serial scherzo is an almost impossible conception, in spite of Schoenberg's attempts in this direction; and when Stockhausen tells the audience to laugh during his *Momente*, the listener's sense of humour is indeed stretched to breaking-point. Is he to laugh at it, or with it? The joke, to be sure, is no ordinary one.

But the monotony of mood and sound is not really a coincidence. Tippett has shrewdly put his finger on the central issue,[1] which was the overriding importance paid by Schoenberg to harmony. The 12-note technique was primarily intended to replace the tonal harmonic system; its effect therefore, as you would expect, was most noticeable not just in its avoidance of all suggestions of a tonic, and of a key,

[1] In *Composer*, April 1965.

but in the absence of those very features which were the chief characteristics of diatonic-chromatic composition—cadences, sequences, Sonata form and so on. Schoenberg, and his successors, sought "the formal possibilities of an absolute music . . . freed from all admixture of extra-musical elements."[1] All trace of the old harmony had to be eliminated; the new chromaticism made no distinction equivalent, for example, to that between the major and minor modes. We note also that the rhythm of counterpoint is something totally foreign to Schoenberg, indeed to German music as a whole, although the 12-note technique is contrapuntal in essence.

The potentially excessive intellectualism of the serial style contains dangers; this would apply in any art, not just music. There has been intellectualism before—in the mediaeval period, for instance; and plainly Bach's music contains a very strong cerebral content. Yet common sense alone calls for a balance to be struck.

The danger of intellectualism in music is twofold. First it causes the listener to be involved only as it were externally. In tonal music, particularly in its formal manifestation of Sonata form, there was entire consistency between the nature of the instruments used, the direction of the harmony, and the temporal unfolding of the music in time; as a result the listener was able to involve himself and identify himself with the musical process without any aural reservations; his intellect agreed with what his ear heard. But with serial music this is not the case. There is no such internal consistency in the music; and therefore no correspondingly direct involvement by the listener; his intellect and his ear are at variance.

The second danger is that the composer may become enslaved to an ideal which will gradually overwhelm him. Intellectualism is not so much a false idol as an incomplete one. Was Bach a great composer because he wrote fugues?

Serialism lacks that warmth which would compensate for its intellectualism; for it stresses the intellectual at the expense of the instinctive. The attempt by some composers to compensate for this process of total intellectual control, by introducing the random, aleatoric element, suggests that the necessity for some such balance is felt.

---

[1] See *Perspectives of new music*, Spring–Summer, 1965.

Next, the claim of historical continuity made by dodeca-phonists is misleading and is based on a false hypothesis. This hinges on whether the diatonic system has "broken up". If it has, then plainly there can be no continuity, and serialism would represent a fresh start; if it has not, then one of the main justifications of serialism vanishes. This question of historical continuity in no way affects the reality of serialism, but only its assessment by the listener. Was it a break from the past, or a continuation of the past? Has the diatonic system "broken up" or not?

Apologists for serialism refer to the "old" diatonic system as though its demise were a matter of undisputed fact. But to assume that something has happened, and to assert that it has, does not necessarily bring it about. 'Atonalism' was a phase which passed. And a glance at the programmes of our concert halls and opera houses is alone enough to provide strong evidence that the idiom of the classical and romantic composers has lost none of its effectiveness for the listener today. Is the contemporary composer right to assume that the diatonic system is dead? For one thing is clear: If he does assume this, he will be breaking with the past, not continuing it. Is it reasonable for the listener, in his turn, to suspend artistic judgement, and to allow that the system is dead for some, not for others? How can this be?

No system can be permanent; the history of art would indeed be dull if this were the case. But notes have a tonality inherent in their physical nature. If a composer totally denies this, he cannot avoid setting up a certain aural antipathy in the listener, which no amount of intellectual explanation can conceal. It is no function of an artist to step down from the platform and act as his own advocate. If the music itself cannot move an audience, then words cannot either.

The greatest misunderstanding has come about through the somewhat loose use of the phrase 'the language of music'. The specious argument put forward by some apologists would suggest that the "language" of serialism merely has to be learnt by the listener, like any other foreign language, for him to be able to understand its "meaning". This proposition contains a dangerous fallacy.

The function of language lies in its conveyance of meaning; that of music in its association. The two are quite distinct.

Language seeks to convey meaning by means of words. Any language is quite patently a limitation, since it does not make use of all the possible formations of the tongue, the teeth and the mouth. If I limit myself to speaking English to an Englishman or French to a Frenchman, it is simply so that, by doing so, I may convey my meaning to him as exactly and fully as possible. Limitation is thus my chief source of strength.

Music exists by association in the listener's aural and intellectual experience. If a composer limits himself to the diatonic scale, or any other scale, and does not make use of other possible sounds, he does so in order to increase the expressive power of his music, and its association in the mind of the listener. His acceptance of a limitation is also a source of strength.

But the analogy between music and spoken language ceases at this point, since notes and words differ in essence, in nature and in function. Notes are complex, their function is associative. The words of poetry are similar in this respect; but the majority of words are single, their function is to convey an exact meaning. It was precisely the treatment of notes in a quasi-logical way, as we have seen, which proved to be a great source of weakness in the dodecaphonic, and later serial, style. The associative nature of notes is not subject to the logical and literal relationship that, generally speaking, governs the meaning of words.

Finally, there is a weakness, or at least an ambiguity of artistic purpose, in later serialism in its treatment of the factor of time. This is not found so much in Schoenberg or Webern. No art, not even poetry, makes such use as music does of the element of time. It is a challenge which has fascinated not only Stravinsky, as we have seen, but every composer of this century, because of its contradictory and paradoxical elements: rhythm and metre; tempo and movement; duration and speed. Time is one of the subtlest of the factors of composition. It plays on the listener's ear in a non-material sense, that is to say through his memory; it is a powerful form-giving dimension in music; it implies movement, direction, purpose.

But serialism treats time like other material elements of music—pitch or dynamics, for example—and in so doing not only misunderstands its nature, or at least treats its nature in a different way from a purely temporal, chronological sequence, but deprives music of one of its main sources of dynamic movement. Time is put on a par with space; duration is serialised. The effect of this is that serial music is a momentary, not a temporal thing; it is static, and lacks the direction that time gives. Nothing that is still can have direction.

CHAPTER TEN

CRITICISM

THE general absence of creative criticism of contemporary music has already been mentioned.[1] It is one of the factors in the rift between the composer and his audience. Yet if the critic is to have a positive function, and if criticism is to be more than journalistic comments or a catalogue of composer's works, it is as a reasoned advocacy of new work that it is of most direct value to the listener. As we have already seen, no apology on the part of the composer can make up for the failure of a piece of music in performance; if his trick did not work, the last thing the conjurer should do is attempt to explain the reason for this to his audience. It is a fact of a composer's life that posthumous explanation, or discussion after the event, are entirely superfluous. And yet before the event the listener may well benefit considerably from a reasoned advocacy by an informed musician. How much better equipped he will be to listen to the music and assess it.

Then again, it is one thing to consider a single new work; it is another to consider the life-work, output and aspirations of a composer. For this a wider and deeper insight into his background and method is needed.

If we wish to obtain a fuller understanding of a composer's intention than his music by itself can give us, the surest way to do this is to let the composer himself give it to us. Even a writer who has studied a composer's work closely and identified himself with it, will not be able to describe at first hand the aspirations, problems, technical setbacks, that have conditioned that composer's work.

Take Schoenberg; a figure of central importance, whatever your viewpoint. Before assessing adequately the 12-note system, it is necessary to discover Schoenberg's creative intention, in the light of his particular situation; it means finding out how Schoenberg himself arrived at, and viewed his new technique. Was it as the inevitable evolution of

[1] p. 4.

atonalism? Was it from the standpoint of experiment, of a deliberate reversal of traditional harmony; or was it from the standpoint of mathematical and logical philosophy? It makes all the difference to our assessment. If the latter was the case, if the basis of the system is not just harmonic/musical but logical/philosophical, we must next ask on what hypothesis it rests; then whether that hypothesis is true. If true, does it necessarily follow that Schoenberg's conclusion is right? If false, could Schoenberg's system still remain valid?

Of those who have dealt with the 12-note system, none could be more painstakingly dedicated than Josef Rufer, one of Schoenberg's pupils. His description of Schoenberg's technique is indispensable for anyone who wishes to study it. Yet he tells us simply what Schoenberg did; not what he set out to do. With the advantages, and disadvantages, of hindsight, Rufer accepts dodecaphony as a *fait accompli*, and describes at exhaustive length how it came about. The all-important question of whether or not the basis on which it rests is valid is never raised.

This fundamental critical challenge has not been fully met. Does this matter? If Rufer accepted dodecaphony as an established fact, so also have countless composers and theoreticians the world over. One may well ask whether it is at all important to find out the basis on which it rests, and why there should be a need for creative criticism to discover the necessity for something which in any case has already been accepted. Is this not like shutting the stable door after the horse has bolted?

However plausible such a line of thought may sound, a closer inspection of the work of serial composers shows that the "acceptance" of Schoenberg's 12-note style is by no means as consistent, unanimous or whole-hearted as might appear at first sight. It has been variously used by different composers. Many have taken this or that aspect of it, and used it each for his own ends. But the single most pronounced characteristic of the development of Schoenberg's technique has been the absence of creative criticism of it; its use by some has been unquestioning, while its rejection by others has been illogical.

In spite of the absence of such enquiry into Schoenberg's intentions, writers have expressed every shade of opinion about Schoenberg's music. Never was there a composer who has given rise to more opinionated criticism, which really only succeeds in telling us more about the person making the criticism than about Schoenberg himself. An opinion is an amalgam of countless prejudices, limitations, experiences, and psychological factors. What matters in criticism is not the writer's opinion so much as his understanding of the composer's aesthetic purpose. The first is self-assertive, and implies that the writer knows the answers; the second is self-negation, and implies that there are still questions to be asked. The first interposes the writer between the composer and the listener; the second invites the listener to form his own judgement.

If then we do not wish a critic to give his opinion, what do we look for from him? A logical conclusion; or, even more important, the logical process which will invite the listener to form his own logical conclusion. By what means will this be achieved? Aesthetic humility, intellectual acuteness, verbal accuracy. It is not the function of the critic to teach a composer how to compose; and it is the very reverse of humility for a critic to reject a work because the composer's aesthetic purpose did not square with what the critic thinks it should have been. Without intellectual acuteness the critic will be unable to understand fully the composer's intention; and without a full understanding of the problems facing a composer, it is impossible to assess the worth of his solution of them. Without verbal accuracy no criticism can be effective; words can mean different things to different people, and, unless they are exactly defined they can mislead.

Let us consider the following example of a criticism of the first performance of a contemporary composition:

"The most satisfying music in the concert was that which came midway between the extremes—Alfred Nieman's Rilke song-cycle for soprano and string quartet. This work's romanticism is basically Schoenbergian, seeking an 'expressionist' equation between literary and musical image and rhythm. Less Teutonically dense than the master, however, Nieman's music could spontaneously effect a transition to a melismatically lyrical manner suggestive of Boulez, and in this its most modern vein could achieve its most moving, if not most personal, utterance. At a first hearing, the work seemed to me slightly longer than was necessary; but I've no doubts about its musicality and humane sensitivity; we should hear more of Nieman's music."

(New Statesman, 26th November, 1965)

This is an extract from a 700-word review of a concert of contemporary music; therefore, the argument sometimes put forward by journalists of lack of space hardly applies in this case. Moreover it appeared in a weekly magazine, which would suggest that the writer had more time for his article than a journalist writing for a daily paper. We may assume that what he writes are his considered views, expressed at some length, and after a certain deliberation.

The general trend of the passage is favourable to the composer. The critic is suggesting reasons why "we should hear more of Nieman's music". Are these reasons convincing? To what extent are we given an insight into the composer's aspirations?

1 The paragraph opens with a value-judgement, given the guise of fact. *"The most satisfying music was . . ."* Therefore what follows is on the level of personal opinion only. A much stronger case would have been made if the writer had allowed the facts to speak for themselves, and left the judgement to the reader. To give an opinion first, and then proceed to justify it, is a reversal of the logical process.

2 *"Basically Schoenbergian"* is a phrase suggestive of innumerable meanings. Does it mean that Nieman is superficially unlike Schoenberg (whatever that means)? Or does it mean that Nieman's technique is a modified form of Schoenberg's? Or that Nieman's music and Schoenberg's music share a common denominator, namely the late Romantic tradition? If so, why not say so? But what precisely is meant by '*Schoenbergian Romanticism*'?

3 ". . . *an 'expressionist' equation . . .*"
The word *equation* suggests the mathematical formula $A = B$, or $A + B = C$, and the use of this term in an artistic context automatically creates ambiguity of meaning. We are not told what the equation is, or what equals what.

Is it one, or more than one, of the following?

   a Lit.(image + rhythm) + Mus.(image + rhythm)
$$= \text{Expression}$$

   b Lit. image + Lit. rhythm = Mus. image + Mus.
$$\text{rhythm}$$

   c Lit. image = Mus. image

   d Lit. rhythm = Mus. rhythm

   e Expr.(Lit.(image + rhythm) + Mus.(image +
$$\text{rhythm})) = \text{Composition}$$

4 Why is the word 'expressionist' in inverted commas? Is the writer coining a new phrase, the corollary of *impressionist*? Does he refer to the German Expressionism that we associate with Georg Kaiser, and other playwrights? All music, without exception, is expressive of something; even Stravinsky at his most dead-pan. The use of inverted commas in this context, like the use of the word 'perhaps' in other contexts, introduces an element of doubt, of self-excuse, of word-searching, which is invariably fatal to the effect of an argument. Either the composition succeeds in being expressive, or it does not. If it does, then there is no need for inverted commas; if it does not, then the word *expressionist* should not be used at all.

5 What is peculiarly Schoenbergian about the fusion of a literary with a musical idea? The influence of literature lies at the very centre of the entire Romantic movement— Schumann, Berlioz, and countless others. What are Schubert's songs if not a marriage of musical and literary inspiration? One might say the same of the Chorale Preludes of J. S. Bach; or, to stretch a point, (but only slightly), of Gregorian chant. It would have been just as correct, and just as profitless, to describe Nieman's songs as 'basically Schubertian', 'Bachian', 'Gregorian'—or indeed almost anything else, from the dawn of the musical art.

6 The phrase '*melismatically lyrical*', if not a tautology, suggests that the preceding section was syllabic—one note for each syllable. If this is the case, it should be said.

7 '*It's most modern vein*' Does this mean that the composition contained veins that were not 'modern'? Or not quite so 'modern'? This is a classic example of a relative term which can mean, more or less, whatever you wish it to mean.

9

By some it can be taken as a term of commendation; by others as an effective term of abuse. A writer needs to make it clear which meaning is intended by him, or else (which is advisable) to avoid the word altogether.

8 The sentence beginning 'less Teutonically dense . . .' is capable of many interpretations. Was Nieman's music suggestive of Boulez because it was in its "most modern vein," or because it was lyrical, or because it was impersonal; or all three? Why should it be impersonal to suggest Boulez, or *vice versa*? Do we or don't we look for a composer's "personal utterance"? If we do, and Nieman's work did not have it, that would appear to go against the argument of the rest of the paragraph; if we do not, then why the need to mention Boulez? It is not clear whether this "melismatically lyrical manner" is moving because it suggests Boulez, and in spite of its impersonality; or because of the spontaneous transition (whatever that means) with which it is introduced; or because it is 'most modern'.

Journalistic criticism is bedevilled by the necessity felt by most writers to give priority to their own opinion. This may well make for good journalism, but its value as criticism is ephemeral. Occasionally opinion becomes so entwined with fact, like bindweed round a flower, that both lose their character and effect. Hermeneutic criticism can only be on the basis of fact, and a writer will not carry his reader along with him unless he first shares with him the facts on which his opinion, we presume, is based. In reality, a writer's opinion is less important than his reportage of facts; which means, in the case of a new work, a description of it.

It is inevitable that opinionated criticisms about the same work, or performance, should be inconsistent; and it is not difficult to point to diametrically opposing views. Some years ago the manager of London's Festival Hall included some examples of mutually contradictory criticisms with the advance notices of concerts for the coming month, under the title *Point and Counterpoint*. It was a diversion, though the criticisms had to do mainly with performances of the established classical and romantic works, which make up the bulk of the London concert season. And so contemporary music rarely appeared.

Critics frequently ignore concerts which contain new or unfamiliar works, with the result that many an important performance takes place quite unnoticed by those who could exercise a most positive influence for good by means of the written word. Clearly, the argument goes, since criticism involves an opinion, it might be rash to commit oneself one way or the other to a new composition; better leave it alone; if it is 'good' it will turn up again somewhere else; if it is not, there is nothing lost.

But occasionally criticism is inescapably confronted with a contemporary work; the writer is clearly ill at ease; he wanders like 'a dream astray at noontime'; in such circumstances he makes his excuses as soon as he decently can, that is to say, as soon as he has given his opinion.

On 24th August, 1966 a performance took place in London of Elliott Carter's *Orchestral Variations*. The next day the event was recorded in two daily papers in the following way:

"German-born American conductor Frederick Prausnitz controlled the New Philharmonia's performance well, as he did in the work of another American composer, Elliott Carter's *Variations for Orchestra*.

The Carter struck (me?) as uninteresting. Its theme was not sharply enough characterised in order to relate it to the variations at one hearing, nor was there sufficient contrast between the variations themselves to hold the attention."

(*Daily Mail*)

"Excellent playing, too, in Elliott Carter's ambitious and closely argued *Variations for Orchestra*, written in 1954–55 when the composer was in his late forties."

(*Guardian*)

Was the work long or short, conservative or serial, conventional or experimental, variations of theme, mood, colour or texture? We cannot tell, unless we already know the work. All we know is that one listener found it "uninteresting", another found it "ambitious"; a third would have found it something else.

With a composer whose stature is not yet established, more directly opposed opinions occur. On 2nd November, 1966 a performance took place of a Welsh composer Alun Hoddinott's *Variants* for orchestra. Two comments were:

"Of the six short movements which comprise Hoddinott's new piece, the last two are labelled Passacaglia and Fugue, and conform recognisably to their traditional models. The comparisons which are thus evoked make the path of such a 'traditionalist' composer harder than that of the self-proclaimed vanguard, in whose work one novelty is readily trumped by another. The 'Variants' disappoints precisely because the traditional challenge, boldly proclaimed, is not fully met. The final movement carries no real finality. Perhaps fatally, the loudest guns are brought into action too early, in the first movement of all. Intermittently, however, one can admire the deployment of themes and instruments, and the unexpected ending of the second movement is quick and incisive."

(*Guardian*, 3rd November, 1966)

"Suddenly Hoddinott is writing tough, purposeful music, original in form and vividly coloured. The six-movement *Variants* make a fascinating virtue of their novel design (three germinating movements, each with a pendant which develops the same material in contrasting fashion), and make up a work about which one can be wholeheartedly enthusiastic without either condescension or special pleading."

(*Observer*, 6th November, 1966)

With a more established contemporary work, the critic can afford to be somewhat less inhibited; he may well consider the performance as well as, or instead of, the composition itself. But even on matters of fact there can be a surprising lack of unanimity. A performance in London of Stravinsky's *Symphony of Psalms* gave rise to the following comments:

"If there was one single thing that confirmed the veracity of Bertini's interpretation of the *Symphony of Psalms*—in the face of a chorus that was much too large and lacking the boy's voices which are part of the work's sound world— it was the preparation of, and the arrival at, the concluding chant. The tempo, so often and fatally misjudged, was impeccable (beyond the claims of a metronome), and felt-through in all its implications for the phrasing of the supernal accompaniment."

(*New Statesman*, 19th August, 1966)

". . . but in Stravinsky's *Symphony of Psalms* it was clear that Mr. Bertini had not taken full account of the echo when he chose his fast allegro for the first movement. On the other hand in the slow "Alleluia" coda of the finale he went to the opposite extreme. Only out of exaggerated deference to the echo could one explain the absurdly slow speed (exactly a third slower than the metronome marking in the score) which practically brought the music to a halt long before the end. A dramatic performance up till then with the Chorus very well rehearsed—better rehearsed perhaps than the orchestra."

(*Guardian*, 10th August, 1966)

For an opinion the listener need consult no one but himself; indeed a direct link of this sort is what the composer wishes. But for information about a work on which such an opinion will be based, an advocate with technical and specialised knowledge is clearly valuable. It is unfortunate however that intellectually conceived music can sometimes give rise to abstruse verbiage; or to put it more plainly, nonsense. There exists a quasi-technical, critical jargon; a newly-fashionable currency of words of ambiguous and questionable derivation, and non-existent meaning. Their sound, and their effect on the reader, is such that one feels they ought to mean something important, if only one knew what. New musical techniques, it appears, need new words to describe them; never mind if no one understands precisely what they signify. Even composers themselves are not always able to express musical concepts, particularly someone else's musical concepts, in terms of words. Let us consider the following attempt at verbal description of Stravinsky's *Movements*:

"This compositional variety is mediated by a highly redundant set structure a second-order all-combinatorial set, each set form is hexachordally equivalent to or totally disjunct from fifteen other set forms, so that one-third of all the available set forms belong to a collection of sets which are hexachordally aggregate forming, that is, hexachordally identical."

Perspectives of new music (Spring–Summer 1964)

If one can believe that, one can indeed believe anything. The important point for the listener is not so much that the writer does not know what he is talking about. In this case the author was the distinguished American composer Milton Babbitt, and we must give him the benefit of the doubt. But he has failed to communicate Stravinsky's purpose by means of words. This is useless writing, not because it is involved and complicated, but because it is meaningless. Words in such a context are precise or they are nothing. The listener in this case would do better to short-circuit the advocacy of Mr. Babbitt, and approach the music direct.[1]

[1] Another similar passage, also written by Mr. Babbitt, is mentioned in *Composer*, Spring 1964, p. 23.

SYNTHESIS

CHAPTER ELEVEN

A CONTEMPORARY AESTHETIC

AN accurate picture of contemporary music cannot be obtained from generalisations, since no individual composers of importance fit snugly and compactly into definitive compartments. To say that this is a century of transition and change is neither helpful nor startling; many previous periods can be so described. Again, to say that this age favours material rather than spiritual values may be partly true, but it takes no account of the many composers who swim against the general tide, and do not drift with it. However, in a sense, it is only from spiritual values that music derives purpose and durability.

Again, attempts to specify and to isolate the work of a particular composer are equally unsatisfactory as a means of obtaining an overall view, because this gives an incomplete account of the pattern of contemporary music.

The *materia musica* as it exists is the stuff of the composer's trade. But contemporary scholarship and musicology have made known to him more traditions and cultures than ever before, with the result that his area of choice is immeasurably widened. Several traditions today, and also several sections within the same tradition, are mutually exclusive; therefore, if a composer opts for one, he will exclude others. What he cannot avoid, however, is a choice; that "speculative volition" of which Stravinsky speaks lies at the very centre of the process of composition. It is no business of the composer to be equally and impartially concerned with every manifestation of music today, and with every tradition, however remote and exotic, from the past. That is the function of the scholar. The composer begins by choosing. This necessarily involves rejecting also. The choice is inescapable; it cannot be delegated and it needs to be made afresh with each new work.

Many contemporary composers modify their idiom according to the nature of the work, and the sort of audience they anticipate. One who, in the concert hall, plays the part of a committed and ardent dodecaphonist may write tonally and non-intellectually when composing a film-score. But such a distinction between serious and light, concert audience and mass audience, live music and background music, betrays a fundamental dichotomy and insecurity of creative purpose. If his idiom really lacks that breadth of appeal and that catholicity which will make it adaptable and appropriate for whatever occasion and for whatever audience, it lacks an essential ingredient which will give it permanent artistic value.[1] No composer of note can afford to be all things to all men, a sort of wandering minstrel whose wish is to suit the requirements of the momentary patron.

A composer's art is an individual creative synthesis of those factors, which bear on his sensitivity and compel him to set out his ideas. Many aspects of music—harmony, phrase construction, form—which in previous ages were instinctive or subconscious, are today openly questioned and disputed. The search instituted by Schoenberg is never-ending, since, where such a thing as harmony is concerned, there can be no finality. The associative power of chordal progressions, particularly when divorced from diatomicism is a mystery which can never be fully explained.

Harmony might appear to be the most accessible, if not the most fundamental of musical elements. It represents the immediate point of contact between composer and listener, which partly explains why it has been singled out by innumerable theorists as a study in itself. The essential clue to Mozart, Beethoven, Wagner, they seem to say, lies in their harmony. Nothing could be more dangerously naïve. Such a way of thinking leads on, logically and inevitably, to the false conclusion that what is chiefly characteristic of contemporary music—or "wrong" with it, depending on your point of view—is its absence of harmony.

But harmony is a secondary, not a basic, element in music. That is to say, it is produced by the interaction of other elements, like perspective in painting. Harmony results from the simultaneous horizontal movement of independent parts, of which chords are the most easily understood manifestation. But the creative process has to do with the primary, not so much with the secondary, elements. Indeed, we might almost say that the secondary elements, of which harmony is the

[1] cf. p. 140, (h),

chief example, are the concern more of the listener than of the composer; and inventing new effects, particularly effects of harmony, is not the same as the creative process, which works with the primary elements and is more concerned with root causes. The creative artist must also be inventive but the inventive one is not necessarily creative. How many inventors of today seek, by taking this or that aspect of the work of Stravinsky, Webern or Boulez, to achieve the status of original creators? When Webern said that music was discovered, not invented, he was speaking for every true composer. The truly original composer is simply the first one to discover an artistic experience, which he makes available for those who come after him to rediscover. But the means which led him to his discovery, which I have called his concern with the primary elements of music, is something which he cannot explain, even if he would. All we can do is point to this or that symptom; aural sensitivity, sense of history, and so on; we cannot analyse the cause.

Moreover, if our response to art, like that of a child to a toy, is a wish to dismember it to find out how it works, we may well find, also like the child, that it is not easy to re-assemble the broken parts. Unfortunately, ours is an age of mistrust, cynicism and disillusion; we do not accept without explanation, and we withhold artistic credit from someone whose work we do not understand. It is a characteristic of our age to take to pieces, to analyse. Yet what is remarkable is not that so much contemporary music is not understood, but that the listener should feel the necessity to understand it. No art exists primarily to be understood; it exists to be admired: to be a source of beauty, not of knowledge. The intellectual process of composition is the concern of the composer, and becomes a thing of the past the moment the composition is finished.

Aesthetic judgement is therefore not to be sought, in the first instance, by analysis. Rather is it to be developed stage by stage, like a composition; first the preparation, then the construction, then the consideration of the finished art-work.

(i) *Preparation*

One of the strongest factors which bears on a composer is tradition. Tradition, as Mr. Goldbeck has observed,[1] is the

---

[1] *Twentieth century music: A symposium* (p. 21).

very substance of music. Music is heard in a context which reaches far beyond the confines of its own duration, or its own physical sounds. A composition is heard with reference to other works of the same kind which have preceded it. Even some terms and concepts, such as Symphony, Chorale, Opera, evoke ideas and associations in the listener, and form a point of comparison, which the composer cannot avoid. Every composer knows this; it is a fact which he ignores at his peril.

A tradition can only start by being geographically localised; later, if it lives, its influence spreads, and even becomes international. After a beginning at one point in time it gradually draws greater vitality from its historical growth. What was originally the technique of one composer, or one group, is taken over and adapted as an aesthetic tenet by others.

In the main, two traditional trends have characterised the twentieth century; nationalism, which has given birth to the development of folk-song on the one hand, and jazz on the other; and serialism. The two trends were united in the second Viennese school.

National traditions are the soil from which spring the composers whose music is international. The cross-fertilisation of one tradition with another has ensured the continuing vitality of the musical art down the ages. Striking contemporary instances of this principle are seen, first, in the life-work and outlook of Stravinsky, whose entire output may be described as the product of conflicting and contrasting traditions, and whose home is everywhere, yet in no one place; and, second, in the interaction between the Viennese school of Schoenberg–Webern and other traditions, such as the American and the French.

National traditions that remain sealed off from external influences are bound, sooner or later, to become effete and lustreless. There is all the difference in the world between the composer who seeks merely to conserve and reproduce an existing idiom or technique, and one who uses it as a means of reaching a wider audience than he otherwise would. A national tradition, if it is to be real, must be dynamic, broadly based, susceptible of change. Many composers have misunderstood or underestimated the necessity of such tradition, have mistaken it for something less, and have set out to make their fortunes in other environments—it matters not where—only to find that by doing so they have put themselves in danger of losing their artistic identity. Schoenberg never once lost sight of his traditional background, which consisted of the German classics. Boulez insists on his debt to the French tradition, particularly that of Debussy.

It is only common prudence for a composer before admitting a powerful external influence to ensure his own artistic stability. Otherwise, he runs the risk of being overpowered by the stronger force. Several composers today, through disdain of national tradition, have sought after the more heady wine of Messiaen, Boulez or Stockhausen, only to find that their own composition then comes to bear an embarrassing resemblance to a diluted form of Messiaen, Boulez or Stockhausen. Their loss is then twofold; first their artistic autonomy, their creative volition, has been forfeited. Any prophetic content[1] in their music is thus obtained only at secondhand, by reference, as it were, to a third party. Second, they find that as their mentor's position shifts, as it certainly will, since no creative composer can stand still, they are left, stylistically speaking, high and dry. They then have the worst of both worlds, since audiences prefer the original to the copy.

Very different, indeed exactly the opposite, is the case of the composer who reaches a stage of artistic stability, based on his national tradition, which allows him with profit to extend the range of his creativity. He retains the creative initiative; and, even if he appears out of date to his contemporaries, and his answers to contemporary problems either wrong or irrelevant, at least they are his own answers. He does not accept someone else's secondhand. He is to this extent more of a true artist. Moreover, he works from a position of strength and will not be at the mercy of the wind of fashion. Such composers of the rank and file have always existed; no healthy tradition can flourish without them.

A tradition that lives and grows will inevitably give direction and purpose to the work of succeeding generations. The German tradition, from Bach to Brahms, exercised world-wide influence, which progressively increased during the nineteenth century, and is still reflected today in the generous respect paid to Webern and his successors. It is not certain that future

[1] See below, p. 259.

generations will be so accommodating; they may well ask what use composers made of this ready audience for their music. Already we can see that the pendulum of musical history has swung decisively in the last fifty years. It is no accident that the period of German domination up to 1900 coincided precisely with the eclipse of endemic musical activity elsewhere, notably in England; and that the re-emergence of music in England, first under Elgar, but more particularly under Vaughan Williams, dates, as we would expect, from that moment when the diatonic/harmonic system of the German tradition began to alter and evolve.

The contemporary European tradition, if not the contemporary German tradition, is serialism. The justification of this phenomenon, and what gives it its artistic validity, is not so much its past association as its future possibilities. Its nature and origin, however, are not in doubt. The discarding of the diatonic/chromatic system of harmony by the serialist school automatically gave rise to melodic and formal problems. Another dimension was added to music, and another criterion for its assessment; this was a kind of logic. The order of the 12 notes in a series was more or less arbitrary; yet significance had to be found for the ensuing pattern of intervals. To ascribe significance to a sound or an interval for its own sake, places a burden on composer and listener alike; this recalls the situation that prevailed before the discovery of the harmonic relation of notes. In the middle ages certain qualities were ascribed to certain modes. The Greeks did the same, instinctively not rationally. But later this imaginative speculation was replaced by a system of harmony based on discoveries into the nature of musical sounds. Now it is not the nature of sounds which has been discarded—indeed, how could it?—but the tonal system arising from it.

If the notes of a theme, or series, are to have significance, this is possible in one of two ways. Either this significance arises explicitly from the interrelation of the notes and their interaction on each other vertically and horizontally; or the significance is assumed to be implicit in the notes themselves. The tonal system was built on the first assumption, the serial system on the second.

We can assume that the nature of musical sound has not altered materially, but only our understanding of it. The strong associative force of notes was well understood as early as the seventeenth century, and the basic principle remains true today, namely that notes imply tonality. This fact is less obvious with notes at the upper end of the audio-frequency range than with notes in the middle. We would, therefore, expect serial composers to avoid middle-register notes; we would also expect them to avoid the use of conventional orchestral instruments, which have not only strong associations with tonal music, but also are rich in overtones; thirdly, we would expect them to avoid the use of such titles for their works as Symphony, Concerto or Chorale, all of which are heavy-laden with traditional meaning, but to adopt names and concepts which have no such association. And this is exactly what has happened.

The force and influence of traditions are external to a composer's make-up. He either accepts or rejects them. But to be exposed to, and aware of, pressures and influences is by no means the same thing as achieving that creative synthesis of style that marks out a Stravinsky, a Copland or a Tippett. All composers share traditional influences, but the creative volition, which is the composer's starting point, is entirely an individual matter.

And the artist does far more than merely respond to, and react to, external events. He interprets and prophesies. The prophetic element in music is the composer's justification for making his music heard; that which makes it relevant for someone else to listen to. This arises from the concern and compassion which the true artist feels for others. He cannot opt out of human affairs, and address others, through his music, from the comfort of his armchair. Creative volition has to do with more than the technique of composition, though naturally it includes this; it encompasses nothing less than the whole of life, and the artist's view of it. Though a tradition starts in one geographical locality, if it is to live its boundaries must gradually widen, until later composers give to it a universality, and their view becomes a world view; or, to use the German word, *Weltanschauung*.

(ii) *Construction*

What gives a composition coherence and permanence is its structure. This is so whether a composer treats the musical elements under the traditional headings of melody, harmony and rhythm, or, as the serialists do, under the headings of pitch, duration, intensity and *timbre*. In each case, form is the essence of the creative process. Every composition gradually assumes a life of its own, and its formal organisation cannot be prejudged. Texture, phrase-construction, variation and repetition, cadence, proportion, are the basic problems of the composer; not so much the invention of startling new ideas. Invention is not composition, as is sometimes made out. The ability to invent new ideas is but a small part of a composer's technique. Far more important is his ability to integrate those ideas into a consistent and coherent structure, whatever style is adopted—whether traditional or *avant-garde*. For, as Varèse once said, "a bad musician with instruments will be a bad musician with electronics."

The process of composition is a double one; first the creative impulse, second the formation of an artistic structure. This duality corresponds with the duality that is inherent in music itself. Only when an idea is taken and placed in a musical context, developed, tested and juxtaposed with other ideas, can we say that the composer has taken over from the inventor; and it is only when this happens that the nature and worth of an idea becomes apparent.

Music either aspires or asserts; these two things are really complementary. This is perfectly illustrated in the classical composers' conception of the 4-bar or 8-bar sentence, made up of two equal, yet incomplete phrases (see Ex. 23). Also in their use of the twin-subject form, the second subject balancing and fulfilling the first, the first being incomplete without the second; the one aspiring, the other asserting.

No art whatever can exist without a creative impulse; but this creative impulse is not by itself enough to ensure a coherent structure. The second half of the process of composition is indispensable. The composer is "prophetic" in the sense that he expresses at the conscious and audible level what others, his contemporaries and possibly later generations, feel only at the subconscious level. He is a spokesman who gives substance and shape to ideas which would otherwise remain unexpressed. And so no lasting composition can contain undeveloped and formless ideas, since the specific function of the composer is to give musical reality, formal cohesion, to the patterns and images that make up the *materia musica*. Anyone with a reasonably sensitive ear and a modicum of musical training, can think of a theme, or note-row, or frequency-series. The composer's function is to construct from that a formal composition.

It is a fundamental fallacy of our age that artists should seek to represent ugliness in the world with ugliness in their art. Even if the subject that inspires a composer is psychologically neutral, the representation in sound of extra-musical phenomena—more usually known as programme music—is the most suspect of all approaches to composition. The composer walks an artistic tightrope, between formlessness and banality. Music has the power to suggest; we do not look to it for description. And if the subject that inspires a composer is ugly or evil, he is under a double obligation to exercise on behalf of the listener that power of interpretation, that is his prerogative, and not merely to reproduce what already exists. The twentieth century is indeed one of violence, war and psychological mix-up. We can say this in no complacent way, but simply to question the validity of that assumption which says that a violent, mixed-up age necessarily produces violent and mixed-up art. On the contrary, it is not the ugliness of an age that an artist would wish to perpetuate. Events themselves may indeed be ugly; but the artist does more than merely represent or reflect such events. For a true reflection of them there is no need for art.

What chiefly characterizes a composition, gives it justification and independence is its structure. Structure is the outward sign of the creative synthesis of the elements of composition. It appeals to the intellectual imagination of the listener in a corresponding way to the appeal of the sensuousness of the sound to his aural imagination. And just as tonality is the result of harmonic movement, so is the structure resulting from tonality, for instance Sonata form, the result of such movement. But there is another sort of structure, one that is more static, based not on the dynamic movement and progression of tonality, but on the juxtaposition of sound-blocks. This is the structure of serialism. It also takes into account the two underlying principles, that the ear takes pleasure in sound, and that the intellect takes pleasure in structure. But it is important, when comparing the two approaches to structure, to remember that tonality is the result of centuries of creative growth and development, which Mr. Goldbeck would rightly call "tradition"; it is capable, because of its long history, of infinite subtlety and refinement; which is not the same thing as complexity. So in seeking to replace tonality, serialism needed not only to replace deeply ingrained traditions and associations in the minds of the listeners, but also to find an adequate substitute for that dynamic structure which flowed directly from tonality.

In the case of synthetic, electronic tone, not only has the composer to work with a material of quite rigid purity and whiteness, but the structure of the composition has to be consciously and deliberately thought out *ab initio*. In no sense does the form flow directly from the sound source itself. As far as the sensuous effect on the ear is concerned, sinus tone is in itself physically primitive, and, therefore, tiring and monotonous to listen to. It is a potential, not an actual, source of artistic beauty. In terms of richness and complexity, it falls short of orchestral instruments, and most of all it falls short of the human voice. If it is to excite the aural imagination of the listener, it needs to be made interesting and varied. Stereophonic reproduction is essential.

Although the formation of an artistic structure can only be the work of one composer, the creative impulse may well be collective as well as individual. It is not difficult to detect periods of collective creative impulse in various moments of musical history; some have already been referred to.[1] In such periods the composer begins his work with a very favourable handicap, as he represents a mood that is generally felt. The heaven-aspiring quality of mediaeval polyphony and Gothic art generally, was the creative impulse of that period; the Mass and the Motet were the artistic structures with which composers sought to match it. In other traditions, with different circumstances, we may find that the creative impulse has not been so matched by an artistic structure of corresponding grandeur. In the case of jazz for instance, the creative impulse far outstrips the forms of its expression; the artistic structures are of a rudimentary nature.

But whatever structure the composer chooses and whatever

[1] See p. 9 foll.

idiom he adopts, the most decisive factor in the establishment of artistic form, is melody. Melody is supreme, and outweighs other factors in importance, because it contains them already within itself. Melody includes harmony, rhythm, timbre, pitch, dynamic, form. It is the basic principle from which the composer starts. If it is objected that a composition may be for percussion instruments only, then that part is thought of as a melody which is predominant at any given moment; the harmony in that case is a harmony of texture and colour; the listener is invited to infer the melodic line from a background that is predominantly rhythmical. Such a conception is in fact a perfectly logical development of the melodic principle, which is that one part should predominate over the rest, and in that one part should be concentrated the essentials of the musical art. Music starts from melody. The minimum requirement for an artistic structure is therefore a single, organised melodic line; such as is found, for instance, in Gregorian chant.

(iii) *The finished composition*

When a composition is finished, its structure complete, a new stage is reached, one that is unique, and cannot be foreseen. Speaking purely practically, as the composer sends his new work on its way into the jungle of the concert world, a lamb among wolves, it must be admitted that its reception depends on luck to a greater extent than he would care to admit. For the sake of argument, however unrealistic it might appear, we must assume that favourable conditions exist; that nothing stands in the way of performance, that the work is played as the composer intended; that the audience was receptive and sympathetic.

It is not necessary to understand a composition intellectually to experience it aesthetically. No more is it necessary to watch the wheels and cogs of a clock moving and interlocking to be able to tell the time. But the aural experience of sound is of precisely equal importance to the intellectual realisation of structure. At every stage in fact the musical phenomenon is two-fold; it is not at all surprising that this should apply to the process of listening as well.

The dual nature of music has already been suggested. To start with, a creative impulse is matched with technique to form an artistic structure. Next, music has an aspiring as well as an assertive character; and one of the strengths of those forms that arose from tonality was that these two characteristics were each allowed for within the same movement. The 4-bar phrase required an answering 4-bar phrase (Ex. 23); the first subject was balanced by the second subject; in the older contrapuntal style, the subject of a fugue (*dux*) required its answer (*comes*).

It is important to differentiate between idiom and structure. In the finished work the composer is able to see fully for the first time whether the idiom he has used is suitable for the structure of the piece. Each of the factors which makes up a composer's idiom operate round a norm; here again music's dual nature is apparent. This can be best shown from two examples, harmony and rhythm.

Rhythm operates round a norm of a regular, metrical pulse; against this is the variety and contrast which comes from irregular, ametrical rhythms. The composers who have most developed this factor in composition are Stravinsky and Messiaen. To sustain a regular pulse, without any variation, would be a negation of the element of rhythm; while to introduce constant rhythmic variation and avoid all regularity, would destroy the norm. Only against the background of normality does variety have any artistic significance. So it is with harmony. The composer needs to establish a harmonic norm, which will be the consonance. To sustain this, and to give it vitality, it is necessary to introduce that variety and contrast which comes from dissonance. Dissonance and consonance are both relative and related; one without the other is artistically meaningless, and juxtaposed sounds are only concordant or discordant in a context. What may be discordant in one composition may be the harmonic norm for another.

Thus a composer's idiom is a reconciliation of contrasts; of consonance and dissonance as far as harmony is concerned; of metrical regularity and rhythmical variety as far as rhythm is concerned. These are merely two factors out of many that go to make up a composition; but in all cases it is essential that the listener should be aware of the norm set by the composer.

The dual nature of the listener's approach is seen to

correspond with the dual nature of music itself. Neither the intuitive nor the intellectual approach is complete in itself. We can all think of certain compositions which require only one faculty for their appreciation. Those works whose appeal is exclusively aural we describe as "easy to listen to"; we wallow in them, slightly ashamed that we should do so, and with such ease, though knowing all the time that the pleasure is both limited and impermanent. Those compositions on the other hand whose appeal is entirely cerebral, we do not enjoy so much as endure. We listen tensely and grimly; we wonder whether perhaps the work contained any particle of aural pleasure which we missed; we are reluctant to admit, even to ourselves, that listening which is purely intellectual is quite immensely boring, or that, where art is concerned, it is unrewarding, because it is incomplete.

Only in the finished art-work can the composer decide whether his idiom measures up to the structure. What matters is the completeness, in every sense of the word, of his composition; the integrity of the idiom; the integrity of the structure; the integrity of the way in which the listener receives the music. Integrity in each case is the result of the reconciliation of contrasting and complementary factors.

A composer is not primarily a musical historian; but the contemporary composer cannot avoid becoming to some extent, as far as his own purposes require, an interpreter of musical history. In the late eighteenth century, the present represented a consummation, a crystallisation of the past; the way to the future was, therefore, both unambiguous and commonly accepted. A study and an assessment of past periods was superfluous for composers of the period. The present was music for Mozart and Beethoven, to say nothing of their audiences; and the present was logically consistent with the past. Schubert was able to write six symphonies by the age of nineteen largely because there was never a moment's doubt in his mind, or anybody else's mind, about the historical rightness, and the artistic validity, of the diatonic system.

No such state of affairs prevails today. Some facets of the present are logically inconsistent with the past; and, before he can put pencil to paper, the composer today needs to choose, and to assess the historical situation.

Since this is the case, and since the contemporary composer

is constrained to synthesise his own idiom, the pattern of contemporary music consists largely of the stylistic development of the individual composer; his wrestling with those traditions and influences which surround him as he searches for that idiom which for him has integrity. So neoclassicism was a particular solution chosen by Stravinsky at one stage of his life; neoromanticism was another solution, which Jolivet preferred. What matters more than this or that solution at a particular stage of a composer's life, is the integrity of each finished composition.

(iv) *Conclusion*

The totality of a composition is the extent to which it reflects the whole nature of the composer and the collective impulse of the listener. If the composer has no spiritual aspirations, his work will lack that creative impulse, without which it cannot live; if he has no assertiveness, his work will lack that uniqueness of physical structure without which it cannot survive. Since art originates in human nature, it clearly has to do with both its spiritual and its material aspects. The idiom and structure of a composition are more material than spiritual; but the aspiring element in a composition corresponds with that individual or collective creative impulse that we have already referred to, and its nature is more spiritual than material.

The examples quoted[1] all derive their force from such basic and timeless issues as religion, freedom and human progress. Now if we accept, as Vaughan Williams maintained, that the composer's rôle is partly that of a servant of his fellow men; if, moreover, we accept that he gives conscious and material expression to the collective and unconscious aspirations of others; and, finally, if we accept that the composer's position today is uncertain, and that he does not belong centrally to his environment, then it can only be that those collective, spiritual aspirations, which in the past have provided the creative impulse for the composer and the justification for his music, are today either lacking or directed elsewhere.

In the absence of a collective creative impulse, the composer is thrown back onto himself. This is patently a source of

[1] p. 9.

weakness as well as strength. While it will ensure for his composition that spiritual dynamism without which his art would be largely derivative and academic, it will not necessarily ensure that his music is relevant, or even interesting, to those who do not share his aspirations. Indeed, he may arouse active antagonism, as Schoenberg did. On the other side of the coin, his work may be seized on by those listeners who *do* share his aspirations, for that one reason only, and the equally important structural and idiomatic aspects of the work may be ignored.

An assessment of contemporary music needs to take into account its material structure as well as its spiritual impulse. Both are equally part of the composer's speculative volition. As far as our understanding of the material structure of contemporary music is concerned, the pivot composer is Webern; not only because of the nature of his style, but because of the subsequent interpretation of his work by later composers and musicians, who selected him as their progenitor. It is a nice point whether Webern himself would recognise and acknowledge his aesthetic intentions from the forbiddingly mathematical and quasi-scientific jargon which fills the pages of *die Reihe*. Surely this account of his work is biased? But as the Cambridge historian G. M. Trevelyan once shrewdly observed,[1] all history is bias.

"We cannot get rid of the element of opinion (or bias); we can, however, endeavour to make it the right kind of opinion . . ."

This is even more true with the history of an art. When a musician considers another musician's work, he can only do so with his own intentions in mind. And it is highly probable that subsequent musicians who wish to assess the *avant-garde* of the 1960's will go back to Webern, where it all started.

The hallmarks of his style are lyricism and an insistence on the sheer musical sound. It is the sound that has fascinated subsequent composers. Yet in his work those contradictions that exist today first come sharply into focus. He was the first to match the auditive perception of sound with the dialectical perception of the *motif*. He was the first to see

[1] *An Autobiography and other essays*, p. 68.

fully the contradiction inherent in any attempt to replace tonality by deliberately ignoring it and by avoiding all reference to it. Tonality had been the corner-stone of form, and the chief effect of atonalism had been not so much to replace tonality with something else, as to weaken, if not to destroy, all formal unity.

Those contrasting elements which belong to music because of its dual nature, are more apparent in Webern than in any other composer of his tradition. Romanticism and Classicism, tonality and serialism, intellectualism and sensuousness, counterpoint and harmony, tradition and experiment. Webern himself achieved that creative synthesis of idiom, that reconciling of opposite and contrasting factors to which we have already referred. It was almost inevitable that out of his composite and sophisticated style, later composers should take this or that technical feature, and develop it to the exclusion of others.

But the integrity of an idiom or a structure demands that a composer should take into account all those aspects which bear on it. The idiom of Mozart or Haydn is not characterised by their use of diatonicism so much as by their treatment of chromatic and dissonant elements. So today, it is not necessarily the adoption by a contemporary composer of a particular technique or system that will give effectiveness to his music, but rather his treatment of those other factors that are foreign to it. An idiom which pursues one aspect of technique, and ignores others, for whatever reason, is lopsided.

In the case of Webern's successors, the divergence in the technique of composition, which followed from their development of different aspects of his technique, produced a confusion concerning the purpose of music itself and the function of the composer. Is it primarily communication, technique, invention, or scientific enquiry? All have been put forward at one time or another. The confusion is not just a semantic one, but a reflection of a more basic uncertainty. Your appreciation of a composition is fundamentally affected by what you think the composer's function should be; and you look for evidence in his work of whatever prime factor you select.

But any understanding of the material structure of a composition needs to be balanced by a deeper experience of its nature; and to understand is not the same thing as to experience. To take an example from harmony, the difference between the effect of the sound of a semitone and that of a fifth can be explained and understood technically by comparing the frequency-ratio between C and its immediate neighbour C sharp, with that between C and the G above it. Such a scientific explanation of the nature of musical sounds, though of fundamental importance to the musician, must not be mistaken by him as necessarily providing an experience of harmony. Nor is it a substitute for that wider appreciation of consonance and dissonance, which is as much a matter of aesthetic judgement as of scientific fact.

If the understanding of the material structure of a composition is external to the listener, his understanding of that spiritual aspiration which underlies the process of composition is of much more direct concern to him. The tradition, the creative impulse that govern the composer can be collective as well as individual, and therefore closely involve the listener. To take three examples from the theatre, the differences between Stravinsky's *Rite of Spring*, Schoenberg's *Moses and Aaron*, and Copland's *Appalachian Spring* are not so much differences of technique as differences of tradition and creative impulse.

In seeking to describe such prime creative forces, we have to consider the contemporary cultural ethos as a whole; and we must ask what is its most characteristic form of expression. If we accept that the composer does not belong centrally to his environment in quite the same way as his forbears did, we imply that music is not the most characteristic and apt form of expression of twentieth century culture. Then what is? We imply also that the things which formerly found expression in music, today find expression in some other way. Then in what other way?

The answer is all too plain and has already been hinted at; our Western culture is predominantly a literal one. That is to say, the sort of questions that characterise our age find their outlet in definition and analysis. Even those fundamental and ageless questions of religion or philosophy, which previously were a source of universal aspiration and inspiration to all people, whether artists or not, today find their expression in dialectical linguistics. Truth and beauty have by no means ceased to exist, but they have ceased to be considered in the same light as hitherto; they have now been made objects of logical enquiry. Things of the spirit have been materialised; religion has been secularised. Even serialism, which might appear to be the most complexly and exclusively musical phenomenon, and is certainly the most widespread tradition in contemporary music, derived from an origin that was, partly at least, logical and philosophical. The twentieth century looks for exact description, realism. This is something beyond the competence of music to provide.

Ours is a literal culture. Ideas are expressed today in the written, or spoken, word, or by means of mathematical or scientific definition, which in previous ages would have found their fullest and most natural outlet in music. The Romantic movement, with all its passion and overflowing vitality, found its natural voice in music; the voice of the twentieth century is its literal realism. Scientific analysis, logical philosophy, historical research, and all the countless intellectual sallies and sorties born of an Alexandrian age, with its self-conscious urge for questioning, discovery, adventure and movement, have for the greater part been accommodated in literature of one kind or another. If the output of books alone were the measure of a culture, ours would be rich beyond compare.

Whereas the tendency of the Romantic movement was to invest words, and other non-musical arts, such as painting, with the characteristics of music, which consist largely of imagery and association, the contemporary trend is precisely the reverse; to invest musical notes and images with the precision and exactitude of mathematical symbols. It is not correct to say that this cannot be done. It can. But it cannot be done without a radical reappraisal of the power and the effect of music, or without artistic reservations on the part of the listener, as long as the memory and the experience of the power of music, that he associates with the Romantic period, remain so strong. That notes imply tonality is as fundamental a *datum* as the principle of gravitation; it is completely understandable, therefore, that composers should meanwhile attempt to discover entirely fresh sonorities, without any of the associations of notes.

If the ideas which most characterise our culture find their strongest and clearest expression, and evoke the maximum response, in literalness, what then is the composer's place? Since the collective creative impulse in our Western society is directed elsewhere, and does not look to music for its chief artistic fulfilment, the voice of the contemporary composer can only sound a personal note, not a collective one. In common with other artists he must discover his individual idiom afresh, each his own. He must by the exercise of his own speculative volition decide both the function and the nature of his art, to an extent that has no precedent in earlier periods of music, such as the polyphonic or the Romantic.

The creative impulse which compels the contemporary composer is born from his innermost mind and convictions. So any permanent validity in his work will be automatically killed by superficiality. He is addressing a minority audience; he is seeking with the totality of his work to arrive at that unity of structure which will call forth an artistic response in the listener. The bigger the work, the more complete the unity, the more far-reaching must be the *rapport* between the composer and the listener. By thus touching the unconscious aspirations of his audience with the integrity of the material structure, and the timeless serenity that belongs to art alone, the composer will give his work lasting significance.

APPENDIX I

SELECT BIBLIOGRAPHY

As a complete list of all the available books and magazine articles concerned with contemporary music would be impracticable, the following is a list of those works which have been directly referred to in the course of this book. A number of them contain their own excellent bibliography about a particular composer or subject.

Adorno, Theodor W. *Philosophie der neuen Musik* (Europäische Verlagsanstalt, Frankfurt, 1958)

Ansermet, Ernest *Les fondements de la musique dans la conscience humaine.* (2 vols.) (Baconnière, Neuchatel, 1961)

Apel, Willi *Gregorian Chant* (Burns & Oates, London, 1958)
Harvard Dictionary of Music (Heinemann, London, 1944)
see under Davison, Archibald T.

Augustine, St. *De Musica*, ed. W. F. Jackson Knight (Orthological Institute, London, 1948)

Beckwith (ed. with Kasemets)
The modern composer and his world International conference of composers at Stratford, Ontario, Canada, August 1960. (University of Toronto Press, 1961)

Beecham, Thomas *Frederick Delius* (Hutchinson, London, 1959)

Bellows, George Kent see under Howard, John Tasker

Berger, Arthur *Aaron Copland* (Oxford University Press, New York, 1953)

Boulez, Pierre — *Domaine Musical* No. 1, 1954

International bulletin of contemporary music. (Bernard Grasset, Paris, 1954)

Penser la musique aujourd'hui (Editions Gonthier, Paris, 1963)

Brandel, Rose — see under Reese, Gustave

Brindle, Reginald S. — *Serial composition*. Introductory textbook. (Oxford University Press, London, 1966)

Broder, Nathan — see under Lang, Paul Henry

Busoni, Ferruccio — *Entwurf einer neuen Aesthetik der Tonkunst* (Trieste, 1907) translated Dr. T. Baker

Sketch of a new aesthetic of music (New York, 1911)

The essence of music and other papers translated by Rosamond Ley (Rockliff, London, 1957)

Cage, John — *The 25-year retrospective concert of the music of John Cage*. Three records of a performance, in Town Hall, New York, May 15th 1958, with descriptive notes. (George Avakian, New York, 1959)

Chase, Gilbert — *America's Music from the Pilgrims to the present* (McGraw-Hill Book Co. Inc. New York, 1955)

Cosman, Milein — (with Keller, Hans)

Stravinsky at rehearsal (Dobson, London, 1962)

Musical sketchbook (Bruno Cassirer, Oxford, 1957)

Copland, Aaron — *Music and imagination*. Charles Eliot Norton Lectures 1951/2 (Harvard University Press, 1952)

Cowell, Henry — *American Composers on American Music—a symposium* (Stanford University Press, 1933) (with Cowell, Sidney)

Charles Ives and his music (Oxford University Press, New York, 1955)

Craft, Robert   see under Stravinsky

Davison, Archibald T. (with Apel, Willi)
Historical anthology of music (2 vols.)
Vol. 1 Oriental, Medieval and Renaissance
Vol. 2 Baroque, Rococo and pre-classical (Harvard University Press, 1950)

Debussy, Claude   *Monsieur Croche the dilettante hater* (Dover Publications, New York, 1962)

Dent, Edward J.   *Ferruccio Busoni* A biography (Oxford University Press, London, 1933; reissued 1966)

Dickinson, G. Lowes   *The Greek view of life* (Methuen, London, 1896)

Dieren, Bernard Van   *Down among the dead men* (Oxford University Press, London, 1935)

Douglas, Winfred   *Church music in history and practice* revised by Leonard Ellinwood (Faber, London, 1962)

Eimert, Herbert   see under *Die Reihe*

Einstein, Alfred   *Greatness in music,* translated by Cesar Saerchinger (Oxford University Press, New York, 1941)

Eliot, T. S.   *Notes towards the definition of culture* (Faber, London, 1948)
Tradition and the individual talent (from *The Sacred Wood*; essays on poetry and criticism) (Methuen, London, 1920)

Ellinwood, Leonard   see under Douglas, Winfred

Ewen, David   *American Composers today* (H. W. Wilson Co., New York, 1949)

Finkelstein, Sidney   *Composer and Nation—The folk heritage in music* (Lawrence & Wishart, London, 1960)

Gilot, Françoise   (with Lake, Carlton)
Life with Picasso (Nelson, London, 1965)

Gray, Cecil	*Contemporary Music* (Oxford University Press, London, 1924)
	Contingencies and other essays (Oxford University Press, London, 1947)
	History of Music, the (Kegan Paul, London, 1928)
	Predicaments, or music and the future (Oxford University Press, London, 1936)
	Sibelius (Oxford University Press, London, 1931)
	Warlock, Peter (Jonathan Cape, London, 1934)
Handy, W. C.	*Father of the Blues* (New York, 1947 Sidgwick & Jackson, London, 1957)
Harvard Dictionary	see under Apel, Willi
Hentoff, Nat	(with Shapiro, Nat)
	Hear me talkin' to ya. The story of jazz by the men who made it (Rinehart & Co. Inc. New York, 1955 Penguin Books, London, 1962)
Hiller, Lejaren A., Jr.	(with Isaacson, Leonard M.)
	Experimental Music (McGraw-Hill Book Co. Inc., New York, 1959)
Hindemith, Paul	*A composer's world.* Charles Eliot Norton Lectures 1949/50 (Harvard University Press, 1952)
Hodeir, André	*Jazz: Its evolution and essence*, translated by David Noakes (Grove Press, New York, 1956)
	Since Debussy—A view of contemporary music, translated by Noel Burch (Secker & Warburg, London, 1961)
Hodin, J. P.	*The dilemma of being modern.* Essays on art and literature (Routledge & Kegan Paul, London, 1956)
Holst, Gustav	see under Williams, R. Vaughan
Holst, Imogen	*The Music of Gustav Holst* (Oxford University Press, London, 1951)

Howard, John Tasker (with Bellows, George Kent)
A short history of music in America (Thomas Y. Crowell Co. New York, 1957)

Isaacson, Leonard M. see under Hiller, Lejaren A.

Ives, Charles E. *Essays before a Sonata* (Dover Publications, New York, 1962)

Jeans, James *Science and music* (Cambridge University Press, 1937)

Kasemets see under Beckwith

Keller, Hans see under Cosman, Milein

Kemp, Ian *Michael Tippett: A symposium on his sixtieth birthday* (Faber, London, 1965)

Kennedy, Michael *The works of Ralph Vaughan Williams* (Oxford University Press, London, 1964)

Kolneder, Walter *Anton Webern* (P. J. Tonger, Rodenkirchen/Rhein, 1961)

Krenek, Ernst *Exploring Music*. Essays on different topics (Calder & Boyars, London, 1966)

Lake, Carlton see under Gilot, Françoise

Lambert, Constant *Music Ho!* A study of music in decline (Faber, London, 1934; reissued 1966)

Lang, Paul Henry (with Broder, Nathan)
Contemporary music in Europe. A comprehensive survey (The Musical Quarterly, January 1965; Schirmer, New York, Dent, London, 1966)
Problems of modern music. The Princeton Seminar in advanced musical studies (W. W. Norton & Co. Inc. New York, 1960)

Ledermann, Minna see under Stravinsky

Leibowitz, René *Introduction à la musique de douze sons* (L'Arche, Paris, 1948)
Schoenberg et son école (Philosophical Library, New York, 1949)

Lockspeiser, Edward — *Debussy, his life and mind.* 2 vols. (Cassell, London, 1956)

Machlis, Joseph — *American composers of our time* (Thomas Y. Crowell Co. New York, 1963)

Introduction to contemporary music (The musical Quarterly, 50th anniversary issue) (Dent, London, 1963)

Malcolm, Norman — *Ludwig Wittgenstein—a memoir* (Oxford University Press, London, 1958

Mellers, Wilfrid — *Music in a new found land.* Themes and developments in the history of American music (Barrie and Rockliff, London, 1964)

Messiaen, Olivier — *The technique of my musical language,* translated by John Satterfield. 2 vols. (Leduc, Paris, 1944)

Myers, Rollo — *Twentieth century music: a symposium* (Calder and Boyars, London, 1960)

Onnen, Frank — *Stravinsky,* translated by M. M. Kessler-Button (The Continental Book Co. A.B., Stockholm, 1948)

Perle, George — *Serial Composition and Atonality An introduction to the music of Schoenberg, Berg and Webern* (Faber, London, 1962)

Priestley, J. B. — *Literature and Western Man* (Heinemann, London, 1960)

Redlich, H. F. — *Alban Berg, The Man and his Music* (John Calder, London, 1957)

Reese, Gustave — *Music in the Renaissance* (W. W. Norton & Co. Inc., New York, 1954), (with Brandel, Rose)

The Commonwealth of Music (The Free Press, New York, 1965)

Reich, Willi — *Alban Berg,* translated by Cornelius Cardew (Thames and Hudson, London, 1965)

Reich, Willi — see under Webern

Reihe, die — A periodical devoted to developments in contemporary music, edited by Herbert Eimert and Karlheinz Stockhausen.

Vol. 1. *Electronic Music*
Vol. 2. *Anton Webern*
Vol. 3. *Musical craftsmanship*
Vol. 4. *Young composers*
Vol. 5. *Reports analyses*
Vol. 6. *Language and music*
Vol. 7. *Form—Space*
Vol. 8. *Musical rotation-technique*
(Theodore Presser Co., Pennsylvania, in association with Universal Edition, Vienna)

Reis, Claire R. — *Composers in America* (Biographical sketches of contemporary composers) (The Macmillan Co., New York, 1947)

Reti, Rudolph — *Tonality, Atonality, Pantonality* (Barrie and Rockliff, 1958)

Richter, Hans — *Dada—Art and anti-art* (Thames and Hudson, London, 1965)

Robertson, Alec — (with Stevens, Denis)
The Pelican History of Music. Vol. 1 *Ancient forms to polyphony.* Vol. 2 *Renaissance and Baroque* (Penguin Books, London, 1960 (Vol. 1), 1963 (Vol. 2))

Roland-Manuel — *Histoire de la musique.* du XVIIIe siècle à nos jours (with 42 other contributors) Encyclopédie de la Pléiade (Gallimard, Paris, 1963)

Rostand, Claude — *Olivier Messiaen* (Ventadour, Paris, 1957)

Routley, Erik — *Church music and theology* (S.C.M. Press, London, 1959)
The Church and Music (Duckworth, London, 1950)
Twentieth Century Church Music (Jenkins, London, 1964)

Rufer, Josef — *Composition with twelve notes*, translated by Humphrey Searle from the German edition *Die Komposition mit zwölf tönen* (1952), (Rockliff, London, 1954)

The works of Arnold Schoenberg. A catalogue. Translated by Dika Newlin (Faber, London, 1962)

Russell, Bertrand — *History of Western Philosophy* (George Allen and Unwin, London, 1946)

Sachs, Curt — *The Rise of music in the ancient world* (Dent, London, 1944)

Schaeffer, Pierre — *A la recherche d'une musique concrète* (Editions du Seuil, Paris, 1952)

Schenker, Heinrich — *Harmony*, translated by Elisabeth Mann Borgese (University of Chicago Press, 1954). First published (Stuttgart, 1906) as *Neue musikalische Theorien und Phantasien*. Vol. 1 *Harmonielehre*. Vol. 2 *Kontrapunkt*

Scherchen, Hermann — *Handbook of conducting* (*Lehrbuch des Dirigierens*), (Leipzig, 1929), translated by M. D. Calvocoressi (Oxford University Press, London, 1933)

The nature of music (*Vom Wesen der Musik*), (Zurich, 1946), translated by William Mann (Dobson, London 1950)

Scherer, Jacques — *Le livre de Mallarmé* (Gallimard, Paris, 1951)

Schoenberg, Arnold — *Harmonielehre*, translated by Robert D. W. Adams (Philosophical Library, New York, 1948)

Letters, selected and edited by Erwin Stein (Faber, London, 1964)

Structural functions of harmony (Williams and Norgate, London, 1954)

Style and Idea (Philosophical Library, New York, 1950)

Schrade, L.   *Monteverdi creator of modern music* (Gollancz, London, 1951)

Schweitzer, Albert   *J. S. Bach* (2 vols.), translated by Ernest Newman (A. & C. Black, London, 1923); *Goethe* (A. & C. Black, London, 1949)

Shapiro, Nat   see under Hentoff, Nat

Smith, Julia   *Aaron Copland* (E. P. Dutton & Co. Inc., New York, 1955)

Stein, Erwin   see under Schoenberg *Letters*

Form and performance, published posthumously (Faber, London, 1962)

Stevens, Denis   *A history of song* (Hutchinson, London 1960)

see under Robertson, Alec

Stockhausen, Karlheinz   see under Reihe, die

Stravinsky, Igor   *Chroniques de ma vie* (Denoël et Steele, Paris 1935 Gollancz, London, 1936) (with Robert Craft)

Conservations with Igor Stravinsky (Faber, London, 1958)

Expositions and developments (Faber, London, 1959)

Memories and Commentaries (Faber, London, 1959)

Poetics of music. Charles Eliot Norton Lectures 1939/40 (Harvard University Press, 1942)

Stravinsky in the theatre, edited with an introduction by Minna Lederman, with excerpts of autobiography, contributions and studies by 22 musicians; list of stage productions, recordings and bibliography.

Stuckenschmidt, H. H.   *Opera in dieser Zeit* (Friedrich Verlag, Hanover, 1964)

Arnold Schoenberg, translated by Edith Temple Roberts and Humphrey Searle (John Calder, London. 1959)

Taneiev, Serge Ivanovitch — *Convertible counterpoint in the strict style*, translated by G. Ackley Brower (Bruce Humphries, Boston, Mass. 1962)

Taylor, C. A. — *The physics of musical sounds* (English Universities Press, London, 1965)

Thomson, Virgil — *The art of judging music* (Alfred A. Knopf, New York, 1948)

Tippett, Michael — *Moving into Aquarius* (Routledge & Kegan Paul, London, 1959)

Tovey, Donald Francis — *Essays in Musical Analysis* in six volumes (Oxford University Press, London, 1935)

The integrity of music ten lectures (Oxford University Press, London, 1941)

Urmson, J. O. — *Philosophical analysis* (Oxford University Press, London, 1956)

Vlad, Roman — *Stravinsky*, translated by Frederick and Ann Fuller (Oxford University Press, London, 1960)

Warlock, Peter — *Delius* (Bodley Head, London, 1923; reissued 1952)

Webern, Anton — *The path to the new music*, translated by Leo Black (Theodore Presser Co., Pennsylvania, in association with Universal Edition, Vienna, 1963)

Wildgans, Friedrich — *Anton Webern*, translated by Edith Temple Roberts and Humphrey Searle (Calder and Boyars, London, 1966)

Williams, R. Vaughan — *National music, and other essays* (Oxford University Press, London, 1963)

(with Holst, Gustav)
Heirs and rebels (Oxford University Press, London, 1959)

Wiora, Walter — *The four ages of music*, translated by M. D. Herter Norton (Dent, London, 1965)

Wood, Alexander   *The physics of music* (Methuen, London, 1944)

Wood, Henry   *My life of music* (Gollancz, London, 1938)

Wörner, Karl H.   *Schoenberg's Moses and Aaron*, translated by Paul Hamburger (Faber, London, 1963)

Magazines and periodicals

The following are among the more important periodicals referred to in the course of this book:—

Composer (Journal of the Composers' Guild of Great Britain)

Contrepoints

Journal of the British Institute of Recorded Sound

La Revue Musicale

Modern Music

Musical Quarterly

Perspectives of new music (Princeton N.J. University Press)

Ricordiana (published by G. Ricordi & Co.)

Tempo (published by Boosey & Hawkes Ltd.)

APPENDIX II

Table showing the proportion of contemporary music performed in various concerts in Great Britain between 1964 and 1966

	Total number of Performances	Number of Contemporary works played	Contemporary British works played	Works by living British Composers
Scottish National Orchestra,[1] 1964/5 season	149	50 (33·5%)	6 (4%)	6 (4%)
Birmingham Symphony Orchestra,[1] 1964/5 season	226	62 (27·4%)	20 (8·8%)	15 (6·6%)
Manchester–Hallé Orchestra,[1] 1964/5 season	195	50 (25·6%)	10 (5·1%)	5 (3·6%)
London–Promenade Concerts, 1964 season	204	62 (30·4%)	34 (16·6%)	20 (9·8%)
London–Promenade Concerts, 1965 season	215	67 (31·2%)	32 (14·9%)	20 (9·3%)
London–Promenade Concerts, 1966 season	202	51 (25%)	28 (13·9%)	15 (7·4%)
London–Concerts presented at the Royal Festival Hall, 1965/6 season	1,028	252 (24·5%)	85 (8·3%)	51 (4·9%)
Overall total:	2,219	594 (26·8%)	215 (9·7%)	134 (6%)

[1] Quoted in *Composer*, No. 15, April 1965. See also Racine Fricker, *The Vanishing Composers* (in *Composer*, No. 13,

Performances of works by living British composers in concerts broadcast by the British Broadcasting Corporation

For broadcasting purposes a distinction is made between 'serious', 'popular' and 'light' music. The acceptance of a new work in the 'serious' category is made, in the first instance, subject to a reading panel. If a work is once rejected, it is most unlikely that a concert which includes it will be acceptable for broadcasting.[1] As far as the acceptance of new works is concerned, out of a total of 203 compositions premiered, or broadcast for the first time, in 1965, 60 were by living British composers (29%). And the following table, which covers the same 6-week period in three successive years, shows the decreasing proportion of time allotted to the work of the living British composer out of the total number of hours of 'serious' music broadcast in Great Britain:

1964	1965	1966
8·8%	7·9%	6·3%

The first and most obvious requirement for the creation of a living musical tradition is that those who have the means to bring it into being should also have the wish to do so. The most pronounced characteristic of the present situation, which is highly unfavourable to the living English composer, is the undue influence exerted by a comparatively small, centralised bureaucracy. That there should be one single selection mechanism for all broadcast concerts, and that all the regions of the country should be bound by this, may well make for bureaucratic efficiency and financial economy, but it is artistically indefensible. Not only is a system which centres all power of decision, and influence, in London, for that very reason a bad system, but, as events have shown, a monopoly of this sort is the greatest single hindrance to the development and growth of a musical tradition in England.

There are two reasons for saying this. The first is that no composition can be adequately assessed merely by being read, however expert the 'reader' may be. There is no substitute for hearing a work in performance. The second reason is that a composer can have no greater ally than a sympathetic

[1] See Gerald Larner, *New music and old scores* (*Composer* No. 17, October, 1965).

performer. The most successful and lasting promotion of new music is achieved first and foremost by individual performers, particularly conductors. We think of Koussevitzky, Stokowski, Beecham, Rosbaud. Wherever such a profitable and creative relationship exists, nothing must be allowed to come in its way; to attempt to subordinate it to the dictates of a bureaucracy will almost certainly stifle its growth; and we can say with certainty that any system which does this is *ipso facto* a bad system.

The policy governing the 'Popular Music' Department is to endorse an already-existing popularity. It is thus quite distinct from the policy governing 'serious' music. The Director of Sound Broadcasting has said[2]: "Our Popular Music Department deals only with music which is currently highly popular." Works included in the programmes are the "current hits and the evergreens of the light entertainment world." New, or unheard music, which may become popular in the future is not considered; this is allotted to the "Light Music Unit", whose share of time is 2%. Over 100 hours of 'popular' music are played each week which, as a matter of policy, ignore the existence of the living composer. Even if we allow this on grounds of expediency, or to satisfy "public demand", it is inexcusable that no alternative broadcasting network is available to put right the balance. As one musician has put it, it is a policy of self-administered asphyxiation.

[2] In a letter to *The Times*, 20th June, 1964.

INDEX

This book is to be returned on or before
the last date stamped below.

9 JUN 1982

20 NOV 1990

-3 MAY 1996

28 OCT 1982

14 JUN 1991

30 SEP 1985

1-2 JUN 1992

28 MAR 1987

CANCELLED

28 MAY 1996

18 NOV 1993

3 NOV 1997

7 OCT 1988

CANCELLED

15 NOV 1988

2 MAY 1994

1 APR 1998

21 APR 1989

CANCELLED

1 9 JUN 1999

12 OCT 1988

-7 OCT 1994

13 OCT 1998

5 OCT 1990

3 0 MAY 2000

6 - NOV 2007

ROUTH

1 2 NOV 2009 2 1 1